The Pueblos

Bill Hillmann

The Pueblos

My Quest to Run 101 Bull Runs in the Small Towns of Spain

Bill Hillmann

Tortoise Books

Chicago, IL

PART I

Suelta

Chapter 1

Origins

It is July 9th, 2014. I am running with the bulls in Pamplona.

A massive black bull named Brevito from the Victoriano Del Rio ranch approaches me on the broad, sunny Telefonica section of the course. His slobbery snout sniffs the air; his wide, tall horns stretch upward above the boulder-like muscles of his pulsing neck. I wave my rolled newspaper in his line of vision and he progresses toward me, his hooves click-clacking on the brick-paved street. *You got him, Bill! Now take him into the bullring!*

As I progress up the street leading Brevito, a group of runners in matching blue shirts gathers ahead of me, clogging the street. Looking back at Brevito as I run, I crash into them. One of the blue-shirted runners gathers his strength and pushes me in the chest with all his might. My feet fly up from underneath me. The runner who pushed me sprints into the center of the street and crashes into another runner, knocking him down.

I fall to the zigzag bricks flat on my back, astonished. The twelve-hundred-pound bull swoops in toward me. He swings his head low and graceful. His big eyes lock in on me as his dagger-like horns aim at my groin.

Another of the blue-shirted runners falls and drops his knee into my chest, and my leg pops up in recoil. Brevito's eye adjusts to the easier higher target of my white-clad thigh. The point of his horn strikes my balls as it swoops upward and digs into my inner thigh. I feel a needle prick, then a vast universe of nothing. I see the girth of his horn embedded in my thigh. Denial screams in my mind. *He didn't gore you!* He lifts me in a majestic lunge. *His horn is just under you!* No pain. I grab my crotch. Cup my aching balls to make sure they're still there. *Thank God! I want to have kids.* His momentum carries us toward the barricades as his foreleg collapses and he falls. My leg sails between the barricades.

As Brevito falls, the horn slides out. I fall to the coarse bricks again. On my back I grab the barricades, pull, and try to scuttle under them. Brevito rises quickly and gores my leg again with a short jab. It sounds like a knife digging through Styrofoam. He looks me in the eye and seethes so ferociously his horn quivers inside me. Then he pulls his horn out and vanishes.

A paramedic named Jesús drags me under the barricades to safety. And for a moment I am alone.

My pant leg is ripped open and my thigh is grotesquely misshapen. When my weight hung from Brevito's horn it ballooned the muscle, so now it looks as if there's a cantaloupe stuffed inside my thigh. The skin is burst open in three triangular ribbons like a Christmas wrapping paper with a dark red hole in the center. I peer into the deep baseball-size fleshy wound, half-expecting it to not be there. *What did you do to yourself, Bill?*

Then a calm voice whispers: *Accept it. You knew this day would come.*

Blood streams down my leg from the second wound and fills my shoe. I crane my neck to see the color of the blood. *Dark blood is good, bright blood is the artery.* I can't see it. If the artery is severed, it retracts up inside. They have to dig inside the wound, find the spurting artery, and clamp it. *You'll bleed to death. Is this how you die?*

The blue-shirted man who pushed me appears behind me. He has short blonde hair; he winces as his veiny arms tremble. The other blue-shirted runners stand by with concern on their faces. He looks down at me.

"It was either you or me," he says in a British accent, a mixture of pain and regret in his voice. A police officer pushes them away. *Are those the last words anyone will ever say to me?*

My stomach aches. I can feel my blood draining from my body and trickling onto the cobblestones. I feel as alone as I have ever been in all my life. Even so, I know that if I do survive this, I will run with the bulls again.

♉

Why, you might ask?

Because I'm a bull runner. A *mozo,* as they call us in Spain. Over the past dozen years, the ancient cultural art of the *encierro* has seeped into my soul. I've nearly lost my life doing this. And that's just part of the experience. True *mozos* know that every time they take to the streets, it could be their last day on this earth. We accept that reality. We embrace it. Because when death runs with you, you feel life in its purest form.

The English-speaking world refers to the *encierro* as "the running of the bulls." But it's much more than just running. *Encierro* translates to enclosure; the animals are released into the street, where the runners try to guide them into the corrals inside the bullring while also keeping the herd intact. The *pastores* (paid herdsmen) wear green shirts and use willow canes to drive the pack forward; they enforce rules. (Such as: no one should ever touch the animals. I've seen a pastore break his willow cane across the face of a tourist who was yanking the tail of a loose steer.) They also control the crowd. The runners run alongside the pack, and the best runners run in front of the pack. When you run directly in front of a bull, he either bashes you out of the way, or decides to accept you as his leader. He follows you—links with you, in a sense. It's called "running on the horns," and it's a thrilling and transcendent experience, a deep spiritual and psychological connection with the animal. I imagine it's like summiting a dangerous cliff, or catching a perfect wave; in short, it is the ultimate in bull running. Once you are running on the horns you try to lead the bull, or the whole herd, as far as you can toward the arena, until the last bull in the herd enters the corrals inside. Some incredibly talented Spanish runners can run three or even four hundred yards on the horns of a bull, though it is very rare.

Sometimes a bull breaks from the pack. This bull—a *suelto* now—often becomes combative, and sees all the runners as predators. The bull wants to fight. Then the best runners must calm and direct that animal, leading it back to the pack, and the arena, with the help of the *pastores*. Sometimes you will see video of a bull goring a runner, and the other runners or one of the *pastores* will come to his aid and grab the tail of the bull. This usually stops the bull from further harming the runner, and stalls him so the runners can begin to lead the *suelto* again. The best runners with *sueltos* often turn circles with the bull to keep him under control and progress him slowly toward the arena. Other times runners will lead a *suelto* in a steady pace with a paper beneath its snout. It is a complex dance full of drama and life-and-death grace, and at times it spirals into a fierce ballet worthy of the greatest stages.

Hemingway's *The Sun Also Rises* is the reason I started to write, and the reason I first came to Spain to run with the bulls in 2005. But it's not why I've returned for more than a decade. The running of the bulls is at once a mythical pagan conjuring of Taurus, a guiding of Christlike sacrificial animals to their Golgotha, and a fun and chaotic adventure into a poetic foreign culture.

Over the years I've found three distinct layers to the world of bull running. First (and most important), the bull itself: *El Toro Bravo*, what we call the Spanish Fighting Bull. They have their own language, both audible and physical, and you must learn both if you want to run well. They are faster than you, they are stronger than you, and they can kill you in a split second. At the same time, they are majestic and noble. They will often try not to harm a runner who has fallen in their path; they might jump over them, or place less of their weight on the hoof that comes down on a body. I've seen, with my own eyes, their most incredible mercy; I've seen them grant life to a runner that was on the tip of their horn.

These animals are astonishingly beautiful. Their fur patterns vary widely; their massive horns are wide and curved proudly upward. The more time you spend with them, the more you understand why early peoples all over the world saw them as gods. There is nothing the Toro Bravo can do that isn't graceful.

A fall, a slip, a leap, a gallop, a turn is a sculpture in slow motion, their mountainous muscle structures constricting and stretching. The sounds of their voices—their cries, their calls—is its own symphony. All bull runners are in love with this animal.

The next layer is the local Spanish and Basque runners, tribal bands from every region of Spain. They range in style, athleticism, and experience. Some are old, wizardly masters whom any twenty-year-old can outpace, but still they manage to link with the bulls consistently, and sometimes the animals seem to slow for them. Then there are the apex runners, who still have the kick to take a bull hundreds of yards up the way, but also the craft to truly connect. And then there are the young rockets, competing desperately to break into greatness; often, like fighter pilots, they crash and burn.

Nearly all of the Spanish runners are standoffish to foreigners. You have to earn their respect and friendship. There is only one way to do this. You have to learn to run properly, and you have to run excellently. When you are running shoulder-to-shoulder with a great Spanish runner leading a Toro Bravo, in harmony not only with the animal, but with your fellow runner and with the encierro as a whole, something shifts. It is a subtle but monumental moment for every outsider who's ever experienced it, and there are only truly a handful of us. The next time you see that Spanish runner in fiesta, he will make a point to acknowledge you. He will be talking about you with the others. People are watching—millions on TV, yes, but more importantly, everyone in the encierro. And if the runners nearest the animals feel they can trust you, they will accept you as one of them. And there'll be no turning back. You will be part of this tradition forever.

Finally, there's the outer layer, the deeply committed foreign runners who have created their own legacy. This foreign tradition has its own literary history; Pulitzer Prize—winner James Michener documented this clan in his books *The Drifters* and *Iberia*. Its true father and originator is a bull runner named Matt Carney, who first came to run in the 1950s. Carney was the first American runner to penetrate the local bull-running circles and become one of them; he also deeply connected with the bulls, leading them up the streets for decades. Along the way, he became one of the greatest runners in the history of bull running, and one of the encierro's most beloved icons. Carney is the face of the lead runner in Pamplona's breathtaking encierro monument, a life-sized iron sculpture in the heart of town that features him running on the horns. There were others like Carney who followed in his footsteps: Joe Distler, Tom Gowen, Bomber, Brucey Sinclair, and Tom Turley, to name a few. Each of them crossed over the threshold and became something special in the culture. They did this in part by running in the small villages throughout Spain. There's no better place to commune with the animals, the people, and the culture than in the small pueblos. By the time of my goring, I'd gotten a taste of this in places like Cuellar and San Sebastian de los Reyes. But it was just a slim piece. I wanted more.

♉

The aftermath of my goring is a real mess. I've experienced some level of success as an author writer and bull runner, but I've never experienced this. Headlines reading "Bull Running Survival Guide Author Gets Gored" spread around the globe. Animal rights activists pour out to claim that I've gotten what I deserved. One friendly and very normal activist emails me directly. "I was so happy to hear that the bull gored you," he writes. "I hope it is very painful. I also hope you die from your wounds." My first instinct is to fight. I lash out at them. But as my anger broils, so does the infection in my leg. I gaze out my hospital room window at the stormy Pamplona sky. *If you keep fighting with these people, you're going to die. You've got to forgive them.* I take a deep breath as morphine drips down the clear tube into my arm. *I forgive you all.*

A warm rush swirls through my leg and my whole being throbs; wonderful shivers run through my neck and back. I begin to chant my Buddhist mantra for my many internet trolls, for their happiness. My karma transforms. An hour later I land an op-ed that gains syndication with the *Toronto Star, Washington Post, Chicago Tribune, LA Times, Daily Mail.* Even *Stuff* in New Zealand picks it up. It is the biggest break yet in my burgeoning writing career.

♉

Ernest Hemingway's *The Sun Also Rises* was the first novel I ever read; I was twenty years old and I read it in one sitting, sipping coffee in an empty library. The book changed my life— it made me want to become a writer and run with the bulls. Three years later I traveled to Pamplona for the first time.

I remember drunkenly sleeping on the curved stone slope at the foot of the Hemingway statue outside the bullfight arena. I lay there, fully clothed and snoring, as the sunrise peeked over the red-tiled roofs of Pamplona. Two officers walked out of the nearby police trailer. One took his billy club and smacked my foot. "*Es hora del encierro,*" he said: It's time for the bull run. The two walked off, chuckling. I took a deep breath, clutched my aching head, and got up.

You probably should know that in those days, I was a destructive monster of a person. Alcoholism fueled my furious spirals into darkness. My family hospitalized me for mental illness, and I was jailed for almost killing a man in a fistfight. But reading Hemingway and setting this goal to come to Pamplona opened a window for me—something to work toward, instead of against.

And so I ran. And the adrenaline of seeing the monstrous and majestic animals up close astonished me. I could have easily become another "been there, done that" tourist, but a few days later, I chose to watch a run from a balcony above the course. Below me an enormous black bull named Vaporoso rammed his horn into the stomach of a portly runner named Xabier Salillas, then picked him up and slammed him against a boarded-up shop. Salillas fell from the horn.

Desire to help flushed through me. I impotently gawked while Vaporoso swung his horn, puncturing Salillas in the chest, face, and thigh. His clothing hung off him in bloody ribbons. A hole gaped below his eye. As hundreds of runners tried and failed to distract Vaporoso, a stoic-faced Spanish runner in a purple-and-blue-striped shirt named Miguel Angel Perez appeared and grabbed Vaporoso's tail, halting the attack instantly. Perez then waved his newspaper in Vaporoso's sight. Vaporoso turned, and Perez sprinted in front of his blood-smeared horns, leading Vaporoso up the street and out of sight. I was in awe of Perez; he single-handedly saved Salillas's life. But I also felt guilty for not running down to the street to help him. That was the moment I knew I had to become one of them—a mozo, a real bull runner.

Deep down I saw glimpses of myself in the Spanish fighting bull—my own fury, my own destructive power. The wrathful sueltos—separated from the pack, ignoring their herding instinct, attacking everything in sight—became very precious to me. I longed to calm and direct one up the path to his herd the same way I wanted to become part of a community, to channel my negative impulses into something positive in society.

I wish I could say that I cleaned up my act right then, but I was still drinking, and at times my anger got the best of me. In winter 2008, back in Chicago, I smashed a nearly full beer bottle over an off-duty cop's head in the midst of a bar brawl. As he wiped away the copious blood avalanching off his forehead, he raised his gun toward me. I peered into the vast blackness of the barrel, then leapt forward and crashed a left hook into his temple. Blood sprayed out like a geyser and spattered my face, but that image of the gun barrel stayed with me.

In 2010 in Pamplona, I encountered a monstrous black suelto named Tramposo peering into his reflection in a dark glass storefront window. I approached him and waved my rolled newspaper in his line of sight. Tramposo's eye flicked with the motion. He snorted and inhaled deeply. An angry bellow rumbled in his massive lungs. His hooves scraped the damp cobblestones as he charged hard toward me. I sprinted up the street. The rest of the red-and-white-clad runners gave ground like a thick school of fish evading a predator. The beast linked with me, a harmonious connection. As I jogged up the street close to Tramposo's sharp horns, suddenly Miguel Angel Perez dashed up beside me. We led the bull together.

After that run I met my friends nearby at Bar Txoko, and one placed an ice-cold beer in my hand. I grimaced as the desire to drink clutched me. I closed my eyes, and the endless blackness of that cop's gun barrel flashed point-blank before me. I handed back the beer. "No, thanks."

Once I finally stopped drinking, the medication I took for bipolar disorder started to work better. I focused my energies into the spirituality of the bull run and, when I got home, into my writing. I began to climb the publication ladder—local arts weeklies, *Chicago Tribune*, NPR. I was mastering the suelto within me and directing my career forward.

The majestic animals drew me until I was running—sometimes shoulder-to-shoulder—with some of the greatest runners ever, directly in front of the bulls leading them into the arena. Most importantly, I ran with and emulated the legendary runner Juan Pedro Lecuona, a big noble Basque runner from Pamplona who would later become a dear friend of mine, frequently visiting me in the hospital after my goring. In 2012, JuanPe showed me the heart of the tradition, and taught me one of my most valuable lessons. We'd been running the horns of the lead bull—me, and bulky JuanPe, in a blue car-racing shirt with Burger King insignia, and his trademark white pants rolled just below the knee. And all I could think was: *With the great! What fucking luck!* A few runners crowded me, and I started to trip on their feet. *Damn!* As I fell, JuanPe, in a split-second act of generosity, reached over and slung his mighty arm through my elbow, keeping me afoot. I'd been thinking of the run as an athletic competition, and when that great runner saved me, it shattered that shallow understanding; I learned that the run is a communal act of teamwork and harmony.

During the bull run on July 13, 2013, I'd encountered a catastrophic pileup blocking the tunnel—people and bulls stacked ten feet high; a tangle of arms, faces, and crying bovine. A blood-soaked horn slid across the throat of a horrified

American. That same helplessness I felt when Perez saved Salillas clutched at me again.

But then the pile broke, and the bulls trampled through. I saw others helping pull the people out of the pile, and dove in to assist. At the bottom of the pile lay five unconscious men. Their mouths gaped, but their crushed chests wouldn't inflate; their heads swelled as if they'd been beaten with baseball bats. I grabbed the worst off, a thin nineteen-year-old boy named Jon Jeronimo Mendoza, and dragged him away. His face was bluish-purple. A group of us picked him up and carried him toward the surgery room in the arena. I gripped his arm and shoulder. There was no pulse in the arm. This negative charge radiated from his limp body, sending sparks of energy out into my hands. Our feet dashed through the white sand of the arena. Suddenly, this hot plasma surged up into his arm and shoulder where I held him; then it disappeared, like the life inside him was running scared, trying to escape. We got him into the surgery room, and they saved his life. The doctors later said he only had a few seconds left before it would have been too late.

♉

I think of that terrible pileup often after my goring, while I walk with the aid of a cane for two months, slowly rebuilding the deep holes in the muscle fiber in my thigh.

And as the first bull run approaches the next summer, dreams of my death haunt me: a dark street; a black bull's horn punctures my chest; I dance along the horns as he rips the life from me. Anytime I think of the coming run, these deep, irreparable wounds from my dreams pulse in my chest and I envision three zigzag lacerations gouged through my heart and lungs. My dead friend Will comes to visit me in a dream. He'd been murdered years ago. He was the love of my sister's life, and the father of my niece. He was family. "Man, Bill," he says. "Being dead sucks. It makes you watch the ones you love through a window, but you can't touch them. You can't help them when they need you. You don't want to die, Bill."

As I sit with my wife Enid at the airport, I realize this could be the last time I hold her in my arms. I squeeze her tight and weep like a baby as I tell her I love her. As I wait in line for the metal detector, I look back at her across the corridor and see our future children gathered around her, wondering why Daddy is going away. I want to drop my heavy bags and run to her, hold her tight and start a new life without the bulls. I sigh. *I gotta see this through.*

July 7th of 2015, I step back onto the course. It surprises me there is no fear, just peace and happiness. But when the run begins, claustrophobia clutches me. As the bulls approach, a runner yells, grabs my shirt, and tugs me. I dart quickly to the side and fall into the oak barricades. The herd rumbles past. *That was total crap. That ain't running in the tradition. You know how to do this.* The only way to truly run with the bulls is to run the exact center of the street and let the bulls find you, then lead them as far as you can.

My runs in the next days descend into cowardly panic attacks. My body is healed, but the fractures in my mind and spirit gape and grow. I want to run, but I'm just incapable.

The night before the seventh run, my friend Dennis Clancy, who is running fantastically, offers some advice. "Don't beat yourself up about it. Just know that if it doesn't happen tomorrow or the next day, it doesn't matter. What matters is that it will happen, whether it's tomorrow or next year."

In the morning I'm scared as I warm up in a dark hallway that leads to the bull-run course. The familiar wounds form in my chest. I look down into the cavernous holes pierced through me by the bull's horn—squirming black holes stretching to my undulating heart. *Why are you doing this?* I close my eyes as the runners sift past, letting me know it's time to enter the street. *Am I afraid to quit? Am I too weak to face that? Fine, I fucking quit, then.* I open the door and step out onto the brisk street. *But I'm gonna run this one last time.* Nervously, I bounce on my toes and think about the bulls waiting in corrals at the edge of town. *Please show me the way…*

I jog in the center of the road as the bulls approach. The claustrophobic pressure closes in around me. A runner grabs my arm and yanks me downward, trying to keep himself from falling. I breathe steadily and look down at my feet pounding the damp cobblestones, and then he lets go and vanishes. The path opens to me. I'm alone. I sprint into the emptiness. The lead animal swoops up smoothly behind me; I can tell by the screams from frightened runners near me, trying to get out of his way; I can feel the gravity of his focus on my back. I glide like the bull does, with urgent, long strides. He links with me. We are one, and I am at peace as I lead him up the way. Then I look back and see him still there, his furry head down, following my stride. I lift my paper to him as he gallops steadily. Then he passes me slowly along my side. His majestic, jet-black shoulders contort. His hooves clap the zigzag bricks in the exact spot where Brevito nearly took my life a year ago. His mighty coral-colored horns bob peacefully near my shoulder. His dark eye acknowledges me as he finds his own way along the cobblestone path and disappears into the arena.

☓

The run I'd decided would be my last is, strangely, the first in a new phase of my bull-running. The next morning I run again, with the bulls from the Miura ranch, and something horrible happens to my friend Aitor.

If my big bulky fortysomething-year-old friend JuanPe is the iconic Pamplona bull runner, then Aitor Aristregui is the heir apparent. In fact, Aitor is like a carbon copy of JuanPe in his youth. Being his generous self, JuanPe has taken Aitor under his wing and shown him how to run well. Tall, thin, and athletic, with a floppy hairdo, Aitor is a guy in his mid-twenties filled with talent, skill, and an untamable passion for his culture. (When he's not running with the bulls, he's also a champion rally car driver.) Everything about the way Aitor runs bulls screams that he is willing to give it his all, and to go out in a blaze of glory.

On that final morning, the Miura bulls surprise everyone. All of them run like lightning. Still somehow young Aitor leads four huge Miura bulls that are on the way to setting the speed record in Pamplona. They thunder up onto us suddenly as I run Telefonica. I glance back as the tall bulls barrel into view. The runner in front of me jogs slowly. *Fuck, they're here!* I smash into his back and we fall. Aitor leads the four bulls down the center of the street. A runner next to him crowds Aitor. A horn hits Aitor's shoulder. He trips and falls. The lead bull tramples him; his hooves dig into Aitor's back.

The bulls ramble past. *Fuck, they were fast!* A childlike voice screams a few feet away. I glance and see Aitor crumpled, lying on his face. *Aitor! Shit, there might be more bulls!* I rush over. He screams in pain and angrily yells at several of us. We pick him up and hand him through the barricades to the medics. *Fuck, I hope he's OK.*

Later I go to visit Aitor in the hospital. He'd visited me a few times after my goring, and it is a great honor to repay the favor. Still, I'm worried. I've been thinking of him as the future of the tradition, the new emerging great. But it turns out the tremendous weight of the animal has broken Aitor's rib, mangled his shoulder, and fractured his spine.

Aitor's parents are there; I meet them, and give him a copy of my memoir with a message of love and encouragement scribed in Spanish. I even donate a fifty-euro bill to his rally car. He and his parents thank me, and I leave wishing him the best in his recovery.

♉

Soon I am back to my normal life, working construction as a grunt laborer in a deep shaft in Chicago.

Construction work is dangerous, just like the encierro. So many ways to die in the hole. I live in the grueling toil, but sporadically I break out of the hole. My memoir *Mozos: A Decade Running With the Bulls of Spain* has just come out; it's sold through its first-run during release week. I appear on TV and radio shows while promoting it; I make it onto the cover of the *Chicago Reader*, and the cover of the Arts section of the *Chicago Sun-Times* with my friend Irvine Welsh. Then an essay

I wrote about returning to run after being gored appears on the cover of the *Chicago Tribune RedEye*, a free daily with a half-million circulation.

I bring a copy of the *RedEye* down into the tunnel with me that morning to read. There's a picture on the cover of me running with the bulls; I hold it up and look up into the blue circle of sky high above as the human filth slides down the wooden shaft walls. A seagull sails high above, a white streak against the powder blue. Then it disappears. I look deeper into the hole below as the men work.

Bottom line is, even though all them dreams came true, you're still a loser as a writer. What'd you make, a few thousand bucks? Can't live on that, Bill. You still gotta crawl around sewers to make ends meet. You're in your mid-thirties, man. If it was gonna happen, it woulda already happened. I squint at the pain of that thought as my coworker Martene hands me up some soggy lagging. I pull it up and slam it on the concrete slab I stand on. *That's not true, Irvine didn't blow up 'till this age. You've got time. So many writers would kill to be where you are in your career. Two books out, an award, big buzz, a bunch of big outlets on your resume. You know you ain't done enough, but what can you do now? Quit? You gotta keep chasing it. Otherwise life ain't worth living.*

I sigh and grab another slimy piece of lagging out of Martene's hands.

Chapter 2

Decisions

I've known a lot of sueltos over the years. But the one that fascinates me the most I only saw briefly in Cuellar my first year there. He escaped the horsemen in the pine forest. He galloped out into the Spanish countryside free for over a week before a farmer shot him dead. I've often wondered what that experience was like for the bull, the incredible freedom combined with the fear of the unknown, and the loneliness he must have felt walking under the stars at night finally seeing what life was like beyond the confines of his ranch and home. For a time he was the truest suelto of all. He'd cut ties with the rules, and escaped into a world of his own creating. He braved everything for his freedom, to live an adventure for those nine sweet days. In a bull's short life, that might as well have been a whole summer.

♉

The urge to run the pueblos still consumes me. I feel like I am running out of time.

In September of 2015 my wife, Enid, confesses she wants to join Peace Corps. She'd mentioned this to me once, years before, and I'd just looked at her as if she was asking me for a divorce. I'd asked her, "Two years? What the hell are you talking about?"

But this time I bite my tongue. I look into her big brown eyes and say "OK."

I step out onto the back porch of our apartment in Little Village in Chicago, sit on a little wooden bench, and spark a cigar. The smoke sifts up in the enclosed porch as the orange alley light bleeds through the back windows. I sigh, lean forward, and put my elbows on my knees. My head hangs down. *Maybe she doesn't love you. Maybe she does want a divorce. Maybe this is her way of leaving you.* I take a deep pull on the cigar and let the smoke sift up in front of my face in this morphing cloud. *What would your life be without her? Alone in your mid-thirties, no kids, no home, no real viable career as a writer. You wouldn't be the hottest commodity. What, go on Tinder? Probably a bunch of weirdos and fakes on there.* Visions of the times I was convinced she was cheating on me flash through my mind. Was it real? Was it just my paranoid insecurities? My bipolar delusions? *Could you really have spent all these years with a woman who doesn't love you? Does she love you, Bill?* I sigh and close my eyes. My heart aches. *Of course she does. You guys have been through so much together. You'd be dead if it wasn't for her love. You never would have gotten this far. She always believed in you.* I sit up straight and look out the porch window to the hazy orange-lit alley. *My God, she let you go back to Spain after a bull nearly killed you. She stood beside you.* I take a puff and blow out a string of smoke. *You have to let her...* I shrug.

You gotta do everything in my power to encourage her to go. This could be the greatest couple years of her life.

Taking a deep breath, I go back in our apartment. She's on the couch with Puggles, our adorable and fat little brown puggle. I sit down and ask her, "Is this your life's dream?"

"Yes, it's the dream of my whole life to volunteer, and help people in poor countries."

"Then do it. We'll make it work."

We hug and squeeze Puggles, and I worry how she will fit into this adventure.

♉

Enid begins the process to join Peace Corps. I help her through everything, including a yellow fever vaccine shortage. Enid tries for two weeks before she finally gives up on finding a shot. The Peace Corps prepares to withdraw her from the program.

I get on the phone and find a hospital that has few yellow fever shots left. We rush over. The skies are dark, and after we park, they suddenly open up. Monstrous globs of hail pelt us. We run into the hospital, and a misinformed nurse tells us they just ran out of shots. I argue with her until finally the doctor comes in and administers the last shot they have stockpiled. We laugh at our luck. I know it's just the karma, forcing us to suffer for what we truly desire.

At one dark point in the process, some Peace Corps-related dental work inflicts Enid with mysterious and unbearable pain for weeks on end. We lie in bed on a Sunday morning and Enid asks me, "Are you going to divorce me if I go through with this?"

Laughter rattles in my chest. I turn and look her in the eyes as the morning light peeks through our bedroom window. "No. I think I'll divorce you if you *don't* go through with this."

Stepping into the kitchen, I pour some coffee from the machine. I mean it too. I don't know if I want to be with someone who is too afraid to follow their dreams, no matter how scary, dangerous, or painful they might be. Entering my writing room, I see the dozens of photos of the running of the bulls covering the entire wall. I sit down and open my laptop. Like all of my adventures in Spain, I know this Peace Corps adventure is something that will bring her deep, joyful memories that will last her whole life. I can't imagine how miserable and empty my life would be without Spain and the run. Our life in Chicago is really only a collection of things: a car, an apartment, and a few items. *Puggles is the only being you'll really miss.* When you let objects and comfort hold you somewhere, you become a slave to them.

Puggles pushes my door open and checks on me, sniffing the air. Then she disappears. *Sorry, Puggles, but we want freedom. We want to live. And luckily my parents and sister and nieces and nephews love you, Puggles, so you won't suffer too much. You'll probably eat way more treats than any dog should.*

I click on my keyboard. Alright, a plan. Save up an incredible amount of money. Head to wherever Third World Latin American country Enid ends up deployed to. Rent a place, and write. I figure I can probably write and complete two books in two years. I close my laptop. My mind races.

I take Puggles for a walk to the nearby La Villita park. We walk up the hill into the park that sits about twenty feet above street level. What does this new plan mean for Spain? Well, Planeta Books, the biggest publisher in Spain, just bought the Spanish rights to my bull memoir. They're translating it, and it should come out this summer. I look across the soccer fields to the enormous Cook County Jail facility; tall fences topped with razor wire surround the big dark red structures. *With Enid in Peace Corps, you can go to Spain and tour your book the whole summer. You could run every run possible for three months! You could probably run a hundred runs in a summer.* I walk swiftly with Puggles happily sniffing the air. *You've run ninety-nine runs so far. You can do a hundred and one. More than double your experience.* Puggles trots beside me with a big slobbery grin on her flat snout. "The media loves outlandish numbers, right Puggles?" She looks up at me, and her big brown eyes tell me she agrees.

I figure the media will get into this. It'll be a great way to promote the tradition. To show them it's more than a one-time, one-day event in Pamplona. I bend down and unhook the leash from Puggles's collar, and she shoots off in a gallop through the small trees at the far end of the park. Meanwhile the inmates play basketball in the gym that sits on second floor in the middle of the building that faces out to the park—shouting and dashing behind the chain link fence. The park and prison feel like a metaphor for my life. *You could continue in the imprisonment of society, or you could escape it altogether, and run wild.*

Puggles finds a pile of goose crap and stoops over it, eating. "Puggles!" I shout angrily, and run after her. She'll get sick again if she eats goose poop.

♉

The *Chicago Tribune RedEye* agrees to let me cover my adventure for them with a series of articles. But I know I need to make serious progress on my ability to speak Spanish. So I hire a tutor named Fernando Martin, who I'd met while taking his class at Instituto Cervantes in Chicago. I book two classes a week with him, and he keeps me on a strict and intense regimen.

Digging in, I work every chance I have. I save every penny from construction, and on the weekends I drive Uber and sell copies of my books to my Uber customers.

Enid leaves that February, and it gets harder being alone. I'm working around the clock with Uber, and it's tough for Puggles. So I start leaving her with my parents. I work every single day and do everything I can, and sure enough I hit my goal for savings.

Evel Knievel attempted more than seventy-five ramp-to-ramp motorcycle jumps over the course of his career—breaking every bone in his body in the process. Jon Krakauer summited Everest, narrowly surviving one of the worst storms in climbing history, and then writing about it for *Outside* magazine. Jane Goodall lived with chimpanzees in Gombe Stream National Park for so long that one troop accepted her into their society. And now I'm planning to immerse myself in Spain and the Basque country, to explore as many of the pueblos as I can in the eighty-four days from June 29 through September 20. I want to experience each town, animal, and event as deeply as possible, and with luck run 101 runs—running just inches in front of the bull horns whenever possible, in the hopes of deepening the world's understanding of this ancient culture, with its roots in the origins of mankind.

I'm also hoping to rediscover my deep passion for the run. Despite the good run in 2015, it's something I've lost touch with since my goring. Assuming Enid and I start having kids, my life is going to drastically change in the next few years. This might be one of the last great adventures that I can experience with pure abandon.

I leave for Spain in June. I'm planning to not come back to Chicago for at least a year. Or, who knows? Maybe never.

Chapter 3

La Visitacion

I roll into Pamplona the evening of June 29' 2016, park my rental car, and hurry like a hungry bull toward the *pintxo* bar to meet JuanPe. *Shit, it took a lot longer to get here than you thought!* I round the corner and see my big strong Navarrese friend standing at a table with a couple of people. He's wearing a blue Nike track suit; he has short-cropped hair and a clean-shaven face, and he grins as I walk up.

"JuanPe!" I barrel up to him and give him a big hug as he chuckles.

"Bill! Welcome. You are home!" His voice is warm.

"Ha gracias!"

"Meet Stephie." JuanPe raises his hand to the tall, blue-eyed blonde next to him.

"Hi! How are you?" Stephie says in an excited Canadian accent, her face glowing in a big grin.

"Nice to meet you," I say. We hug, and she gives me a kiss on either cheek. *Jeez, she looks like Vanna White.*

"And this is Alfonso." JuanPe motions to a meek but intelligent-looking guy with black spikey hair and a mischievous smile. We shake hands.

"The famous Bill Hillmann." He grins. "Nice to finally meet you. I thought you'd be a giant from the way JuanPe talks about you."

I giggle. "Thanks! Sorry for disappointing you. I do that a lot."

"Let's get a *pintxo*," Stephanie says as she motions us inside. The Basque call tapas *pintxos*, and they do a terrific job with them. A wide colorful variety of several dozen *pintxos* sit stacked up on display racks atop the bar. I pick a nice hunk of bread with some orange caviar and an anchovy on top, and a toothpick holding it all together. As we eat, they explain that they have formed a business together called Heart of Pamplona. Stephanie rents out several luxury apartments she owns throughout the old section of town, and JuanPe and Alfonso do tours with her clients. They've decided to team up and handle my book release event and the publicity to follow, and hopefully get some attention for their business in the process. My official book release has been scheduled for the events room at Corte Ingles in Pamplona. Planeta decided to change the title of my memoir to *Corriendo con Hemingway*, and I was fine with that.

JuanPe grins at me with a sparkle in his eye.

"I have a surprise for you, Bill."

"What is it?!"

"Guess who will be speaking at your book event?"

"Jeez, JuanPe, just having you be part is honor enough. Who?!"

"Javier Solano!"

A shudder of nerves flares in my stomach. *Javier Solano? The voice of the encierro?* He's the main host of the national TV broadcast. One of the most respected and beloved people in the culture. I stammer, speechless, my eyes darting around the table.

"Bill, he has read your book."

"No!" My eyes bug out.

"Yes, and you will meet him tomorrow."

You're going to meet Javier Solano? I can't believe it. *What if he hates it!?* My mind races. *Could Javier Solano actually like something you wrote? No way, get real. He's just doing JuanPe a favor.*

"JuanPe, my friend." I grab hold of his big meaty shoulder. "Thank you."

"Bill, it is just the beginning." JuanPe raises his glass. "A toast to a great summer and a great book, and *mas importante*, great friends." We raise our glasses and clink them together.

♉

I end up staying at one of Stephanie's rental apartments near Plaza del Castillo. The next day we all meet up around noon with a *Diario de Navarra* photographer near the Hemingway statue beside the bullring.

"This is a good place for a photo shoot, isn't it?" Stephanie asks.

"Yeah!" I giggle. "During my first fiesta I had nowhere to stay, so I slept on the stone here at Hemingway's feet." I lie down on it as we wait. "It's actually really comfortable."

Stephanie grins and fields a call on her cell phone. *Man, you were just a dreamer back then, a crazy kid who wanted to be a writer. Well, something's come of it anyways.* The white-bearded photographer shows up on a big motorcycle. He tells me to climb up on the Hemingway statue. I stand on a little stone shelf above my sloped bed. The *Diario de Navarra* photographer tells me to lean into Hemingway's chest. *Guess you've come a long way, Bill.* The sun filters through the leaves of the tree branches above, and a little break in the shade splatters light onto both our faces as the cameraman snaps a few shots.

I climb down and thank the photographer and he pulls away on his motorcycle. *Well, it's probably a little story, one small photo, but it's nice to get some attention for the book.* Stephanie is back on the phone, this time with the journalist set to interview me.

I lie back down on my sloped bed and look up at Hemingway floating above. *Hmph, you and me, we've gotten twisted up over the years. I know your grandson John and your great-grandson Michael. They're terrific people, and good friends.* I giggle, remembering my goring. *You had a view of my goring, you know, it was right over there.* I point to the spot in Telefonica just a few dozen yards away. Suddenly I am looking in that deep wound, listening to the blood trickle down my leg and filling my shoe, wondering if this was how I'd die. *Michael Hemingway came out of nowhere. He's not a big burly Hemingway like you, he's kind of a skinny awkward teenage kid. He is a good photographer, and he was shooting right there. He looked at the wound and almost puked. Then he squealed in a high-pitched voice, "My god, Bill! You've been gored!"* I giggle. *I'll never forget it, Papa.*

Michael was a Hemingway, and he'd still had some of that old real stuff in him. He rushed to me, knelt down, and held my hand. I asked him to translate with my medic, a big bald-headed guy named Jesus. He asked Jesus if it was the artery, and if I was going to die. Jesus reached into the gaping wound and felt the artery with his finger. He told Michael, and Michael told me. "No, Bill, the artery is intact. You're going to live."

Sometimes you have to wonder. I close my eyes, lying atop my old bed. *All the things that had to happen to make that single moment. It's ludicrous. If you wrote that scene in one of your novels, Gertrude Stein would have screamed it was too unbelievable. But that's San Fermin. Its magic has no use for believability. It brings us crashing together, whether we like it or not. Ain't that right, Papa?*

The reporter shows up, and we walk to a nearby bar and sit down for a talk that Stephanie translates. By the end, the reporter, Nacho, grins excitedly, thanking me eagerly for the interview. He shakes my hand firmly and rushes off to write the article.

♉

We head over to the event at Corte Ingles.

My book follows my decade-long journey running, developing into a real runner, and finally coming to the conclusion that my destiny wasn't to become one of the great and true bull runners, but to be a witness to them, and to tell their story to as much of the world as I can. Needless to say, I'm anxious about whether I've done a good job.

Nerves course through me as the room fills. *This is your first time public-speaking in Spanish. Chill, you got it all written out right here.* I look at my paper with my written and rehearsed presentation. *But you gotta pronounce it properly, or they won't get any of the frickin' jokes.*

As the start of the event draws near, Javier Solano shows up: tall, regal, and thin, with a white beard and mustache. *Holy shit, he's really here!* He slowly works his way across the room toward me. *Javier Solano. The voice of the running of the bulls.* He looks at me and grins. He ran really well in his youth, so he sees deeply into the heart and soul of the tradition, and speaks like a father to all the younger runners. I look at him bashfully. *My god, I have so much respect for you, and you read my book! Oh shit, what if you didn't like it?*

Javier Solano shakes my hand.

"I enjoyed your book very much," he says.

I recoil. *Holy shit!* Shock courses through me.

"But there is something, though, that I have to tell you," he says.

OK, here it comes, Solano putting me in my place. It's fine, I'm ready for it. He looks me in the eyes with a stone-cold seriousness and leans in, peering down at me with his paternal brown eyes. "You have to know that you are one of them."

I freeze in that moment, dizzy with shock. Tears well up in my eyes. *Really? Me? The goofy construction worker from Chicago that got gored?!* I look away and shake my head no. No. I sigh and look back at him humbly.

"Thank you, Javier."

He pats me on the back and walks off to say hi to JuanPe. *Jesus, did that really just happen? No, he's just being nice. OK, why would he say it if he didn't mean it? Because you're JuanPe's friend, and you have some good pictures running. Maybe that thing with Jon Jeronimo Mendoza, but anyone would have tried to help that kid. You just happened to be there. Oh man, Solano just said that to you. Holy shit. What an honor.* I sit down at the presentation table. Shivers surge up my back. It means everything and nothing, all at once. I know I am not one of the true and great bull runners. I look out into the audience filling with runners, reporters, and friends. My calling, my duty is to observe and retell the truth of the real runners to as much of the world as I can. I am a witness.

The room fills and the event starts. Javier and JuanPe say very nice things about me and the book and as the event progresses it is my turn to read my little speech. It goes over great. The audience laughs at my corny jokes, and when I get to the part about my gratitude for JuanPe, I glance over at my big strong clean-cut friend and see a few tears sparkle in his eyes. He rests his elbow on the table, covers his brow with his hand, and wipes them, as people in the crowd sigh and point. He blinks a few more tears back and giggles, embarrassed. *Wow, you even got JuanPe to tear up?! Damn, guess you're better at Spanish than you thought!* I look over at him and grin, and he grins, and I can see all the things that made us strong friends. The event concludes with a big applause.

Afterward a young pretty Pamplonica with light hazel eyes comes up to me to sign her book.

"I loved your book," she says. "I think sometimes we take for granted our own culture. I wondered why would this man from the USA be so moved by it. The book, it awakened an interest in the bulls in me. I drug my boyfriend to an exhibit on the encierro last week." She giggles. "We wouldn't have gone if it wasn't for you and this book. Thank you."

I thank her as the emotions of the moment swirl through me. *Are you dreaming?! Did a pretty and young Pamplonica just come up and thank you for writing your book, and give you credit for changing her mind about the bulls? Fucking Bill, you crazy fucker, you did it.*

Stephanie, Alfonso, Juan Pedro, and I go for a drink at a nearby bar, and I thank them.

JuanPe seems a little upset that Aitor didn't show up. "I told him to come!" JuanPe says.

"It's OK, he's a kid, he was probably out with his friends or had to work or something." I sigh. I haven't seen Aitor since he was in the hospital, after his trampling.

"He's on the cover of the book with you! You wrote very nice things about him. You honored him."

"JuanPe, it's nothing."

"It's something to me," he says angrily.

I squeeze JuanPe's big shoulder. "JuanPe, thank you so much for putting this event together, it made so many of my dreams come true."

He grins and lets it go. We finish up, and I crash out in Stephanie's apartment.

♉

The next morning, JuanPe sends me a message on Facebook. He wants to show me something, and is waiting for me across the street at a little bakery, drinking his morning coffee. I rush downstairs, and as I walk up to him, he raises that morning's *Diario de Navarra*, the biggest, most prestigious newspaper in the region. There I am leaning against Papa Hemingway's chest in a huge photo that spreads across the front cover. I burst into laughter. Is that really me and Hemingway on the fucking cover of *Diario de Navarra*?!

JuanPe hands me the paper. I take it. I shake my head and close my eyes, then open them. Fuck, that's me. *Are you fucking dreaming?* I pinch my forearm.

"You aren't dreaming, Bill. It's you," JuanPe says, and we both burst into laughter.

JuanPe buys me a coffee. It's the first chance we've had to relax and hang out without the pressure of looming interviews and events. We make little jokes and chitchat. Alfonso shows up and guffaws at the cover. JuanPe just keeps laughing and shaking his head. My Spanish has come miles since the last time I was here. Tears sparkle in his eyes again. JuanPe tells Alfonso, "I can't believe it, this is Bill, we can talk." We talk about all he's been through over the past year—how he lost two dear family members, how the factory he'd worked for for twenty years, had closed. I pat him on the back. Our friendship's always been strained by the language, so it's nice to simply talk with my friend.

We go up to Stephanie's rental apartment for another interview, this time with Navarra.com, a high-traffic website for the region. As we wait on the interviewers, JuanPe decides to show off his flexibility. He swings his leg up and taps a chandelier with the toe of his shoe. "Fucking JuanPe!" I chuckle. "You're one flexible motherfucker!" JuanPe grins proudly. It is impressive for a fortysomething guy. I guess you can't lead bulls two hundred yards up the street for twenty-five years and not be an incredible athlete.

Alfonso stands up excitedly. "I can do it too!" he says, and swings his leg up. It comes a foot short of the chandelier, and we hear the ripping of fabric: he's torn the crotch of his pants.

"Haha Alfonso! Stick to the cultural research, buddy!" We all double over in laughter, and I loan him a pair of shorts.

The interview goes great, and I feel awesome as I say goodbye to my friends and head toward my rental car. I walk down the winding cobblestone streets of Pamplona with the epic balconies looming above and the bright afternoon sun pouring down on me. *You gotta get out of town. This shit is too crazy. Fucking, like, four of your lifetime dreams came true in twenty-four hours. It's like your success is driving you forward, but all you want is to escape like a suelto.* I switch gears in my mind; I'm thirsty for a run. *A hundred and one bull runs in one summer, baby. You got this. But you gotta get going now or you'll never get close!*

I wish I had someone back home to talk to about all the incredible things that just happened. *It's OK, you can call Enid later. She won't give a fuck, though. She hates this shit.* My brush with death in 2014 really took a toll on our marriage. We even split for a few weeks. She already didn't like the run, but now she hates it so much that I can't even talk about it in her presence without her tearing up or getting furious.

I hang my head as I walk through the cool shaded street on the way to my rental car. *It's hard, because the run is something so dear to you.* I rub my achy chest. *It's one of the things that make you special. You've got a lot to be proud of: everything you've been through, this deep connection you have with this culture. You're absolutely in love with this world. Fucking Javier Solano knows who you are, for Christ's sake!* I pass two old ladies carrying their groceries. *It's the reason the biggest news outlets in the world want to talk with you. And you can't share it with the woman you love.* My throat aches with emotion. *She wants nothing more than for you to quit. Maybe one day. For her.* Resentment rises. *She's so damn angry about it, though! So miserable about this thing you love. Maybe she isn't the one for you.* I step into a sliver of deep warm sunlight peeking through the curved streets. *Stop it Bill, you love her more than this. You just gotta be patient.*

♉

I jump into the rental car with the thrill of the adventure pulsing in my shoulders. My main target on this short voyage is the fiesta of La Visitacion in Fuentesaúco. I plug it into Google Maps on my phone, and head out.

As I drive, I comb through my research in my head. Fuentesaúco is near the border with Portugal, in Castilla y Leon. I scratch my head. *What do they do there? Oh yeah, farming. Cereals and chickpeas. The famous Garbanzo of Fuentesaúco. And hogs and dairy cattle, of course.*

I soar along the highway with the sun baking the fields around me. This bull run in Fuentesaúco is apparently different from any of the others I've visited or even heard of in Spain; I try to imagine it from the videos I've seen on YouTube. It begins with what they call an *espantes.* The Saúcanos congregate at the edge of town in the morning. Horsemen guide the bulls and steers in big circles around the enormous Reguera meadow, which is fenced in. The horsemen try to guide the herd through a passageway into town. The young Saúcanos—brave and a little crazy—stand in the way, and try to scare the bulls back into the meadow. This can go on for hours, but eventually the herd breaks through and into the streets where the bull run starts. The origins of this tradition are pretty blurry, but it was first documented around four hundred years ago.

Fuentesaúco is around four hours away, though, so I've put together a list of bull runs I can hit on the way there. First up is Lardero in La Rioja, just barely outside of Navarra. It's a fast-growing town of ten thousand people, and they have a run scheduled for the afternoon.

I take a wrong exit, and Google Maps starts recalculating. I speed to make it on time, racing into town like a frantic lunatic. I see some red barricades, park hastily in a lot, hop out, run to the barricades, and climb in.

Luckily they're running late. As the organizers prepare to open the big red metal corrals, the streets fill with young men. There are big wooden obstacles, a staircase to nowhere, and a waist-high square platform. I'm standing near a teenaged greaser with slicked-back blond hair and wild green eyes.

The corral gates swing open and a *vaquilla* pours out, her hooves scraping the cobbles. Then she shoots straight at the greaser and I. We dash with her hooking for us, and bail to the barricades as the *recortadores* career in splendid loops around her. Then the greaser and I lead her to the section with the platform; we hook a hard turn behind it that she can't follow with her four legs. We high-five, panting, as other *recortadores* circle her and the crowd roars like football fans. The greaser's balding hippie-looking father calls to him from the barricades to be careful, and the greaser gives him a dismissive wave and grins at me. Then we're off again blazing, with her following us into the far section. Then some steers bring her back into the corrals. Then they release a bull, and he is after us, and we are diving behind the staircase laughing like maniacs while hippie-dad pleads from the barricades. *Sorry Pops, there's nothing that can stop your boy now!* We are deep in the joy and rush of bulls chasing men—the scent of dung, the scrape of hoof on stone, the screams and cheers, the rasp of breath in their massive lungs, the stabbing of their horns into the air near our backs.

After the fifth animal I pull out my phone and check the time. *Damn, you gotta hit the road or you won't make Fuentesaúco in time!* I step to my young greaser friend and reach out my hand. He grins his mad grin and I know he's sick like me, sick in the best way possible. He grips my hand and I tell him, "It was fun."

He shrugs, not understanding how I could leave this magic afternoon. I nod, knowing he'd come with me if he knew. I bail through the barricades as his father yells out again from the barricades, trying to bring a bit of sanity to his kid. *It'll never work, old man! That boy is one of us.*

The urge to stay pulls at me as I jump in the car and shoot out of the lot. I get back on the highway and tear off toward Portugal. *How should you tally those runs you just did for your count? Your snobby little British and American critics are going to cry foul if you count each time you ran the horns. But hey, it was extremely fucking dangerous! You were just a few feet in front of their horns! And there were some long runs!*

"330 Kilometers to Fuentesaúco Zamora..." my phone announces.

They weren't encierros technically, but the bulls and vaca would tear off on hundred-yard gallops, and you were running in front their horns for strong stretches. A lot of bull runners and ninety-nine percent of your biggest critics run their whole lives and never run in front of a bull or vaca like you just did. Ah fuck it, you just gotta think some more about how to count them.

And then: *Fuck!* I realize I was in such a hurry to get out of Pamplona that I never wrote the name of the town near Fuentesaúco that had the run scheduled for that night.

I drive and drive as the skies get dark, and I look up the town's name once I get closer: the place is so small that Google Maps centers the pin way out in the middle of a cornfield.

By now it feels like it's the middle of the night. I pass a cluster of houses and drive through the dark field on a narrow road, and suddenly Google Maps announces: "You have arrived at your destination!"

Fuck, this isn't it! And you've only got five minutes before the run starts! It's gotta be that town you just drove through! I pull a U-turn and fly back in to town and find the course; I follow it to a big sandy lot filled with thousands of people, and park, and scramble out of the car to join the runners.

A bulldozer brings a red metal container out of a big metal barn. The container says "Cañero." They open the container, and Cañero barrels out, big and black and furious. He thrills the crowd, careening in large circles before smashing into the metal fencing. It bends to his will as the crowd shrinks back from him. Then he tears into the streets as we sprint off before him. He inspects every nook and corner with his curious snout and jagged horns. I dash before him in one desperate moment, and bash into a fellow runner looking for an escape. We grab each other's arms and hold each other up before bailing to the fence together so the bull can pass by. Laughter bursts out between us as we walk behind Cañero, grinning at our fortune, our history as runners bound forever, even though we may never see each other again. For the next several minutes, Cañero runs up and down the course as I step out through the fence and re-enter in front of and behind him. I finally exit for good with Cañero hot on my tail. He booms into the metal fence behind me as I stare at him. I watch him sniffing for my scent. *It was fun, buddy! But I gotta go now.*

Back I go, back to the rental car. Back onto the road.

Shooting off the highway, I arrive in Fuentesaúco about a half hour before a night run is set to begin. I park and hurry through a line of festive stands selling T-shirts, toys, balloons, drinks, and snacks. I wander the hilly and twisty streets of Fuentesaúco until I come upon a square with a big stage. Electronic dance music thumps through the thousands dancing in front of it. *This is a hell of a party!* Red and blue vertical metal barricades line the wide street that cuts through the square; the surface is covered in three inches of sand, and the street curves off downhill. *What the fuck is gonna happen now?* I have no idea. Memories of all the different runs from earlier in the day flash through my mind like a discombobulated highlight reel. Solano's voice saying: *You are one of them.* JuanPe holding up the cover of *Diario de Navarra* at the coffee shop, grinning. There I am leaning on Papa Hemingway's chest, like a dream I've dreamed a thousand times.

You gotta share this fiesta! I turn on my live feed video on Facebook. "I'm here in Fuentesaúco! About to do a night run…" My eyes glow wildly, and my mind flows open into a joyful nebula of mania.

"Donde esta el encierro?" I ask the locals when it's done, and they point down the hill.

I walk down the curved street. In the distance, a gigantic Plaza de Toros seems to float in the sky. Bright arena lights hover above it and cast the exterior of the structure in darkness. A brightly lit mouth seems to gape open at the base of the structure; it's vomiting out a long hill of dirt. *My god, that's the tunnel into the arena. You've seen this in your dreams.* Déjà vu, images of my recurring dreams: an old American man guiding me through my future, and the afterlife of bull runners. My heart races as I walk toward it and up the steep hill of the *callejon*, the tunnel into the arena. In the Plaza de Toros, the klieg lights blaze white as dozens of recortadores stand waiting in the sandy arena.

"What's going to happen?" I ask a young Saúcano.

"Dos toros. Un toro primera y un otro dispues. Va en la calle." He points to the steep downhill tunnel out into the streets.

Bill, you gotta run this fucking callejon! I set up at the mouth of the *callejon* inside the arena. I'm gonna lead him right down this hill.

The first bull explodes through the door, huge and beautiful and dark. He bows his head and makes several big circles in the ring as the recortadores dodge him closely. I start down the hill that flows through the tunnel, looking back, anticipating his approach. The bull emerges into the mouth of the tunnel just up the hill. He sees me and gallops downward as I twist into a sprint. We enter the shade of a tree that blocks the streetlights. I glance back as he melds into the blackness of the shadow and disappears. I sprint as hard as I can as the street brightens and flattens out. The bull thunders after me, emerging into the electric light.

Humongous tufts of long fur sprout on his narrow face. His thick white horns aim at me like spears.

I dive between the vertical metal slits of the fence. He rumbles on and disappears up the hill into town, with the locals slipping through the fence on both sides of the street just as he reaches them.

I run a few more times before exhaustion falls on my shoulders. I'm done. I head back to the car.

The tires and the sides of the rental car reek of urine. I figure at least twenty people must have peed on it. I drive away and park out in the wheat fields, and crank back my seat, and sleep.

♉

The next morning, I get up and walk down the long sloping hill through the pretty town to the Reguera meadow, a walled-off grassy spot about the size of six football fields. Thousands of spectators line the wall; I hear several converse sternly about a bad goring that had taken place the day before. Meanwhile bulls and steers are galloping in a big slow circle all throughout the center, along with nearly a hundred horsemen. There's a ten-story metal electrical tower in the middle, and six thick cables spanning overhead. Several big trucks with trailers filled with Peña bands and spectators line the adjacent fencing near the entrance to town. *This shit is epic!* I giggle eagerly as I climb over a fence into the meadow.

A soap-colored bull called a Jabonero breaks from the pack, and several skilled and brave recortadores make turns with him near a fence on the other side of the meadow as I stand near the entryway to town. I can't get too far away from the entrance, or I'll miss the bull run.

The horsemen scoop up the Jabonero and drive the bulls toward us. The animals fan out wide. Two peppy black bulls flank the Jabonero, who is trailing them with his tongue dangling low. The steers gallop on both sides of the bulls. The dozens of horns in the pack seem to twist together like a tangle of thorns as they surge toward us with the horsemen driving them from the rear. The brave young Saúcanos hold their ground, waving and yelling; I get caught up in the swelling excitement and wave my arms as the bulls charge us angrily. *Holy fuck, they ain't stopping!* I give ground as the Saúcanos stand theirs. At twenty yards away, the eyes of the two black bulls enlarge; they let out a scared bellow and the herd folds. It peels off in a dusty swirl, back into the horsemen, back for another huge loop around the meadow. A couple middle-aged Saúcanos laugh at me and pat me on the back.

The spectators' cheers swirl all throughout the fencing. Later, the bulls run into a hilly section and surround several spectators. The black bulls chase some, while others dive for cover and many retreat to the fence. A brown bull locks onto one fat guy, who sprints around the base of a green hill. The bull dips his horns and the fat man makes a fantastic panicked *corte*, narrowly avoiding the gouging horns. I giggle as the crowd rejoices. *That's one lucky fatso!*

A creaking sound stirs behind me. I glance back as they swing open the metal gate to town. The horsemen gather the herd together and try to push through the wall of Saúcanos near me again; the Saúcanos hold their ground, with me amongst them. One skinny teenager beside me beats his fist on the chest of his white soccer jersey as the bulls turn and gallop away.

Afterward, the spectators retreat into town to watch the encierro along the streets as runners move to take positions throughout the course. I jog up about fifty yards from the gate. Houses line one side of the wide course. A long fence lines the other side, keeping the animals from a vast agricultural field. A more complex area sits further up the course, with a four-foot drop to a small square. Past that, a narrow uphill urban street climbs to the corrals.

The horsemen and herd thunder at the Saúcanos trying to block their path. The herd pierces their spirited wall and splinters the Saúcanos to the sides, and the animals enter the streets. The herd charges toward us, with the horsemen following beside and behind in a big dusty stampede.

I run with a group of brave Saúcanos. As we sprint, the pack catches up to us.

I glance back: the Jabonero is galloping deeply, mouth agape, with his slimy light purple tongue dangling below. Next to him: a tall steer with asymmetrical horns. The rest of the pack charges at their hindquarters.

After fifty or sixty yards, my lungs start burning. I hit the fence as the pack thunders past. Ahead, two black sueltos dislodge from the pack and begin to zigzag the course. *Fuck, this is gonna get interesting.* I cautiously jog behind them. One gets to the ledge near the square, leaps down into it, and lands badly. Several ladies scream from the balconies and *barreras*. He stands up. The cries of the townswomen watching agitate him. He swings his head around in angry circles as he looks up at them. *Don't like the sound of them screams, huh, buddy?*

Skirting him, I come up beside the lead suelto and run his horns with the Saúcanos. His black face bows as he stubbornly scrapes the pavement with his hooves. Sweat beads off our faces in the midday sun as we entice him to charge, only to have him spin and retreat toward his brother, who is giving similar difficulties to another twenty Saúcanos a few dozen yards down the narrow street.

As our bull makes his chaotic spin, I climb over a fence, and the angry suelto passes me. (I find out later that this is where the bad goring happened the day before, the one I'd heard the locals talking about: a bull broke this fence, and tossed an old man in the street who couldn't get away fast enough. A nineteen-year-old boy came to the old man's aid. The bull turned on the boy and gored him savagely for nearly a minute—inflicting wounds that would tragically end the young man's life; the bulls giveth and taketh in this world, and we must bow to their will.)

I climb over the fence back into the street and lure the second suelto with the young mozos. When we arrive at the corral, the fence stands closed to keep the other bull in. *You gotta get outa here, Bill, this is too fucking crazy!* My lungs burn and my legs throb, and I want to sleep in a bed for a long time.

An hour later, they release several more bulls into the street from the arena, and I run them half-heartedly. I hit the fence with a bull hooking for me in a cloud of dust. *Jesus!* I heave exhaustedly, watching as he climbs the hill like a rocket. *You ain't really slept in two days. Fuck it, you're going to Hotel San Francisco.*

I hop in the car, shoot over there, quietly check in, and sleep for a long time. I feel much better when I wake.

♉

As I drive back across the country toward Pamplona, the sandy mountains surround me and I feel nearly satisfied. There's just one more run on my list for this little trip. Novallas...

When I arrive, the town is asleep. *How the hell is there nobody in the street? No sign of a fiesta, nothing.* I drive around looking, and finally ask a woman walking with her two small children where the Plaza de Toros is.

She looks at me like I'm insane. "There isn't one."

"Is there a bull run today?"

"No, there is no fiesta here today," she says, and hurries off with her children.

Fuck, the website musta been wrong. Oh well. I go to eat at a little bar. Several old men sit at the bar drinking their afternoon away. I get online and google Novallas, and it says on the Fiestanet website that there is, in fact, a fiesta. *What'll it hurt to ask one more time?*

I look up at the old bartender. "Is there a fiesta in Novallas today?"

He scratches his stubbly chin. "Yes, there is a fiesta in Novallas."

"Today?"

"Yes, in an hour, you should go."

"But isn't this Novallas?"

The old Spanish men all turn from the bar, guffawing and shaking their heads as the bartender giggles.

"No, this is Novillas!" They all burst into a hearty laugh.

I thank them, pack up my computer, and shoot out the door, heading to Novallas like a flustered young dumb bull. I'm laughing at myself the whole damn way.

Novallas is a precious little pueblo about half an hour away, with a population of just 807. I find some grey metal barricades right away, park, run over, and climb in. The corrals look like a garage, and there are people milling around the street. *Guess you got some time to kill.*

I walk down the long curvy path, past a little park where people are gathering to watch the bulls and vaca run through the street. The midday sun cuts the street in two, shade and sun. *Sol y sombra.* I grin as I walk; the street rapidly narrows until it is nearly too narrow for a car to drive down. This town is breathtaking. I peer up at an elderly man smoking a cigar on a balcony. He converses with various others on balconies throughout the street. Flowers sprout up from planters hanging on the railings. Makeshift little wooden walls stand in front of the doorways to the homes along the path, like the passageways in a bullring. An old woman and her grandchildren set up to watch from behind one. I stroll the impossibly narrow curvy path until it ends in a small square and takes a hard right turn into an uphill shady street that empties into a small bullring with makeshift bleachers surrounding it.

As I walked back to the pretty section, a group of boys aged ten to fifteen fill the street in a worried gang. A rocket shoots off near the corrals. Doors bang open in the distance, and the hooves of a vaca crackle on the pavement. The boys' faces show everything. *Look at them.* I grin at one frantic little black-haired boy with spectacles, hyperventilating. *So brave and so afraid and then brave again, and of course they're always brave, especially while they're afraid.* The vaca gallops toward us and we scatter to the fence as I laugh at our fear. *She's just a curious young girl, with a narrow brown face and twisty horns.* The boy with glasses heaves beside me, holding the bars to the barricades, relieved he's safe.

"What, are you afraid of a little girl?" I ask him.

He shakes his head yes.

"Yo tambien!" I agree as we laugh.

After a quick breather, I ease into the street and run with the boys and the vaquilla for an hour, sprinting down the narrow street below the flowers and children and elderly couples, who are watching as if they're peering down from the heaven. The little boys run with all their hearts, their urgent eyes darting up to me as they try to keep up, as if in the years to come I will be the one observing from the balconies and even later from above.

A *peña* (a communal party group) in a garage that opens onto the course gives me a bowl of Rabo de Toro. I thank them and take a bite of the delicious, hearty stew. *I think I'm in love with you, Novallas.* I finish the bowl before dashing back out to run on a full stomach of beef.

Finally at the end of the *rese bravas* they release all the animals at once. We run up the street into the arena and the animals dash across the sand into the corrals, a furious mob of thrashing horns. And suddenly it is over. I walk around shaking as many of the young boys' hands as I can, telling them, "You are very brave!" and meaning it.

As I walk back to the car, a big grin spreads across my face. *How fucking lucky are you that you found Novillas! Wait, no. Novallas!* I hop in the rental. *Adios, Novallas!* I pull off exhausted and happy, heading home to Pamplona.

ŏ

With adrenaline still coursing through my body, I gallop back to Pamplona at full charge and do an interview with *Diario de Noticias*, a big local paper. Afterward, Stephanie invites me to her place to stay with her family for a couple nights.

Stephanie's pueblo of Mendiaroz is tiny, old, and gorgeous. It sits in the middle of hay fields, with a big stone church in the center. I arrive and find Tom Turley sitting on their back porch with a blanket over his head like monk.

Turley is one of the greatest American bull runners ever, and is beloved amongst the Basque people. I look up to him a lot. I sit on the couch across from him and listen as he tells stories about hurrying to get in line for churros after epic encierros. I just watch Turley talking. *Am I ever gonna be great like you?* An image of Turley running back in 2004 flashes in my mind. He fearlessly leads this massive black Jandilla bull around the curve and up Estafeta street, running in his green, red, and blue running sweater, his eyes darting back ferociously behind his sports goggles. Another historic run. That bull later gored Julen Madina in the tunnel and nearly killed him. *What a fucking legend you are.* Turley breaks between Spanish and English effortlessly in his self-deprecating way. *But look at his humility and kindness. He's playful like a damn little kid. Never pounding his chest or bragging. Just a humble mozo. Fuck, ain't that a trick? He'd never count runs. Maybe this whole counting runs thing is stupid. Maybe I'm hurting myself, rather than helping. Call it off kid! Haha. Too late to quit now. Maybe the core runners will forgive me for counting. Let it slide because I'm trying to bring positive attention to the encierro. I'm doing this for them too. I hope they know that.* Turley stands up to leave. I stand with him and shake his hand, and he looks me in the eyes with an older-brother smirk.

"Good luck," he says with a wink, and heads back to Pamplona.

Relaxing, I lounge on the back porch with Stephanie's teenage son Tazio, a sweet blond-haired kid with a big heart, and Kiliki, Stephanie's soon-to-be husband, a handsome burly Basque guy with soft eyes. We survey the scene. A big hill rises up behind her house, filled with golden hay. As we chat, suddenly two small bucks spook from a ravine and ramble up the golden hill with their heads swaying, looking fearfully back toward us before they're eclipsed by the crest of the slope. I think of my family, my parents and my brothers and sisters. They're all settled down, with families of their own. *Their encierros were long ago. You're the last one, the suelto of the bunch, still out here roaming the Spanish countryside, living your adventure.* I miss them. What would life be like if I'd settled down early like they did? Who would I be?

After some tossing and turning, I fall asleep alone in their extra room.

The next day a big spread comes out in *Diario de Noticias* with me posing between the horns of a stuffed bull.

I move into my hotel, a twenty-minute walk from the heart of Pamplona. I lie on my bed and journal a little, trying to tally my runs. *If you count every time you ran on the horns of an animal for more than ten yards in those three days, you'd tally about forty to fifty runs, but that's not fair, and it isn't an accurate picture of what you did.* I sigh as I scribble in my notebook. My whole pursuit in this is to explore the many different forms of the world of the bulls, and to get close and commune with the animals, and if I make the effort to get to a new town and they release an animal into the street, and I run in front of that animal closely, I will consider it a run for the sake of this endeavor. So heading into San Fermin I count twelve runs, and if I'm able to run all eight runs during San Fermin, I will have twenty by the end of fiesta and be on target to make it to my goal of 101. *That's fair right? And who really amongst the real runners cares about numbers anyways? Only the handful of egomaniacs. This quest isn't about status, or breaking some silly record. This is a pursuit of an extraordinary number to deliver to the English-speaking world, to show there is way more to the running of the bulls than meets the eye.*

Sure, the purists will argue that those reses bravas are not what the Spanish people call encierros, and they're correct. But you're not counting encierros. You're counting bull runs, and that's how you define them. The funny thing about it all is, some very knowledgeable Spanish runners will argue that even Pamplona is not a true encierro, because the animals are not released into a field and brought to town by horsemen. Those purists will argue the only true encierros are in places like Medina del Campo and Cuellar. They claim that the most famous encierro of all during San Fermin in Pamplona is not an encierro but a *translado*, a transition of the animals from one pen to another; they also argue the run in San Sebastian de los Reyes is also just a *translado*. This would be considered sacrilege to most serious runners, but these purist Spanish runners have a right to their opinion and it is not my culture to argue. The Spanish and Basque love to argue these kinds of things, and I leave it to them to define what a true encierro is. I'm counting bull runs, and I've got twelve down, and eighty-nine left.

I close my notebook and lay it on my chest. Let's roll...

Chapter 4

Pamplona

I stand naked in my hotel room, wet and warm from the shower like a newborn calf. My white and red clothes for Chupinazu, San Fermin's opening ceremony, lie out before me on my bed.

First I pull on my red boxer briefs with the black bull across the crotch. The running of the bulls in Pamplona. It's the greatest, most prestigious bull run in all of Spain—the World Series of bull running. I slip my arms through my white dress shirt. My big dark tattoo of a seagull flying through a galactic nebula spread across my chest—a symbolic manifestation of my visions as an artist. It's an image of freedom and liberation and regeneration devoted to my beloved grandfather, Da, who'd passed away of lung cancer when I was a little boy. Da suffered and joyed in manic depression and passed me the curse and blessing. I peer into my reflection in the mirror remembering him slicking his hair back in the bathroom when I just a kid. *Da, you'd have loved this fiesta, it was made for people like us. I hope you somehow visit me and see and feel all of this with me. The joy and sadness, the light and dark, life and death. I've never felt sadder or more happy than here, never felt more alive than in this fiesta. That's why Hemingway loved San Fermin, he was like us too, Da. Maybe you wouldn't have run, like Hemingway didn't, but you would have run through some of these amazing women, I'm sure.* I grin at my muscular reflection as I button the white shirt. *But I'm taken, so I won't. I'm here to run, Da.*

Eight consecutive days of morning bull runs. The best bull runners from all over Spain are here now, getting ready. Pamplona purchases the biggest bulls from the finest ranches, a different ranch for each day. I pull on my white Nike running pants; they fit snugly on my thick thighs. *The entire world media is here. The biggest outlets, preparing to photograph, write, and film it.* I take a deep breath and look at myself in the mirror, my form all wrapped in crisp white. And now comes the red: my sash *penuelo* and red gym shoes, lying there on my disheveled bed. The National Spanish encierro broadcast airs to millions. It always receives the highest ratings for its time slot. I grin as the energy of San Fermin courses through my whole body like a rocket about to shoot into the sky and burst. *The whole damn country grinds to a halt each morning to watch these magnificent bulls gallop through this gorgeous town.* I pick up my silky *penuelo*. *I've been wearing this puppy for years. Everybody thinks the running of the bulls in Pamplona is a been-there, done-that vacation. Dummies. It's not their fault, I guess.* The media outlets around the world broadcast clips from the run on July 7, the first day of runs, which is probably why most foreigners think it is a one-day, one-time-a-year event. *They have no idea.* I fold my penuelo to form a wide triangle. *I mean, it's OK if you're one of them, dear reader. It's not your fault, you don't know better.* I tie my penuelo in a slipknot around my neck. *But if there's one thing I can impress on you with this book, it's that the running of the bulls in Spain is much bigger than that. There are eight runs, one per day in Pamplona during San Fermín and there are thousands of bull runs held all across Spain each year. Nearly every single little town has some form of bull festival.* I giggle and sit down. *Even in Catalonia, where they recently banned bullfighting. But bullfighting had no cultural heritage there. Franco imposed it on them. But even in Catalonia, most towns still hold* correbous *events where they place tar balls on the horns of bulls and light them on fire then they run bulls through the streets and sometimes the bulls die from exhaustion. Didn't know that, did you, PETA? Or was that one of the things you've worked to suppress in the media in the States?* Correbous *is a centuries-old, beloved tradition in Catalonia.* I pick up my red sash and tie it around my waste so two long strands dangle down my thigh to my knee. *The media in the US does a piss-poor job presenting Spanish bull culture. They bow down to the influence of animal rights groups like PETA which, of course, went around killing thousands of puppies and kittens in their death van. But oh, no! Don't talk about that! Haha, that was murder! Pets deserve better treatment than normal animals, because human beings love them and the pets trust and love human beings as well. PETA lied to the owners of those pets, saying they were going to find them adoptive homes, when in reality they were murdering them before their death van even pulled away from the owner's house. Killing pets under false pretenses is a crime, you hypocrites! Slaughtering cattle is not.* I pull my tan cap on. *All PETA does is lie about this place.*

This mass misinformation is the main thing I've set out to battle with my writing. I want to call out the animal rights activists and media for their racist ways. *Look, Spain has a rich and complex culture of running with bulls in the streets, one that is thriving to this day. And it predates Christianity. Didn't know that, I bet!*

An image of the PETA protests in the town hall square flashes in my mind. It used to be a big parade of naked people, but it's been shrinking for years, now it's just a few dozen paid models who dress up like bulls and cover themselves in red paint. I see them lying there, playing dead on the cobblestones draped over each other. I giggle. *Everybody has the right to protest, I guess.*

(The thing is PETA and the people who support it aren't bad people. I actually agree with them on a lot of issues. I love animals: wild animals, pets, cattle. My family is full of hunters and conservationists. My father's dedicated hundreds of thousands of dollars to conserve animals in Africa because hunters, of course, are the greatest donors. They hunt through the African Professional Hunters Association. Poachers fear no one more than Professional Hunters because they are legally bound to track, capture, or kill any poachers they encounter in the wild, and the trophy hunters are obliged to help. No one is more devoted to protecting wild animals than hunters; if PETA would work with hunters, rather than peddling false narratives, the animals would benefit exponentially.

My father had a lifelong dream of killing a trophy African buffalo. I can see him now, with his white hair and mustache above his jagged jawline, grinning between his two massive buffalo mounts with their furry faces, wide noses, and curvy horns; I can see my father now, the pride glimmering in his blue eyes.

I have my own bull mount, Brevito. He's hanging on the wall in a restaurant in Cuellar, noble, black, and massive with his tall wide horns. I will see him soon.)

The town's official San Fermin brochure catches my eye, and I pick it up off my desk. Even in Pamplona during San Fermin—flooded with a million tourists from around the world—the traditions are alive and well. JuanPe will be running, and Aitor is supposed to be as well, despite the trampling he took last year; there will also be other great runners from the area like Sergio Colas, El Boti, and Dani. And fiesta isn't all about the run. Numerous other festivities are taking place throughout the day, including the parade of the giants (a series of huge hand-crafted statues which actors march and dance with through the streets), religious processions, a wood-chopping competition and tug of war in the bullring, traditional musical acts, and cultural dancers performing throughout the many squares and stages set up in town. It is impossible to attend everything, but it's good to see the real Navarrese culture is thriving within the madness of the international tourist crowd; the fiesta Hemingway visited in the 1920s is alive and well.

I put the brochure back and pick up my memoir from the table. White, silky cover with flaps. On the cover photo, just the fiery little black bull (Denunciante, which means "Whistleblower"), Aitor, and me. Aitor just ahead of me, tall and thin like a gazelle, ready to lead the bull with me. It's so perfect. I'm so glad they didn't cut Aitor out of the photo.

Let me tell you a little more about my young friend, Aitor Aristregui Oloriz.

Around twenty years ago, in a town outside of Pamplona named Huarte, a little boy named Aitor was watching the running of the bulls on TV with his family as JuanPe and Julen Madina led the animals into the arena. Aitor looked up at his grandfather and said eagerly, "That will be me one day, Grandpa! I'm going to do that!" *You were right about that, kid.*

I rub my thumb across Aitor's face on the cover as I sit on my bed. This photo, it's a special one, from 2011. But it only tells one small slice of the story. I'm leading Denunciante in the center of the street, with nineteen-year-old Aitor just ahead of me, preparing to run the bull into the arena. In the moments after the photo, I entered the tunnel with my rolled newspaper below the bull's snout; Aitor, just in front of us, twisted back and placed his newspaper across mine. That's when our paths truly crossed. But there was a lot more to Aitor's run.

About forty yards before they'd reached me in Telefonica, Aitor was leading Denunciante when a runner in front of them lost his balance. Rather than going around the standing man, Aitor leapt. His leg miraculously swung up over the man's shoulder, his crotch hit the man's shoulder, and somehow his foot swung down in front of the man and landed well on the cobblestones. Yes, you read that right: Aitor hurdled a standing man with a bull's horn a couple feet behind his back. You think you know about athleticism? You don't know nothing about athleticism until you see Aitor run bulls. (Aitor continued to lead Denunciante; the man, luckily, escaped harm.)

I slip on my original edition red, white, and black Nike Air Jordans. *Aitor's like the young Michael Jordan of bull running. Before the rings—winning slam dunk contests, taking over games in flashes of brilliance, dunking on Pistons, smoking Larry Bird and Magic Johnson, proving every game that his era is arriving!*

After the leap and just before the cover photo, Denunciante had encountered me stubbornly running the center of the street about a hundred yards from the arena. Aitor and JuanPe blew past me on either side. Denunciante's horn tip pushed into my back and slid across it, then pushed my shoulder. Denunciante then crashed into several runners near the final bend into the arena. I accelerated and established connection with Denunciante. I led him. He nudged my back with his horn. I barely maintained balance as my foot bumped his slobbery mouth on the backswing. JuanPe crashed into a falling runner and nearly fell into the barricades, and he lost connection with Denunciante. This was a hundred yards into Aitor's run, and Aitor still found a way to reestablish connection with me and the animal in the tunnel. Accomplishing that while running full sprint through the utter chaos of Telefonica is just impossible. It was then that we crossed our papers below Denunciante's snout, and became bonded as only bull runners can.

As we entered the arena I cut away, and Aitor ran straight out into the sand in front of Denunciante. The packed twenty-thousand-seat arena erupted as he cut off to the side. In that moment it was like Aitor was telling the arena, and all of the fiesta: I'm going to be a great runner! It was his first truly great run in Pamplona; all told, he'd led Denunciante for around two hundred yards. He'd doubled my run, or more! He's been on the path of greatness ever since, and we've been friends since then.

I get up and look in the mirror one last time. *Hah! My penuelo!* I take it off. *Total amateur move to get caught with your penuelo on before El Chupinazu!* I tie it around my wrist and head out toward the heart of town.

Anothe image pops into my head: Aitor screaming last year, after the Miura trampled him. I wince. *Fuck, I hope he's OK. It would be so fucking tragic if he lost a step, or couldn't run like he used to. Broken back is a serious fucking injury.* The doctors placed Aitor on bed rest for a month, and he wasn't able to return to work for several months.

I walk along the nice stone citadel. *I really hope Aitor's healed and can come back from this. What a miracle if he does. He's the best young runner in all of Spain, and he's got a great spirit. He's the future of the tradition. What would happen without him? The tradition would take a major loss. But even beyond all that, he's a great guy and friend. I just want to see him happy and healthy.*

I turn the corner. A huge four-story illustration of JuanPe running with the bulls covers the whole side of the gigantic Corte Ingles. *Hey JuanPe! Good to see ya, buddy!* I giggle. I wonder if Aitor will ever be up there like that, an iconic runner. Hopefully.

♉

The whole city clad in white seems to be drawn magnetically toward the heart of town, a massive migration that thickens the closer I get. I used to go into town hall square for Chupinazu. But fuck that, it's total chaos—a claustrophobic mosh pit of sangria, with big blow-up beach balls flying overhead. Sometimes fistfights break out in the middle of it. There's always a few drunken Aussie girls passed out and crowd-surfed to the medics lining the edges of the square. People always mistake the chaotic images of the ceremony for the tomato fight in Valencia but I hear La Tomatina is much tamer than the Chupinazu in San Fermin.

I slip into the big mob of partiers and step to the edge of Plaza del Castillo. *Man, I'm just gonna hang here.* Plaza del Castillo fills with a sea of white and red, but mostly families and locals. This is nice and relaxing. The city's set up big screens showing the live national TV broadcast. Images of the Chupinazu at town hall fill the tall screens. A big fight erupts in the town hall square between two groups of Aussies. The families near me groan and frown. The fight continues for several minutes. Big shirtless meathead Aussies bash each other as everyone else retreats. Tears drip down the face of a little girl on her father's shoulders. I sigh. Pamplona's popularity has its price.

The fight simmers down, and the joyful murmurs of Plaza del Castillo return. We all raise our red penuelos to the sky as the clock strikes twelve and the big balding mayor steps onto the balcony of the ornamental façade of town hall. Colorful flags flow in the breeze all around him. He grips the blue foam microphone, his big chest heaving under his white button-up shirt.

"Viva San Fermin! Gora San Fermin!" he bellows as the crowd echoes the "Viva! Gora!"

The mayor takes a stick with a smoldering lighter at the tip and lights the fuse of the stick rocket aimed out and up over the crowd. The flame crawls up the fuse and ignites the big rocket. It shoots way up into the air, with a smoke trail flowing behind it. I watch it pierce the sky above La Perla and pop. The whole of fiesta rejoices. Two parents kiss in front of me as their children bounce at their feet. Then they tie each other's penuelos around their necks. My heart aches. I wish Enid was here. The whole Plaza cheers; we all tie our penuelos around our necks, where we'll wear them for the rest of the festival. A mad inescapable riot of thundering joy surges through the thousands of revelers. The horns and drums of a nearby Peña marching band kick up and begin their drunken parade. I fall in with them, following them to Estafeta street. Buckets of water pour over the balconies and avalanche in a white spray down onto cheering mobs on the cobblestones. Sangria flies and bursts up all around as a group of teenagers battle, laughing and chasing each other as the Peña band's leaders wave their huge white banner overhead. I close my eyes and look up to the channel of blue sky above the balconies as the glorious crescendo erupts all around me. *It's begun!*

After the sun falls I meld into the night. Estafeta alive with revelers, their white clothes soaked pink with sangria, jumping, singing, dancing. A stupid one-euro green fedora bouncing atop a filthy skinny man's head, his eyes wide with drink and the carnal exhilaration of San Fermin as he tries and fails to kiss a pretty Australian blonde, then laughs with his head craned back and aims for another. Big-breasted women walking tall, swaying on their heels arm-in-arm as their large hair bounces, wildly triumphantly with the knowledge that everyone wants them but deep down, no one will ever truly have them. A massive drum marching band beating heavily, dancing in unison a bouncy side-to-side hop, their beat crackling over the chaos. A drunken mob dances with them low-low-low, bowing at the knees only to jump up and resume the cacophonous march: But to where? To the core of San Fermin, and they can't stop won't stop until they arrive, and when they do finally arrive they are nowhere and everywhere in an endless timeless vacuum of NOW-NOW-NOW forever and ever eternally. Viva San Fermin! Porque en San Fermin no hay nada y tienes everything in one enigmatic momento.

And a quart of beer crashes into a thousand pieces, littering the cobblestones that bulls will gallop atop in a few hours. *Better clean that up guys.* A small street sweeper eases slowly through the bedlam. *What are you doing still up, Bill? This isn't for you no more. You had enough to drink for one lifetime. You have something in the morning to do, mozo.* A breathtaking young Basque woman with porcelain brown skin walks slowly past me. Her deep olive brown eyes peer into me like they are the gates of the heavens slowly opening as she lingers. *She could be yours, Bill,* the voice of an old man whispers in my ear. *No, no...* I close my eyes and see Enid sleeping in bed. *It's time to rest. The encierro is coming.*

♉

I wake at six a.m., prepare, and head out on the street wearing my tan cap, all-white pants and shirt, my red and blue suspenders, and my penuelo. I walk the half mile from my hotel to town, shivering in the cold rainy darkness.

I arrive onto the bustling course and grab a coffee and croissant just off of Cuesta Santa Domingo. Tension flows through the packed bar. I go out and warm up on the side street. Then I enter the course, waving to friends, avoiding others. JuanPe materializes; he spreads his arms wide, his chest puffed out for a hug. He leads me into a bookshop, where I buy a paper at the table on the sidewalk next to the door. My book sits on a big display, right at the entrance. *The damn book is everywhere!*

JuanPe grins at it and pats my back as I roll my newspaper. "Don't roll it," he tells me. "This is how the Navarrese people do it." He takes it and folds many tight folds like an accordion, so when you hold one end, the rest opens like a fan. "So if you have to escape." He releases it, and the newspaper opens into a nice big falling distraction for a bull to gouge at while you cut the other way.

We are quiet in the dim light of the store. As the time nears, JuanPe and I walk down to the small opening in the wall near the beginning of the route. Workers place a one-foot-tall idol of a red-caped San Fermin inside it. We sing, petitioning the saint to protect us. "San Fermin perdimos…"

And then we are off, knifing through the crowd toward the end of the course. At town hall, thousands of tourists cram in and block the way. A small file of us follows the mayor and police as deep as we can into the mess. We wait a few tense minutes under the big clock on town hall until the police line breaks and they let us through. We walk down Mercaderes. A seven-tiered wall of photographers stand, kneel, and lie behind the barricades at La Curva, Dead Man's Corner, Hamburger Wall, where for years the bulls have slid and crashed before the long uphill straightaway of Estafeta. I lose JuanPe as we pass the great head *pastore*, Miguel Reta, whose handsome weathered face smiles as he sits atop the barricades in his green-colored *pastore* shirt, with his long willow cane sitting in his lap. He waves to us mozos as we pass him.

We head up the long canyon of Estafeta. *You beautiful beast of a street.* The marvelous ornamental balconies climbing each side of the cliffs are full of families and photographers; Basque flags and flowers hang from the railings. We walk the wet streets nervously. Another police line stops us at the first intersection, and the rowdy runners in front begin to bounce on their toes and sing "Olay…olay olay olay…olay ooolay…" The police line breaks and we advance up Estafeta. I pass the great runner David Rodriguez from Sanse, who's in his white shirt with two large bright green patches at the chest. I shake his hand; he seems nervous. I continue on and arrive at my starting spot: the place where Estafeta widens just before the buildings give way to the wide-open curved path known as Telefonica that leads down into the arena.

I shake the hands of my friends: Jose Manuel in his blue-and-white striped shirt, who I'd run the horns with many times. Then the big Basque runner in the green plaid shirt, the one who'd led a pack of bulls a hundred yards into the arena with me in 2010. (His massive hand swallows mine.) I cross the street to my friends, the Pamplona Posse: Galloway with his white beard, his orange-and-blue striped shirt and red bandana; Gary in his red and blue stripes, with his stubbly face and deep blue eyes. We shake hands and hug. Now I'm ready.

The rocket soars into the sky and bursts. The bulls are in the street now! We bounce on our toes, arching our eyes to see as far down Estafeta as possible. Panicked waves of runners shoot up and filter through our waiting bodies. One fat Irishman smashes into me and almost knocks me down. Then the rush pauses, then another rush, then a break.

As the camera flashes move toward us, I break into sprint. I run the center of the street. The thunder rises behind me as I enter the bright sunlight in Telefonica. I glance back, and as I do I drift to the side, and a small pile falls in front of me. *Fuck!* I leap, but my foot snags on a kid's back and I fall into the pile. The herd rambles past, hooves crackling; the bells swinging from the steers' necks bang and then surge past, and it is over in those few furious moments.

0 and 1, I guess… I shake off my bumps and bruises; I look around for the injured and find none, then walk up the street and squeeze into a bar so I can see the TV replay.

Pushing my way in, I arch up on my tiptoes and see Aitor on the screen; it's his first run in Pamplona since fracturing his spine, and he's leading the first bull. *YES!* His short brown hair whips around as he dashes in his long, elastic way, holding his fanned newspaper before the big black bull's snout. *No way!* My chest swells with joy and my arms tremble with adrenaline. Aitor guides the animal nearly two hundred yards, all the way into the arena. As he enters the sand, he throws his head back in elation. His narrow angular face spreads in a great smile at the heavens. *My god, he's back!*

I head over onto Estafeta and find Aitor. He stands tall in a new shirt with the image of an old man on it.

"Felicidades Aitor!"

"Gracias Bill!"

"Que es este." I point to the image of the old man.

"Es mi Abuelo," Aitor says sadly.

"Oh, I remember," I say. He'd posted about losing his grandfather on Facebook. "What a wonderful thing to do," I tell him.

"Gracias, I dedicate my runs this summer to my grandparents!" he says, and grins through the sadness.

I look at him proudly. *What a great kid.* I give him a big hug. Aitor is back, strong as ever.

"I'm sorry," Aitor says. "I wanted to go to the event for the book, but I couldn't. I was out of town working."

"I don't care, Aitor! Come on. We're gonna run some bulls this summer, brother!"

He looks at me, surprised.

"No pasa nada," I say. "I just care that you are back and healthy! Mañana mas!" We wave goodbye.

I don't know it at the time, but JuanPe right then is still mad and hurt that Aitor didn't come to the book event. It doesn't bother me at all; for me it was an epic and monstrous success. But a rift has formed between Aitor and JuanPe. It's ludicrous, because the most important part of my book was about observing the tradition being passed from one generation to the next between the two of them. They'd run together for several years, sometimes in complete sync on either horn of the same bull, and at other times JuanPe leading the first, and just feet behind him Aitor leading the next as if they were a repeated image, two historic Basque runners mirroring each other. My most treasured memories of my time in Spain are of observing them in those historic moments. And now they aren't talking. They miscommunicated in the run; they're starting to smash into each other and push each other and yell at each other. It's a catastrophe but I'm too swept up in my own problems to notice; if I did, I'd explain to JuanPe that it isn't a big deal that Aitor couldn't come, though I don't know if it would help. There's more to it, of course. JuanPe's going through a lot of changes. He's had a terrible year. Now he has to work both as a *mulillero* in the day (dragging the dead bulls out of the arena with a team of horses) and a bus driver at night. He doesn't have time to sleep, and trying to run on no sleep is dangerous. There's also this feeling that even though JuanPe's still a very great runner, maybe the torch has already been passed. It's nothing to be ashamed of; Julen Madina, the great runner of the 1980s and '90s, passed the torch to a young JuanPe twenty years ago. Julen remains a great runner to this day. But this new transition seems to have turned dark.

On the third morning, I run into Telefonica, the big wide stretch before the bullring. The herd approaches. My fellow mozos surround me on all sides. *We're tight! Too damn tight!* One runner beside me loses his footing, and several of us collapse to the cobblestones with him.

First a steer passes over me—his white furry hooves clawing at my arms. As I try to roll to the barricades, a bull's hoof crashes into the back of my head. The sound's like an L Train roaring down the tracks. I fall through my body into a dark pit, into the tunnel of sound.

I look up and see the white leg of a steer stepping on my calf. His cloven hooves rip the flesh as he strides on. I struggle back into my body and crawl toward the barricade as the rubber soles of the runners slam into my back. Several fall on me, deflating my lungs. *I can't breathe!* I bring my arms close and lift myself on my elbows and continue. They roll off me. I grab the wooden barricades and a medic pulls me under.

I heave for breath as a fellow runner speaks to me. I can only hear his voice broken and morphed, indecipherable, like the parents in the Charlie Brown movies. I sit on my backside and hold my knees as blood oozes from various places: the back of my head, my forearms, my knees, my calf. The pain takes me to a hollow and lonesome place. My gut aches. I meditate: Nam Myōhō Renge Kyō...Nam Myōhō Renge Kyō...allowing the pain to flow through me. *Tell me how bad it really is.* Then the chaos of a suelto approaches Telefonica. I stand. *You gotta get back in the street.*

I step through the barricades into a flock of young Spanish runners. They erratically cut in and push each other. Panic courses through me: an image explodes in my head of me tangling with runners and falling to the pavement as Brevito approaches, aiming his massive horns. *Fucking assholes, calm down!*

One tall young Spaniard in a long-sleeve blue jersey grabs my shirt at the chest and won't let go. I grip his wrist. The bull nears us as David Rodriguez turns him in a small loop.

An image of my thigh wound flashes through my mind, the inner thigh ballooned outward from where my whole weight hung from the horn. The hole like something exploded from within my meaty thigh, the wound running so deep there is no end. Nausea swirls in my stomach. I break the Spaniard's grip on my shirt and step out of the street. On the other side a regretful horror fills my stomach. It's the first time I've stepped off the course intentionally with bulls in the street in a very long time.

The big black suelto passes, with David Rodriguez and David Ubeda leading him. I start to step back on the street behind the bull when suddenly a second brown suelto roars around the bend, the black splintered tip of his horn slashing a foot from my stomach. I freeze with my foot on the barricade as the wind from the charging animal whips past my face. *He'd have killed you. You'd be dead if you stepped through a second earlier.* I stumble back, dizzy. *What the fuck are you doing? What the fuck are you thinking?* All the dark gravity of the earth swirls up and grabs hold of me.

My world turns grey. A lead blanket falls on my shoulders as exhaustion drags me down until I can't walk very far without having to sit down and rest. I head toward my hotel, worried about my book sales. I walk down the center of a green park like a sad and lost suelto longing for the steers and horsemen to come find me and show me the way home. The shade from the tree branches hanging over my head chills me to the point of shivers. *You'll never make the bestseller list. You'll never write for a living.* Another memoir on the bull run came out that year by a Spanish author, journalist, and runner named Chapu Apoalaza; *7 de Julio*, it's called. *Look at Chapu's book. It's on the verge of hitting the Amazon Top 100 bestseller list!* Exhaustion forces me to sit on a park bench halfway to the hotel. *Chapu's book is selling because Chapu is a real writer, and you're just some fucking crazy American who got gored. That's all you'll ever be, some news blip from the past.* I slump forward with my head in my hands. *Who were you fucking kidding with this crap?*

I lie in my hotel room the rest of the day nursing my wounds—trying to regroup. My spirit feels like it's pinned to the white bed.

♉

I soldier on. The next morning as I walk up the wet cobblestones of Estafeta street with the other runners, my eyes follow the smooth dark gutter in the center of the street. My feet step on either side of it as a small stream of black water runs down it. *I don't give a fuck if I die, I'm going to run. I'm going to fucking run, for real like in the old days.*

As the chaotic ramble of hooves and men approach, I twist into action. The bobbing horns of the lead bull appear beside me as the pack surges past. I sprint after them and two of the bulls suddenly fall as they try to make the final bend into the arena and crash into the barricades. The two bulls attempt to stand, their legs straining like they're stuck in mud. I slow and wave my paper under the snout of the brown bull as he gathers and rises. I run slowly in the center of the street as the other runners grab at my shirt. I feel the gravity of the animal behind me. *Finally.* The bull links with me. We are one. Our spirits and minds connect into this surging force both bovine and human. I dash before the bull into the tunnel. One runner with curly blond hair screams at me angrily as he yanks on my sleeve with all his might. *Motherfucker.* I lose balance, falling forward. I barely keep on my feet as I stagger through the tunnel. All the runners around me seem to squeeze the air out of my lungs. I push into the back of the runners in front of me with both hands. Several fall as the bull gallops close behind me. As I enter the light of the arena, I fall into the sand and contuse my knee as the bull gallops out into the arena. That injury (combined with the trampling from the day before) makes me limp the rest of the day.

Wandering near Bar Windsor in Plaza del Castillo, I bump into a seventy-year-old white-haired American man with an enormous drunken smile on his reddened face. His name is Tom Gowen, and he is a Pamplona institution. The Spanish, Basque, and the foreign regulars all know him; he's one of the greatest American bull runners ever.

Gowen invites me to play a game called Chino with him and a younger wealthy socialite Englishmen who used to be my friend. The game is about reading your opponents; everyone is given three coins, and you have to decide how many coins you want to keep in your hand or pocket. Then once everyone has decided, they hold the coins out in front of them in their fist, and you have to guess the number of total coins that are in all of the fists.

As we guess, Gowen tries to teach us. Someone takes my ex-friend away after a few rounds, and it's just Gowen and me. He peers at me, with his blue eyes and weathered face and deep raspy voice like John Wayne's. Then Gowen's Basque girlfriend Maria ushers Tom off for a date. Gowen grins and tells me, "We'll finish this one of these days, kid," before disappearing back into the white mob of Plaza del Castillo.

I drag my aching body through the happy faces of fiesta like a ghost meandering amongst the living. The joyful music burns in my ears. I wrestle cringes into grins as national TV crews interview me and my face appears in nearly every national news outlet in Spain. You'd think that would make me smile; instead it crushes me like a tin can, empty and useless.

"You're everywhere!" a friend tells me, and hands me a national magazine with a big spread of me and the book. "That's not a review, it's just publicity," I mutter, checking my Amazon rank on my phone, expecting it to explode. Instead it just sits there, like garbage floating in a murky pond. *You're nothing, Bill. This is all a façade. You're a fucking loser. You suck at writing, you suck at running, you work in the asshole of Chicago with people who hate you and are going to get you killed, your wife essentially left you, most people crack cruel jokes on you when they hear your story. Nobody gives a fuck about you. Why would they? You're a piece of shit.* My body trembles weakly.

I walk past a bar in Plaza del Castillo; all the TVs show my image speaking to a million people all across Spain. "I love this culture, it changed my life." My book flashes across the TV screens, the outlandish picture of me leading Denunciante, a culmination of six years of honing my craft as a runner and taking incredible risks, wrapped up in the ten years of slaving away to write it. My lungs struggle to inflate. The bright sun lights the plaza as this heavy darkness swells up around me and grips me like the jaws of a huge black beast. *It's nothing, it hasn't changed anything. You're still miserable, useless, you.*

♉

Meanwhile, Aitor continues to run incredibly.

I bump into him and his friends after the run one morning, and Aitor's spiky-haired best friend Xabi Mintegi invites me to have breakfast with them. They take me to Aitor's nearby hometown of Huarte. We stop at Aitor's house to see his parents; they have a pretty apartment with a beautiful bull mount and photos of their son running with the bulls in his magic way. His parents have just woken. His mother comes to Aitor in her pink robe and sleepily gives him a small kiss. His gregarious father greets me with a big grin and shakes my hand eagerly with his big soft hand. They remember me from my visit to the hospital the year before, and are very warm to me. I also find out they are famous local musicians.

"Teo!" Xabi says as a fat grey cat appears and jumps from one lap to the next as we sit on the couches in their living room. He plops on my lap, I pet him. His thick silky fur is incredibly soft.

"It's Bill, Teo!" Aitor tells Teo with a big grin on his face.

Teo leans up and nuzzles his soft cool nose on my cheek. I laugh.

"What a great cat!"

"Watch this!" Aitor says, getting Teo's attention with a small plastic toy.

Teo's eyes widen, and Aitor tosses it down the long hall. Teo runs after it. He gets to the toy and, concentrating very hard, takes the plastic ring in his mouth. Then he brings it back to Aitor, very slowly and thoughtfully.

"It's impossible!" I say.

"He taught a cat to retrieve!" Xabi tells me.

"This guy speaks the language of animals better than humans," I say as we giggle.

Aitor rewards Teo with a tiny piece of *jamon* and a warm pet as Teo nuzzles his head into Aitor's hands. It's more than just bravery and athleticism. He truly loves animals; he understands them, and they can feel it.

Afterward, we head to a nearby bar for breakfast. The Huarte crew consists of about ten young guys in their early to mid-twenties. They crack crude jokes on each other. Xabi leads the assault, asking the guy beside him with mock seriousness, "And when are you going to let me take your sister on a date, you asshole?" They laugh and explain Xabi's question to me, and I shake my head and wave my finger "no" at Xabi as they all burst into laughter.

But Xabi is also very heartfelt; he seems to have leadership qualities of his own within the group. I grin at them; they're all runners of varying ability levels and seriousness, but there is no doubt they all love the tradition. We all eat our eggs and ham and potatoes, and these big slices of tasty soft bread with a hard dark crust. We eat our meals quickly, but the heaviest kid at the table can't finish his plate. He has well-manicured slicked-back hair and some flashy jewelry.

"You're the fattest one and you can't finish your eggs!" I say, and the table bursts into laughter.

His jaw drops as he glares at me. I blush, trying to hold in my laughter. I'm about to apologize when Xabi laughs at him and slaps him playfully on his bulky chest, then pinches his chubby face in his hand. He scowls at everyone, his chest heaving as he tries to choke down the rest of his eggs.

Highlights of the run appear on the TV screen. The guys mockingly call Aitor a show-off, and he sheepishly grins as the footage shows him leading another set of bulls into the arena. I smile at Aitor. *Damn, I want to run like that again, and lead the bulls with Aitor but I'm just blowing it this fiesta. I just don't got it in my heart. Well, he's got it under control.* I pat Aitor on the back.

I look around the table at the young men grinning and messing with each other. These guys, they're all bonded by their love for their tradition. The fat pretty boy belts Xabi in the arm with a mean punch as Xabi recoils, laughing mischievously and gripping the impact point. *Look at them, the tradition is alive and well. Who fucking cares if you run good anymore? I mean when is enough going to be enough, Bill? When you get gored again, when you get killed?! These guys, they've got it. They're living it. It's alive and safe with them. You got this book launch taking your focus, and that's fine. Just let it go, man.*

As I go to pay, Aitor disappears and comes back, and tells me mine is paid for. I protest, then just thank him. Aitor tells me not to thank him. He takes me outside and there is his father, smiling in the morning light from the driver's seat of his fancy car. A nice watch glimmers on his wrist as he gives me a thumbs-up. I thank him, and the rest of us ride the bus back to Pamplona, grab some ice cream, and splinter off into our own paths.

After filming yet another national TV interview, I walk around the Plaza de Toros and suddenly feel compelled to write. I sit at the foot of the Hemingway statue. Suddenly Chapu Apoalaza, the guy with the other book, appears out of thin air. His long light brown hair and puffy full beard glow in the sunlight as he grins at me.

"Bill, how are you, my friend?"

"Chapu, congratulations on all your success."

We shake hands.

"And you too! I see your book everywhere!"

"You're gonna make the bestseller list," I tell him.

"Oh that, well that's not very important to me. I have money. What's important is that my book can change the conversation around the bulls in Spain for the better," he says, and pats me on the shoulder. "Suerte a mañana, mozo."

"Igualmente!"

Chapu walks off, grinning in the afternoon light. *Come on man, snap out of it!* I write in my notebook at Hemingway's feet as the masses of happy Sanferminos walk past me. *Who cares if you make a bestseller list?* The warm sunlight breaks through the swaying leaves overhead and kisses my hand as it writes. *Some authors just have it in their magic to make a list. Maybe you do, too, but even if you don't, making it this far is no small miracle, and the fact that you've made even one Pamplonica change her mind about her culture is a staggering triumph. Maybe your fading running ability isn't such a tragedy.* A jolly drunken old Basque man limps past me with his wooden cane. He squeezes a copy of *Diario de Navarra* in in his free hand. *Maybe this is your transition to your dream coming true: writing for a living. Why feel shame when you run bad? That's crazy. Just let go. The tradition is in good hands. Look at Aitor and his crew, they're taking the torch into the next decade. And you've been here to witness it, and to tell the tale.* A group of little boys follow one of their fathers toward the Plaza de Toros. They bop and giggle excitedly as I write in the notebook. *And maybe with some luck, a little boy somewhere in Pamplona is watching Aitor Aristregui lead the bulls into the arena this year, and urgently telling his grandfather, "That will be me one day, Grandpa! I'm going to do that!"*

♉

Sadly these joyful epiphanies are rare, and take tremendous effort to dig up over the rest of my San Fermin. I limp physically and spiritually through to the final day. I go down to town hall for the Pobre de Mi closing ceremony. Everyone holds candles pushed through plastic cups to catch the dripping wax. We light the candle as the year's champion Peña band climbs up on the stage in front of town hall.

The heavy lead blanket of sadness squeezes around my whole body so that I can barely stand or breathe. The band plays the Mexican folk song "El Rey," and I remember Enid playing it for me as we sat on my roof in Mexico City looking out at the flickering orange streetlights climbing the black mountains that surrounded us. *I want to be with you, Enid.* I see her joyful face and sweet thick lips. *I want to kiss you, baby.* I sigh as the song ends. I just need to lie down for a few weeks.

The new song kicks up and the crowd sways, singing "Pobre de Me, Pobre de Me, San Fermin terminó." I sing along sadly. *How are you going to last another two months in Spain? You got another eighty-one runs to do. What a stupid fucking idea. You'll never get it done.* A pretty Basque girl in a red vest sings and cries near me; the waving candlelight turns her tears in golden droplets sliding down her face. *You should just quit and go home now. Or maybe you should just fucking kill yourself.* I giggle at the massive black abyss of death lurking just out of reach around me always. *Not yet.* I look at the thousands of candles like stars floating in the heavens and I feel like the loneliest suelto of all.

☿

The day after fiesta ends, I walk down to Plaza del Castillo. I sit at Bar Windsor, sip an espresso, and try to get a grip on what I need to do next. The heavy lead blanket lies on my shoulders as I write in my journal. Depression, it takes away the hope for joy. It blinds you.

A sparrow hops on my chrome table, he glares at me angrily with his beak open. *Look, snap out of it, you pussy! You have a duty to keep going.* The sparrow hops and flies away, leaving a nasty little orange turd where he stood. *Look at how fucking lucky you are! This should be paradise for you, and here you are moping around. Just go and try! Please, at least try. And maybe the bulls will grab hold of you again and you'll run up the street linked with them like the old days. Or maybe not. But that isn't even what's important, you asshole! What's important is you continue to observe and tell the stories of this tradition that's radically transformed your life for the better, this tradition you love so fucking much.*

Tom Gowen's gravelly voice sparks up behind me. "There he is…"

"Hey Tom, how are ya?"

"I'm OK, kid. How 'bout you?"

I force a smile.

He sits down at the table beside me. "I've been keepin' an eye on you this fiesta. Seeing you struggling. Trying to get that black dog off your back."

I look into his weathered face.

He grins. "He gets me too, sometimes."

"Yeah, he's still there, man." I squeeze my traps and roll my neck.

"He's a son of a bitch."

"Yes, he is."

"The mania never bothers me. I know how to deal with that. But the black dog, he can keep me down for months."

"I just can't shake him."

"Well hey, here's my number." He writes it on my notebook. "If you need somebody to talk to, I'm here."

"Thanks, Tom."

"I live right here." He points at his door. "Red door, fourth button."

He gets up and starts across the square. I watch him go. *Wow, I didn't know Tom had bipolar disorder. Shit, what a nice thing to do.*

I check my email. Dyango wrote me, telling me to come to Cuellar. I pack up and go back to my hotel to close out.

Standing in my hotel room, I stuff my stinking clothes into my backpack. Dyango Velasco is my dear friend from Cuellar. He befriended me on Facebook and started sharing videos of his town's incredible fiesta. They release the bulls into a pack of hundreds of horsemen, then they gallop into a pine forest, then they walk and trot seven kilometers into town. And at the edge of town, they gallop down this big hillside into the streets where the runners wait to take them through the winding streets into the Plaza de Toros. I first came there in 2012, and it was greater than I'd imagined. Dyango was a great host. He's a fiery guy, built like me: strong girthy legs and compact upper body. I stuff my dirty white running pants into my bag and see his long straight black hair and excitable eyes. He's a bull sculptor working mostly in lost wax iron casting. He honored me a few years later with the Divulgation Award for my writing on Cuellar which appeared in the *Chicago Tribune* and *Outside* magazine. I keep the sculpture on my desk at home. An image flashes of us running Cuesta San Francisco, his eyes a light, waiting out the lead bull as I gave distance. He is like me in other ways too; he is very intense in his friendships, a bit of a borderline personality. People like us just feel more intensely than others, and are deeply hurt much more easily. It's a blessing and a curse. He took a bad goring in the mid-thigh a lot like mine, but the bull tossed him and flipped him and he smacked his head on the street. Just another mozo like me with a few marks to show for it. I tie up my big green bag and throw it over my shoulder. *I really miss you, Dyango. I can't wait to see you, my friend.*

Chapter 5

Navas de Oro

I buy a weak black plastic trunk to carry my box of books, load up, and walk toward the train station. I stop at a stoplight, and when the little green man starts walking I tilt the trunk with the box of books strapped in it so it can roll. The plastic creaks and threatens to break. I pause, looking back at it, and it wobbles and falls over. *Fuck, you shoulda never ordered these stupid books. Order a hundred you'll sell 'em at fiesta! Yeah, fucking right. Now you're fucking stuck with 'em.* I pick it back up and continue exhaustedly to the station in the bright afternoon sunlight as this serious darkness clings to me.

You try and tell people, "I'm depressed," and they say, "Why? Cheer up!" So you force a smile; you even believe for a few minutes that that's all you need to do, cheer up and look at the bright side! I force a fake grin at the brutal sun. *Yeah, right.* Three minutes later the hellish doom returns, stronger than ever. I stop on the walkway and lean against a little concrete wall, breathing heavily. I look off the sidewalk at the Ebro river flowing past an arched bridge; a big white swan squawks and honks in the peaceful stream.

Fucking depression...it's a tide that comes every few months. There's no stopping it, no willing it away or ignoring it. If you ignore it, like a tide, you'll sink and drown beneath it. I take a deep breath and spark a mini-cigar. *All you can do is try to float to the surface and survive it, without fucking killing yourself.* I giggle watching the bird sip at the water. Running with the bulls is nowhere near as dangerous as surviving bipolar; about one in ten of us kill ourselves, and almost half try. I pull on the cigar, load up, and trudge on.

I buy my ticket and post up at a table in the bar inside the station. A cool weathered-faced old man sips a beer at the bar, and my parched mouth aches for a sip. *No, you ain't falling off the wagon.* I sigh and close my eyes. *How long is this fucking depression gonna last this time? A week, a month, three months? Who fucking knows.* Jesus, my neck is stiff. I lean back in my chair and arch my stiff neck backward; it cracks and pops and suddenly BONG! I smash the back of my head against the metal rim of an empty keg sitting behind me. I burst into a befuddled laughter. *Man, you got some weird karma.* Then these strange buzzing sensations swirl along my neck and the back of my head. Energetic sparks pop in my mind. *Is this fucking mania? You got a lot of writing to do. Man, get going on the* Trib *piece!* Ideas for the story flick through my mind: my runs, Aitor, the conversation with Chapu. *You gotta be kidding me, are you snapping out of this? Wait, so a bull kicks you in the head, you fall into a hopeless hellish depression, now you bonk your head on a keg and suddenly you're manic?* Images of all the concussions I gave and received in boxing and college football flash through my mind. Puking over a toilet, the flickers of blind spots in my vision. Maybe this mood shit is connected. I've got a lot of bipolar on my mom's side but maybe I've got CTE a little too…I was a strong side linebacker, delivering tremendous blows on big-ass offensive linemen. Junior Seau, the violence, the suicides: suddenly they aren't just some outside tragic story line. *Could you have that? Boxers get it, too. Fuck.* I don't even want to know…

I board the train and shoot through the countryside like a young bull who doesn't know why or where, just that he needs to run away from everything. But I do know. It's a long trek out of depression, and Cuellar is the perfect medicine.

♉

Outside the Valladolid train station that night, a fancy black luxury sedan pulls into view. "Bill!" The smiling face of my dear friend Dyango Velasco emerges from the driver's-side window as he rolls to a stop. Dyango's long black hair whips around as he gets out and hugs me with his stout compact frame.

"Congratulations! The book is doing great!"

"Thanks, it's going alright, I guess."

"I can't wait to show you all the runs around Cuellar. Peñafiel, Tudela de Duero, Iscar, there is so much to show you!"

"I can't wait either Dyango! Thank you so much."

Thank god for those Spanish classes! I can actually understand most of what he's saying! He's like my damn cheerleader or something. I guess from the outside, the book does look like it's doing great. I guess it isn't that bad. Most writers would kill to have that kind of publicity for their careers. I glance over at Dyango talking eagerly as he soars through the night. I guess I just really needed a friend.

Dyango checks me into a hostel in Cuellar built under a twelfth-century cathedral. I have the whole facility to myself. An ancient white stone well sits in a big courtyard near the entrance.

"There aren't any runs right now, but I will take you to see the towns you'll run later in the summer," Dyango says as he leaves.

"Great, thanks!"

"I'll pick you up tomorrow, we'll go to the pool."

"OK."

Dyango takes me with his wife and young daughter to the Cuellar aquatic center for a relaxing day. I dive into the big pool. Beautiful grey birds swoop over the water. Their undersides glow blue in the reflection from the trembling surface. Cuellaranos leisurely swim and then relax on the lawns around the pool. *How the hell'd you end up here, completely immersed in Cuellar, your favorite little town in the world?* Dyango jumps in and we race across the pool. It's a tie; we laugh heartily as we grip the ledge and gasp for breath.

"I smoke too much for this," Dyango says.

"Me too!"

Dyango is working a lot of hours, so during the coming days I wander Cuellar. Tight, winding, and hilly streets string through the town like veins. I climb upward toward the castle. The big white castle walls spread wide with manicured lawns and a road flowing in through a big wide arched entrance. The Duke of Albuquerque's castle. I walk through the entrance; it opens into a massive courtyard surrounded by a big tall fortress wall with lookout points atop it. I pay a few euros and climb up on the wall. I read from the plaques the castle was built between the thirteenth and eighteenth centuries, and is a mixture of Gothic and Renaissance architecture. Originally it was the Duke's home, but later it became his summer home, and later the castle was largely abandoned. *What, it wasn't big enough for you, Duke?* I glance up at the heart of the castle; several spires climb into the sky. A wooden balcony stands high above the fairgrounds and gardens below. I imagine the royalty strolling the balconies in their crowns and elegant gowns. During the Spanish Civil War, Nationalist forces used the castle as a war prison, and as a hospital for prisoners suffering from tuberculosis. *A prison? Wow.* I look over the courtyard. *That's a pretty prison.* Today it functions as a high school and a tourism center. I look out at the town with its cathedral spires poking up out over the red tiled roofs that slope down the hillside. Out on the horizon, the agricultural fields coat the terrain in orange and yellow and green. I identify the *embudo* where the hundreds of horsemen gallop the bulls and steers down the hillside into town during fiesta. *Where's the corrals? Somewhere way out there. I wish the encierro was on for today!* The thought surprises me. *Could you run a bull run today?* I loosen my shoulders: the lead blanket doesn't feel too heavy. *Maybe.*

I pass a big poster showing the colorful eight-hundred-year-old document of the pope's edict. My eyes trace the elegant calligraphy. How must that have looked, the priests running the horns on Cuesta San Francisco! It is such a complex statement, a nuanced contract: the people can have their pagan tradition, but we must keep the clergy from it. Was it fear that the priests would muddle their sermons, and insert the pagan stuff? Why couldn't the pope just ban it? *Because people like Dyango would have stood up and fought with all their might to protect it. Because deep down we all know it is part of us. It is deep down in our collective unconscious. We ran; we lived by our ability to run to control these animals, to kill and feast on them.* I see furry *Homo erectus* leading an African buffalo into the swampland in the Oldivia Gorge, desperate to feed his clan. His mind calculating his escape, keeping himself linked with the horned monster behind him, risking it all and knowing all of the stakes. Then I see the Blackfoot buffalo runners driving the animals towards the cliff, the ones dressed as wolves growling and slowly moving toward their prey. The buffalo stomp their feet and snort as the hundreds of eyes peer at them fearfully. The buffalo runners dressed as calves easing in to their places quietly behind the herd. The grassy drive lane rising up to the heavens above…

I snap out of it and head downhill along the winding streets in Cuellar.

♉

Cuellar is a stellar town; I find solace bouncing around the bars writing, eating tapas, drinking coffee and sparkling water. I bump into old friends and make a few new ones. Then I hear from Craig Stables, a big tall jolly Englishman with blond hair, a fair complexion, and the big strong body structure that hints at his former professional rugby days. Stables has lived in Cuellar for years with his family. He runs the English Academy of Cuellar and invites me to come speak with the kids at his summer camp, so I visit the next day.

The summer camp happens on the second floor of the school in the center of town. I walk the hall past the doorways where the kids recite English.

The little ones are really excited to talk with me. One little blonde-haired girl with blue eyes is especially sweet, she nervously tiptoes up to me. "Are you really from the United States?"

"Yeah!" I say as her eyes bug out exuberantly.

I make a little presentation to the kids about why I love Cuellar, and about my book. One of the pretty teenage camp workers who'd just passed her proficiency in English test translates for the kids.

"It's very important that you all should know, you should be very proud of being from Cuellar. It's one of the most precious and greatest pueblos in the whole world," I tell them.

"We are! We are very proud!" The little kids squeal and jump up and down.

They clap and that is it, we walk out and take a nice photo on the stairs of the main entrance. Several little boys get together and approach me.

"Will you run with us during fiesta in the kids run?"

"Yeah, I promise I'll come run with you guys."

They bounce away excitedly to go play soccer. I take a deep breath and feel the joy rising in my chest. *Man, you haven't been this happy in a while.*

I thank Craig and his soon-to-be wife Reme eagerly, and wander off to kill some time. I walk to the park; my chest aches. A little crack seems to open up the dark lead block of sadness in my chest, and a tiny little yellow flower seems to sprout up from it. *Cuellar, you mean so much to me. My first quest into the pueblos. That mystical dusty haze engulfing the stampeding animals like a bright orange avalanche of primeval glory. Dancing with the old women in the streets before the sueltos come then enticing them up the street with the Cuellaranos in a ballet of death and majesty. And now the people are unveiling themselves to me, embracing me with softest kiss on the cheek.* I walk down the winding slope of Cuesta San Francisco with the sunlight blazing through the channel; so many of my dreams have come true in this tiny precious town. *Cuellar, you have to know, I love you.*

That night Dyango takes me to Peñafiel. We drive over and I see a big narrow mountain rise up in the horizon with a pretty castle sitting atop the ridge. We pull over by the pens and have a couple sandwiches and chat in a park by the river. Then we drive in through the impossibly long bull run path, with a nearly kilometer-long straightaway that's about forty yards across.

Finally we park near a tight banking right turn on the course, and walk around another bend. About eighty yards down the ancient buildings, an opening gapes like a parking garage. We turn into the tunnel and enter the dark passage like a pair of uncertain sueltos. We step through into a beautiful sandy square with a red wooden bullring in the center. The epic Peñafiel castle seems to float above it in the distance, lit bright with white lights atop the blackened mountain. *Oh yeah, I'm running this tunnel next month.*

"It's unique, the square is all made of just family homes." Dyango points to all the buildings lining the square. "They build some bleachers, but not much. The rooms that face out into the square are actually owned by the town and they are rented to people. So, say you live there…" (He points at a house with a big balcony.) "During fiesta, people just come to your house, knock on your door, and you have to let them in and up to the balcony! Hahaha, it's a unique place."

"Extremely unique! And very beautiful." I point up to the castle floating in the sky above. "I want to share these places with the whole world, Dyango."

"Good." He grins proudly.

He takes me to Iscar the next night. Their beautiful domed arena emerges from the dark trees on the horizon. It looks like some kind of a beautiful alien mosque.

"Iscar and Cuellar, they're very close, and they have a rivalry. Cuellar had the biggest bullring in the area so Iscar, they built this." He points toward the arena. "With just over six thousand seats. Forty or fifty more than Cuellar."

"How many people live here?"

"Six thousand."

"So there's a seat for every person in the town!" I guffaw. "That's like Chicago building a sports arena with three million people to outdo New York!"

"Yes, that is Iscar, but there are many excellent runners from here, and they have a very strong fiesta with a *suelta*, and an *embudo* with horsemen like Cuellar. It is an excellent fiesta."

"I can't wait. Jeez, that's only a few weeks away."

We laugh and open up to each other as we walk toward the beautiful arena gates. I giggle. This friend of mine, who represents so much to me: god, now that we can communicate, he's come alive as a person. Complex and full of moods and tenderness and that pure rural love of the bulls. We stop in front of the big tall metal red-and-yellow bullring doors.

"Gracias Dyango." I pat him on the back. "This means the world to me."

"In three weeks maybe, you will lead bulls through this tunnel into the arena."

"With luck."

"*Con mucha suerte.*"

"*Exactamente.*"

As we drove through the dark woods between Cuellar and Iscar, my mind drifts. *What a good friend. He understands my mission, to help present his culture in its highest, most beautiful form, and he's grateful and eager to help. This time he's giving me is his gift to his culture and his town too. What a cool guy.*

♉

I hang around with Craig and Dyango at the local bars, and suddenly the book starts selling really well. After a few days in Cuellar I've sold fifteen books in person.

I wake from a nap and get ready to head out. *This big stupid box of books is shrinking, finally!* I stuff a few more copies in my backpack and head back out. I bump into Stables at Bar Paralex, his favorite bar around the corner from his house. He sips a beer from a small glass.

"Bill! I've found out about a bull run tomorrow, do you fancy it?"

"Hell yeah! Where is it?" I sit down with him.

"Navas de Oro, a small town, but it should be fun."

"This will be a blast!"

We drive out the next morning in Craig's truck through a series of fields.

"Navas de Oro is a tiny town," Craig says as he shifts gears. "Just over a thousand people, it's about fifteen kilometers from Cuellar. It's a farming town. Livestock, agriculture. But most of the people, they work in the factories in the area."

We drive through the lush pine forests that surround the town.

"You know what, they've got an important observatory; it's called the Pegueras Observatory. They've made some important discoveries on variant stars, I think."

"Cool..."

We get to the course early and walk it. The narrow path zigzags the small town. The rusty fencing at each intersection doesn't match in shape or color.

"Man, them fences don't seem up to keep a bull in," I say.

"Yeah, the bulls break the fences all the time in these small towns." Craig hikes his blond eyebrows up.

"Wild..."

We round the final turn toward the small red Plaza de Toros, and the pavement transitions to a dusty dirt two-track path. Weeds and grass patches sprout up in the middle. Rusty barricades line the sides.

We walk into the metal makeshift bullring. A few grassy patches litter the sand ring. *Man, this is just like* The Sandlot.

"You ever see that movie, *The Sandlot?*"

"No, what's it about?"

"It's about these kids. They play baseball in a sandy abandoned lot." I laugh. "They get in a bunch of trouble with a dog."

"Sounds like a fun film."

"Yeah, but it's about the purity of kids' love for baseball."

"It would probably be like kids and football for us in England."

"Yeah exactly." I sigh. "Man, I've been looking for that, that pure joy I found in the run, ya know?" I crouch down and scoop up some sand. "I lost touch with it." I let the sand fall from my fingertips as Craig crouches down next to me.

"Maybe this is the place you'll find it again, Bill."

"Maybe."

Taking it all in, I look around the dusty ring and out through the opening onto the two-track. A light-brown rabbit nibbles on a blade of grass near the barricades. *Maybe, maybe this salt-of-the-earth town is the place to find it.*

Craig pats my shoulder.

"Come on, let's go see the suelta."

They release the bulls from their metal bull boxes way outside of town into one hundred or so horsemen. We drive out and get there just in time. Craig backs into a parking spot between two pine trees.

"Man, this is nice. With Cuellar, the sun is barely rising when they do the suelta. What time is it?"

"It's ten."

"Haha… nice and relaxed."

A small firework pops in the blue sky and the bulls tear out of a big blue box and gallop through the center of the field. The horsemen turn with them and stir their steeds into gallop. The mass of animals and men blaze through a thick cloud of salt-white dust toward town.

Craig pulls out and drives back toward town, but the bull-watching traffic jam catches us and we barely make it back in time for me to run. I jump out and run alongside the last bull, and he passes me before the two-track. I watch him gallop into the ring on the dusty path.

Craig grins and asks, "Did you run close?"

I smile and shake my head. "Not really."

"Maybe tomorrow?"

"Maybe."

A funny thing starts to happen in the post-fiesta week: my memoir starts to sell on Amazon. It slowly climbs the rankings until it hits 207 in all books, and the second-best-selling memoir in all of Spain. I watch the sales rank bob up and down throughout the hours. *Somebody's reading it, I guess.*

Craig, Reme, and sweet blonde nine-year-old daughter Bethany return with me to Navas de Oro the next morning. This time we skip the release in the fields and just hang by the bullring. They take up spots along the barricades along the two-track, and I move up a couple streets into the town where the path widens into a small diamond-shaped square with a big circular concrete fountain in the center.

A big pack of steers with a few bulls snug inside them approach. I run a little, but they ramble past me. Then another suelto approaches. A group of mischievous *recortadores* prepares to engage the bull. Like most *recortadores* they wear their hair spikey and slicked back, golden necklaces hanging from their necks. They look like the kids in *The Bronx Tale*. The bull stalls in the center of the square and bellows exhaustedly. One *recortador* in a bright-yellow soccer shirt walks to the fountain, dips his hand in the water, and splashes it towards the bull. Froth dangles from the bull's open mouth as he raises his nose and his big nostrils sniff at the fountain.

"Are you thirsty?" the recortador calls to the bull as the others laugh. *I bet he is,* I giggle. The recortador stirs the water with his hand and splashes several big waves at the bull; the water wets the pavement at the bull's hooves. The bull trots over, sticks his head in the fountain, and slurps the water loudly as the spectators laugh and clap from the street and the windows of the homes lining the square.

A small sand-colored dog jogs up with his bald owner. They approach the bull cautiously. *Watch your dog, buddy!* The dog carefully observes the bull, crouches low, and looks to his owner for direction. He's a smart little guy. The bull finishes his refreshment break and begins to trot toward the dog. The dog interacts with the bull thoughtfully, like any serious runner; he enters the bull's space at times, and other times gives distance. The bull charges ahead, and we lead him around the bend; the dog trots between me and his owner, right in front of the horns of the bull. As we near the dirt path with the bull, the dog's owner calls to him and they fold to the side and pause as the bull trots past.

The old emotions stir in my chest again, and I let the bull get close. I jog with a small pack of runners around the bend of the two-track in front of the bull. When the bull hits the dusty path, he accelerates into a gallop, and we break into sprint, leading him. I glance back, and the dog and his owner follow the bull closely, like pastores driving the bull. We ramble all the way to the arena. I cut to the side and hit an exit in the ring. They open the corrals, and the bull crosses the ring and trots in. My heart throbs with excitement. *Well, that was fun.*

A commotion rambles out on the two-track. *Fuck, there's another one!* I run back out as the last bull approaches the square; we lead him onto the two-track, bouncing on our toes. As salty dust flies up around us, the warm pulse of the encierro enters the crack in my chest and splinters spread throughout it. I fall into a dream I once knew. A deep awakening spreads throughout my entire being—a warm shivering throb. I pause with several locals before the animal as his hooves dig into the sandy dirt and we shoot off like a flock of birds—one being again, one encierro. *This is it, Bill. Remember? This simple joy...* We dash into the sandy arena as the hundreds of spectators roar in elation for us; the bull enters at our backs as if drawn by some cosmic harness.

Stables grins and pats me on the back. "I saw it all. Good couple runs, and I got it on tape, too. But I've got to say, that dog outdid all of you!"

"He sure did!" I giggle as we walk in to watch the recortadores make their circular dashes with the bulls inside the ring. Craig's daughter Bethany plays with a little bull doll and is very happy to watch the recortadores' fierce and exciting exhibition. She cheers as the recortadores make their impossible cuts in front of the bulls' horn tips, arching their backs over the bulls' heads and throwing their hands in the air. *Even the little half-English half-Spanish girls love bulls.* She twists the furry black bull on her lap, imitating the bull in the ring. *I guess these traditions are going to survive after all.* A recortador arches his back as the bull jumps upward, gouging his horns: a narrow miss. Bethany stands and cheers "Olé!" Her eyes beam bright behind her cute pink glasses. *What an amazing place this is.*

As my bus pulls off from Cuellar a few days later, I watch my favorite pueblo drift away, feeling like a suelto reluctant to leave a new haven. *Thank you, Cuellar...Jeez.* I'm feeling healed: mentally, physically, and spiritually. I've deepened my old friendship with Dyango, and I have a new one now, with Craig. *Fuck, I can't wait to get back to Navarra for the bull run in Tudela.* As we roll along the highway, Peñafiel's castle floats atop the horizon. *I'll be back to see you, too...*

Chapter 6

Tudela

Riding the train to Tudela, I go online, and there's an article in my Facebook feed about Julen Madina being injured in the bull run that morning in Tudela.

A group of guys sitting a few feet away find the article too.

"Look! Julen Madina was hurt by a bull in Tudela," a skinny guy in a Real Madrid shirt says.

His smug blond-haired friend giggles. With a snide sneer, he asks, "Yeah but what about the bull?"

"Stupid, Julen is a great runner, come on."

Well, I guess even some of the douchebags are anti-taurinos. I glare at the giggling blond douche's head. *Julen Madina is one of the greatest Basque bull runners in history, you asshole, not that your own culture matters to you at all. And he's a dear friend of mine.*

Trying to let it go, I pull up the video. The footage of the bull run in Tudela is incredible. Aitor Aristregui leads two bulls over two hundred yards into the arena, then he thunders back out into the street and finds a black suelto near the halfway point of the course. Aitor guides the very reluctant lone bull in fantastic fashion for a quarter of the course.

I pull up another clip. Aitor yells at the other mozos to give him space as he gets ready, then he takes his paper and slaps the pavement with a loud *crack*. The sound and motion ignite the bull; he charges, and Aitor leads him for thirty yards before the bull becomes combative again. *Damn, Aitor can handle sueltos, too?!* Near the tunnel, the bull makes an awkward turn and Aitor jumps up on a solid wooden wall and climbs over. *Good move!* Julen Madina's round shaved head and small loop earrings materialize as he shouts to the bull. *Julen is a beast!* The bull charges him and Julen leads the bull through the tunnel. The bull hits Julen as he leads the animal onto the sand arena. *Fuck!* Julen topples in a sandy splash. As the massive black bull passes over Julen, he dips his horn and scrapes the tip along Julen's ribs and breaks several. *Fuck! Well, at least he wasn't gored.* Julen rolls to his knees, and as the bull turns and comes back for him, he gets up and runs—dodging the animal's charge. *Good, he got up! Hopefully it isn't that bad.*

My eyes shoot at the blond guy who'd made the stupid dismissive comment. *Julen Madina is a fucking master runner, you idiot, and a friend and teacher of mine.* The urge to punch the blond douche in the back of his stupid head trembles in my arms. *He's sixty-one years old.* I sigh. *He's been flirting with retirement for a few years.*

I research the location of the local hospital. I gotta go visit him.

♉

My train pulls into Tudela in the night. The course goes straight past the parking lot of the train station. My hostel is behind the bullring. I shrug and walk along the barricades of the bull run as it winds through the pretty and clean town. With a population of about thirty-five thousand, Tudela is the second-largest city in Navarra behind Pamplona, and it's the second major bull festival in Navarra's summer fiesta season.

Populated since the early Stone Age, Tudela is situated in the Ebro Valley, and it's witnessed many battles. Even Napoleon Bonaparte fought here; he won the Battle of Tudela during the Peninsula War. I slog along, exhausted by the long trip. *I guess I'm in a battle too. Gotta fight my way out of this depression and back into the heart of the action.*

♉

I get out on the course early and bump into Aitor and Xabi Mentegi; they greet me warmly.

"Incredible run yesterday, Aitor!" I hold up the cover of that day's *Diario de Navarra*; it shows him in front of a suelto.

"Gracias." He grins humbly.

Xabi rolls his eyes as I giggle. Aitor's running must give Xabi a heart attack.

Xabi points at me. "You understand, today isn't a normal run. *Dos encierros*, two runs today. Three bulls, then a minute later, three more bulls."

"Really?"

"Yeah and three of them are Muira!"

"The second set," Aitor chimes in.

"First set, Fuente Ymbro."

"Wow."

I limber with them on the course. Good thing I got Navarrese friends! The many teenage bull runners of Navarra gather around nervously and stoically. *Tudela must be a place for the young guys to prove themselves.*

The rocket pops in the distance and I run and get lost in the runners and animals. The first set thunders past me.

Then I ready and run again as the second set approaches. A horn lunges toward me through the running bodies. I dive to the ground near the barricades. My hands brace me, but my momentum carries me forward, and the top of my head smashes into the big vertical post of the barricades with a loud *crack*. I black out as a sharp pain stings my neck.

As I come to, I notice an old toothless man sitting on the barricades above me; he points at me and laughs. *Fuck you, old man!* I roll under the barricade into the grass. *Well, I guess it was pretty funny.*

I wander around in a daze. I ask some of the older guys, "How is Julen? Where is he?" No one seems to know. I pull my cap off. There's a dark red circle of blood in the inside center. I go to the infirmary inside the Plaza de Toros, and the doctors give me one lucky stitch in the top of my head.

After I get stitched up, I head out. I've decided to walk the five miles to the Tudela hospital and see if I can find Julen there. I take a wrong turn; the compass in my head spins wildly, and I feel like a lost bull. I ask an old lady in a white wig for directions, and she points up a long winding hill to a roundabout. *Julen, my dear friend, you were one of the great stars of my book. A true inspiration for me, a father to all the young runners.* I get to the roundabout and ponder my next move. *I watched you since the beginning, your shaved and hoop earrings gleaming in the morning light—running down Telefonica with bulls at your back, dominating sueltos, and this was in your fifties when you'd lost more than a step, but you'd gained experience and knowledge like an old monk.* (You may think you need incredibly speed to run but no, when you have the craft, timing, and skill like Julen you don't; you could almost walk them through the callejon.) *Julen, you hypnotized the bulls and whispered for them to slow and run with you, and they listened as if their grandfather had called them to go for a walk.* But that was only Julen in his older days. Julen in his youth was a smoldering comet, rocketing up Estafeta street, blazing past the best. One morning Julen did the impossible and ran bulls from La Curva all the way up Estafeta, down Telefonica and then into the ring. But it wasn't all triumph, it never is; there was the goring, the fateful day in 2004 when the Jandilla bull Trigueno stabbed his mighty horns into Julen five times in a pileup, nearly taking his life. Still he stormed back the next year, running like magic, as if the bull had never touched him. *Julen, you're like some mythical being; there's a spirit of boundless power like the bulls injected life into you, and everyone you ever touch can feel it.*

I step along the sloping sidewalk, moving through sprinkles of shade from the young trees that line it. Julen is a judo master as well, and the only man in Spain who could beat him was also the great runner who came before him, Atanasio, a man whom Matt Carney called "The Seventh Bull" because he was built like one, dark-skinned with a broad hairy chest, and he ran like a Toro Bravo too. In the 1970s he was a complete dynamo, but eventually he passed the torch to the young Julen. Julen kept the flame safe for many years, until the 90s, when it came time for him, too, to pass the torch to the young JuanPe. Julen showed JuanPe the way, and the two remained dear friends, *maestro y estudiante* to this day. Julen is a *maestro de maestros*, a master teacher and guru of the highest order. And when that man looks a young runner in the eyes, they know that he loves them, he loves us all.

I near the big brick hospital. *Maestro, I hope I find you well.*

One of the doctors doesn't want to let me in to see my friend. He squints at me suspiciously with his mean dark face.

"Are you one of those anti-taurinos?"

"No! I'm a bull runner!" I pull my book out of my bag. "That's me running in Pamplona! Julen is my maestro. He visited me when I got gored a few years ago."

The doctor shrugs and lets me in.

I step into the dark room. Julen lies in bed. Exhaustion makes his eyes squint, pain trembles in his face.

"Bill," he says weakly, raising his eyebrows.

"Is there anything I can do for you, maestro?"

"No, no, *tranquilo*, Bill," he says. "Sit down." He winces painfully. "They'll transfer me to a hospital near home soon."

"Good! I'm glad."

I should make this quick. I take out a pen and the copy of my book and write a heartfelt inscription, wishing him a swift recovery and thanking him for everything he did for me and for my whole generation. *Man, I want to brighten your spirits. It must be tough when you've run incredibly for forty years. How do you let go of something that brings you so much joy? Man, how the hell am I ever gonna let go of bull running? When is enough enough? Aw hell, I'll keep running as long as my body lets me, just like you.*

I give him the book, and he thanks me.

Man, I bet all the runners are worried sick who can't be here.

"Should we take a picture together, so everybody can see you're OK? Like the one we took when you came and visited me!"

"Yes, sure, OK."

We get ready, and Julen thinks about it and then takes my book that is sitting on his food tray and puts it on his chest. I shrug and take the photo. It's a little dark, and we try a few more times, but we can't get a good picture in the dark room.

We shrug and agree it's OK. We hug, and I leave him to rest. I post the picture, figuring it'll be good for everyone to know he was OK and had visitors.

♉

I walk back to town and take the train to San Adrian. They have a reses bravas scheduled for that afternoon. San Adrian is a town of about six thousand located around thirty minutes from Tudela. Situated between the Ebro and Ega rivers, the locals are called Aguachinaos because much of the land is floodplains and they've had to build an elaborate network of canals and irrigation ditches. What little dry land they have is dedicated to asparagus.

The celebration in San Adrian is to honor the holy relics that they house in the town; legend has it they have the powers of restoring vision.

After an expensive cab ride, I walk into the town, past an ornate pink town hall with a green garden park surrounding it. I find the course, a twisted series of streets with a variety of big wooden obstacles for the animals to navigate. Near the corrals, I step into a bar and sit down for a water and a cortado. A lesbian couple in the bar begins chatting with me; they find out about my book and buy the copy I have in my bag. I sign it for them. Proud Aguachinaos, they travel with a couple children to see the bulls in a variety of towns and explain that what is about to happen in San Adrian is a reses bravas but "You can run with them too, especially at the end when they run all the animals through town."

I leave my bag behind the bar and get on the course. They release three animals at a time into three different stretches of the course and I play it safe at first, staying down by the bar, which is the most beautiful stretch, a slow winding narrow cobblestone street full of balconies that feeds in to a triangular courtyard with a series of obstacles. One obstacle is the stairwell to nowhere, a ten-foot-high red staircase that peaks then goes back down on the other side. They release a rowdy brown vaca in our section and she gallops the full stretch, then retreats along the narrow street and is reluctant to come back to the courtyard with us. I jog out with my rolled paper and entice her. She sniffs at the air and turns away. I close the gap between us and she spins and charges hard. I sprint before her horns directly toward the stairwell to nowhere. A dozen teenage Aguachinaos sit on the steps and as I approach they squeeze to the side to make room for me. *Here I come!* I leap up and land on the fourth step as the vaca rambles around the stairwell. The little boys pat me on the back as the onlookers cheer. I giggle as the adrenaline trembles through my thighs. *Man, I fucking love this country.*

A vibrant sensation courses through all of my body; it is warm and electric. I fall deep into the wild dream of horned beasts set free in the streets of Spain. Sweat beads down my face and arms as I lead the young bulls and vaca back to the recortadores for the next hour with the teenage Aguachinaos. Our shouts and dashes meld with the animals' charges; we lose ourselves in the ancient physical language of man and bovine until we became like flowing mediums for our ancestors. At one point exhaustion strangles the tubes in my chest and I sit down on the stairway to nowhere. *My god, how the hell am I still going?* Then the vaca tears off down the long curved straightaway with the pretty balconies under the thin stream of blue sky. A strong mania swirls in my mind for the first time since Fuentesaúco. In mania I don't need food, water, or rest. My mind and body strike a high gear and my limits crumble around me as I flow forward after my desires. I leap off the stairs and run after the vaca and bring her right back. Her foamy mouth bellows, a foot away from my backside. I leap up onto the stairs, this time landing on the seventh step with the young Aguachinaos squirming for cover.

I run like mad for two hours straight; sweat pours off me and soaks my running shirt. I'm expelling a tremendous weight of negative emotions in this whirlwind of action in a narrow street in a small town far away that I may never return to except in my dreams.

I move up the street to the middle section and stop to watch on the fence with my Aguachinao lady friends. A big brown bull that must have been a three-year-old rampages around the street near us. An elderly lady sits on the ground cross-legged, resting her elbows on the bottom run of the wooden barricade. Suddenly the bull charges our barricades and hits the fence in front of the old lady. Then the bull twists his horns and pushes his whole head and horns through the space between the planks and puts his slobbery snout in the old lady's lap. I lunge in, grab her by her arms, and drag her to safety as she gasps in shock. It takes the bull some violent twisting to get himself free from the barricades. Afterward everyone takes an uneasy look at the safety of their watching position. *Yep, that's how people get killed watching from the barricades.* I step back into the street to run with the rowdy bull.

After the last animal enters the pens, I say goodbye to my friendly Aguachinao family and sit in the bar for a while eating tapas. These little dots pop up and float through my vision. *Ah fuck, I got a migraine coming.* I hop a cab to the train station and sit nauseous in the empty station. I grip my achy stitched-up head. *You gotta slow down, man.*

♉

The next morning I wake up nauseous. I climb up on the barricades in Tudela and don't run much. I bump into Aitor, Xabi, and the guys afterward.

Aitor made the cover of *Diario de Navarra* again, and we chide him. Xabi guffaws and smacks the cover photo of Aitor leading three bulls around the final bend into the arena.

"He's the fucking Cristiano Renaldo of the encierro!" Xabi shouts in his flustered gregarious way.

"No way, he's the young Pele of the encierro," I chime in as everybody giggles.

"You coming to San Adrian or what?" Xabi asks.

"Yeah, do you want to come with us?" Aitor says.

"Sure," I say with a shrug.

We pack into the car and drive over—busting each other's balls the whole way. We eat breakfast in San Adrian at a long table in the street and prepare for the run. A stunningly beautiful curvy girl with dark eyes and long straight almond hair stands out in front of the bank she works at; she seems to be showing her stuff off for Aitor and Xabi.

Xabi nudges Aitor. "Go talk to her, she wants you!"

"No, leave me alone," Aitor dismisses him, bashfully.

"Hola!" Xabi says with a wave and she waves back with a cute little wink.

Trying to stay conservative, I set up to run on the last straightaway into the arena. Aitor, Xabi, and the guys set up before the curve in front of the bank. *Oh yeah that definitely isn't to impress the knockout, supermodel girl or anything.*

I wait as the bulls approach, watching the corner. Aitor rounds the hard banking turn on the horns of the lead bull. He seems to fly before the horns, not touching the ground. *Now he can fucking fly, too?!* The bulls approach, and I run alongside them and don't get too close.

Afterward, we gather up and they blow off the bombshell as she bats her pretty eyes at them through the window of the bank, her phone in hand, ready to exchange Instagram handles probably. I watch them giving her glances back. *A lot of hot chicks must throw themselves at you guys to let that one slip by.*

I giggle. "Thanks guys, I'll see you tomorrow in Tudela."

Aitor stops and looks at me confused. "Come on, we're taking you back to Tudela."

"No way. It's out of your way."

"No, doesn't matter."

Holy shit. I touch my achy head. I do feel like shit.

"OK." I shrug and follow them to the car and they drive me all the way back to Tudela. I thank them heartily before they pack up and head home to Pamplona. I watch Cristian's car zip out of sight up a curvy street in Tudela. *I gotta fucking pay them back somehow.*

♉

The next morning I wake up feeling good. I sip my morning cortado in a bar near the plaza. I gotta fucking put a plan together. *OK, what if I just get up on the barricades and watch for the bulls to approach? Once they get close, I'll hop down and run along the inside of the last curve. When the bulls swing wide and smash into the barricades, maybe it'll open up for me?* I scratch my head. *Fuck it, it's worth a shot.* I slam my cortado and head over.

I hug the thick wooden barricade as I stand on the bottom rung about fifty yards from the last curve. The pack shoots into view down the street. Aitor leads the lead bull as the pack fires up the narrow course. As they close in I jump down and run along the barricades. A steer shoots ahead of me at the curve. I look behind the steer and three black bulls soar into view with white-clad Aitor jogging in the middle of them. I run into the center of the street. Aitor syncs up beside me. We run in front of either horn of the lead bull, linked with it. We lead the three bulls into the arena and dash off to the side as they ramble across the ring. A few seconds later, Xabi leads the final bull into the arena in his black sweatshirt, waving a red penuelo in front of the bull's snout.

Aitor, Xabi, and I meet up and embrace in a joyful three-way hug on the sand. Then Aitor looks across the ring and darts off to lure the last unruly bull into the pens. Xabi and I guffaw and shake our heads at Aitor.

"Fucking Aitor!" Xabi says.

"He never stops." I giggle.

"Never gets tired!" Xabi guffaws.

Aitor comes running over, smiling broadly.

"Don't you ever get tired?" Xabi asks, exasperated.

We giggle and head to the stands to watch the recortadores. Aitor just never quits on anything in a bull run. I watch him grinning in the stands beside me. He's a damn dynamo.

♉

The next day in Tudela, I climb the barricades again and drop down as they approach. As I run the inside of the curve, a black bull soars into view, skating on his hooves, then falls and slides on his belly for ten yards. I wait as he climbs to his hooves. *Like stealing candy from a fuckin' baby.* He rises and gallops and links with me and I run him into the arena. A couple seconds later Aitor barrels into the ring with three bulls hooking at his tail.

With warm elation rising up off my body, I look up to the big circle of blue morning sky high above the arena. *These are the runs I've been hoping for.* My disappointments in Pamplona fade from my mind. I suffered a lot to break through with these runs, it was a goddamn war. *Man, this is so fucking sweet.*

Afterward I bump into my friend Raul Lasierra, a tall, friendly, heartfelt guy with a big mop of black hair. He works at the Toro Passion ranch not far from Tudela. He also is involved with the Encierro Exhibition that travels around the world and has a really fun virtual reality game that really makes you feel like you're running an encierro.

"Are you going to San Adrian?"

"I don't know, maybe I'll take the train."

"I'll drive you, come on."

Raul and I cruise along the highway.

"Man, you had a great run the day I got trampled with the Cebada Gago!" I tell him.

"With the suelto, it was a fantastic feeling."

"Man, it was just you and him on the TV screen. When I saw it I shouted, 'RAUL!!!!'"

"These moments, they stay with us forever, Bill."

"Damn right."

We eat breakfast in San Adrian with Aitor and the guys. As the bulls approach I run the lead pack into the arena with several young Aguachinaos. Afterward, I thank Raul and stay in San Adrian and run with the vaca and bulls all afternoon. One tremendous vaca charges the huge metal dividing gate and explodes through it. The gate pops right off its hinges and smashes down flat on the street. They set it back up and she knocks it down again a few minutes later. The crowd reels as I shake my head. *She's a fucking menace!*

I can't afford a taxi, so I walk down the shoulder of a highway for an hour past all the water ditches and channels in the farmland as the sun sets on the horizon. My feet plod along the roadway like the hooves of a tired suelto trying to get home. The high-speed traffic whizzes past me as I hug the guardrail.

The final morning in Tudela, I plan to use my new strategy of hugging the inside of the curve, but something tells me to hold off. The bulls hug my side of the fence and instead of jumping down, I climb up and watch the run for a bird's-eye view of Aitor leading the bulls down the street with the young Navarran runners struggling to run beside him.

I walk through the pretty town of Tudela after the run, feeling fine. *No shame in not getting in the action. Look, this is a dangerous summer but not a crazy get-yourself-killed summer.* I've got a lot of objectives in this trip. I gotta observe the towns and see the bull run from every angle, I have to stay healthy enough physically and mentally to run the whole summer, I need to promote the book, and of course I've gotta stay a-fucking-live! And there's no shame in running a bull run on the fence.

As my train pulls away from Tudela toward Pamplona, I tally my run count. *Forty runs in a month. Not bad.* I'm on track, but I need to keep at it if I'm gonna hit one hundred and one.

I close my notebook and watch the epic Navarran country flash past my window. *But look, these are just silly numbers, just like your stupid Amazon sales rank.* We soar past a muddy ranch full of vaca. There is something to be said for goals, but when you set goals and you push yourself to reach them, sometimes they blind you. All you can see is the goal; you fixate on it so much you can't even feel the marvelous world around you. Other times goals can help you through the doldrums, and every once in a while, goals can push you to the limits of the experience.

Chapter 7

Lodosa

My friend Graeme Galloway writes me an email. "Don't miss Puente la Reina! It's a fantastic run! It's the home of the most dangerous bar in the world!"

I look it up, and sure enough Puente la Reina is scheduled for the next day. It's is a little village of three thousand people just outside of Pamplona. It literally means the Queen's Bridge, and is named that because Queen Muniadona, the queen of Pamplona, built a beautiful six-arched stone bridge in the town in the eleventh century. The town and bridge are an important point on the Camino de Santiago pilgrimage route.

My bus soars into the electric light of a long concrete tunnel with three deep green peaks of the Pyrenees looming above. I jump off the bus and gallop into the main square, then trot through the corridor of an arched overhang that runs beside a temporary red bull square full of sand with wooden bleachers surrounding it. The corridor empties onto a street full of partiers. Some barricades and a swinging metal fence sit near the intersection with the square.

"Is this the bull-run course?" I ask a drunken guy dressed up as pirate with a patch over his eye.

"Yeah...yeah, but it's only vaquillas," he slurs and motions down the long narrow street.

What do we do with a drunken sailor? Ask him advice about an extremely dangerous activity. I head out into the narrow cobblestone street that slopes slowly downward, slipping through the boisterous partiers as the falling sun lights up the old façades on the two-hundred-yard straightaway in a golden sheen. *Man, this is a sweet little pueblo.* I pass many open doorways of bars and homes; metal barricades with vertical bars stand in front of the doors so people can squeeze through but the vaca can't. *Fuck, are they going to keep the bars open during the run?!* I remember a video Graeme made years back where he ordered a gin and tonic, then walked through some vertical bars and crossed the street holding it as several vaca thundered past him. He giggled at the camera. "This is the most dangerous bar in the world," he said in his regal Scottish brogue.

Trying to get a feel for things, I walk all the way down to a turn in the path at the base of the Queen's Bridge. The pretty bridge soars up in a big arc. *Man, what if the course didn't turn and the vaquilla went over the bridge!* Imaginary vaca gallop up the narrow path. I examine the sturdy stone blocks. *I bet the Queen's Bridge could handle it.* I go around the corner and see the pens and hear the vaca banging the doors with their small horns. I make little calls like a bull; the banging stops, and then one of the vaquilla lets out a faint call. I giggle. *She must think I'm a suelto.*

On my way back to the bull square, the locals drag handmade chest-high square wooden shields out of the bars and clubhouses and homes that open onto the course. Four or five wooden grips stick up out of the top of the shields, and the bottoms lay flat on the cobblestones. Old women and children stand behind the shields and hold them up, peering down the street where the vaca will come from any minute. *Are they gonna stand behind those things when the vaca come?!* Navarra is a fucking wonderful place.

"Bill!" somebody shouts happily. I look; Aitor sits on a high window ledge with a big smile on his face.

"Are those old ladies gonna stand behind them shields during the encierro?" I point at two fat old women in flower-pattern dresses sipping plastic cups of sangria and holding up a purple shield with their free hands.

"I think so." He nods and giggles.

"Incredible." I shake my head at them. "You gonna run?"

He squints. "It's ugly to run with the vaca, this is for the little boys."

I shrug. "I don't care! I'm running, man!"

Aitor laughs.

An older man in a nearby doorway sings a raunchy *jota* with a big, deep, and powerful voice as men with weathered faces crowd around him and laugh at the lyrics.

Three young teenage boys walk the center of the street nervously; two look Basque, the third looks of Indian descent. They pass a green bottle of beer between them. The Indian kid seems to be working up his will to run. *Grab your balls, guys.*

Suddenly six black vaquilla shoot around the corner near the Queen's Bridge and gallop our way down the center of the street.

The partiers hurry behind shields and squeeze through the metal vertical bars in front of the open doorways.

The three nervous little boys position themselves in the center of the street and bounce on their toes watching the horns of the vaca charging toward them. As the vaca close in, they run; the Indian kid runs closest, whipping his head around watching the vaca and shouting to his friends. *They're trying so hard, they're so damn brave!* I wait, and as the boys pass me the gap between them and the vaca opens. *I can't help it!* I dip in between the boys and the vaca and lead the vaca for a while, then cut out.

Aitor walks up, shaking his head at me and rolling his eyes.

"What? Come on, this is my only chance to run here!"

"It's for the kids…" Aitor sighs.

We head over to watch the vaca in the bull square with the recortadores. I pat Aitor on the back. *That must be what it feels like to be Aitor running bulls in Pamplona. The five-foot gap between the rest of the runners and the horns of the bulls must seem like a square mile to you. He probably thinks, "Look at those guys trying so hard to run good…let me show them how it's done."* Aitor rests his arms on the wooden bullring wall, watching fondly as the vaca tears around the ring.

We watch the bull dodgers incite the vaca to charge, cutting a half-circle as the animal approaches. Then they narrowly evade the vaca, arching their backs over the heads of the animals as the vaca gouge at them with their twisted horns.

I run with the boys on and off for an hour. It's like a tiny paradise—the three young boys striving all out, getting closer and closer, falling and picking each other up, with Aitor grinning and watching from a window ledge high above like a ghost of their future peering down into the ghost of his past before it all exploded for him on Estafeta like the great dawn of a new era in the encierro. And me hiding behind the wooden shields with the giddy old ladies and children, then dashing out and stealing tiny sips of this great stream of ancient humanity always just past my grasp, but my thirst always growing as if there was an endless void in my soul for this foreign world, so familiar, this great escape of my life that sends me deep into my original identity.

Then the mood shifts. The Indian boy struggles so fiercely to run close and lead the vaca; his eyes and face strain as if he is drowning in raging rapids. He directs his friends, who support him. They approach me. I cut in behind him again. This time he slows to equal me. This little guy has steel balls. And we run shoulder-to-shoulder leading the vaca. I grin at him and pat him on the back. *Good work, kid.* He glances at me urgently, then looks back at the horns of the vaca bobbing close behind us. *He wants it so bad. Let him have it.* I peel off as he takes the vaca up and around the bend into the ring, his small swift body melding with the rambling black vaquilla. I grab my bag and take off for Pamplona with one last glance back at the three boys working the vaca up the street. *It's like it means the whole damn world to them.* I turn and walk through the stone corridor. *I hope it does, guys. Keep at it and I'll see you in San Fermin in a few years...*

♉

Stephanie Mutsaerts invites me to stay with her and her family in Mendioroz. By the time I get there, I'm exhausted and a little depressed. Her sons Tasio and Oliver invite me to play a game of two-on-two basketball with their friend.

"Sorry guys, I'm too tired." I relax on the back-porch couch. As they walk off, something tells me: *Go play with those kids.* I jog over and catch up with them. The court sits on the side of a tall beautiful chapel. I pair up with blond-haired Tasio; he's fourteen and the younger brother and much more heartfelt and angelic then his older brother Oliver, who's seventeen and more athletically built, with short curly hair. Oliver's a bit of a rebellious and mischievous knucklehead.

Oliver bounces the ball and chides us.

"We're gonna kick your guys' asses!"

Tasio flips a switch, and a mean competitive streak sparks up. I smash the boards and Tasio sinks some nice shots. We brutalize Oliver and his friend and win by five points.

"So who got their asses kicked, Oli?!" I chide them as Tasio and I slap each other five.

"Yeah," Tasio pipes in.

"OK, OK, you got lucky." Oliver follows us with his head hung.

"Your little brother beat you, Oli, that must be embarrassing, no?"

Tasio beams a big boyish smile as we walk back. *Well, you're even more tired now, but you sure ain't depressed no more.* I pat Tasio on the back.

"Campeon!"

♉

The next day I drive out to Lodosa for the festival of Emeterio and San Celedonio, two martyred Roman soldiers who the Romans beheaded after they professed their belief in Christ. Lodosa is a midsized town of nearly five thousand people in southwest Navarra. JuanPe took me there in 2014, and our friend Miguel Leza showed us a nice time. I've had trouble keeping in touch with Miguel because of my erratic travels, and I'm hoping to bump into him.

I arrive about twenty minutes before the bull run is scheduled to start, and none of the barricades crossing the streets are up. *Fuck, did you come on the wrong day?* I park and go for a coffee at a café on the course. When I walk back outside, the town workers are swiftly erecting the barricades. Runners flood in just fifteen minutes before the bull run starts as the locals fill the barricades and balconies to watch.

Where the hell should I run? I inspect the course. The last section comes out of a long, wide straightaway and banks a hard left turn. Then sixty yards down, it makes a hard right turn, running alongside the big yellow and burgundy bull arena, then another hard left into the tunnel into the bullring. I shrug: *fuck it, I'll run it.* The rocket pops in the sky and the bulls thunder up the way. The lead bull passes on me on the final turn with Aitor leading it. And I run into the arena between the first bull and a second pack.

Afterward I bump into Miguel Leza, a dark-skinned guy with slicked-back salt-and-pepper hair, clad in white with a green penuelo.

"How are you?"

"I'm fine, I'm glad you made it." He hugs me and kisses me on the cheek. "Welcome back to Lodosa."

Miguel takes me all over. Lodosa isn't the kind of Navarran town that is spectacularly beautiful from the first moment you see it. Her beauty is elusive, but when she is ready, she shows herself to you in all her splendor. We pick up Miguel's dog, who is old, leashless, and well-behaved. Then we walk to a pretty riverbank with a park and picnic tables.

"The young lovers, they come to these benches at night and…" Miguel makes some crude humping motions as I burst out laughing.

Past the park, the huge stone arched bridge of Lodosa spans the wide Ebro river.

"Pretty bridge."

"Yes, yes, this bridge was very important, many wars were fought over it. And many unwanted babies were made right here." Miguel taps one of the metal picnic tables.

We follow the dog through a wooded patch. *Here you go again, hanging with the locals. You're a lucky SOB.* Miguel's friendship is a lot like that bridge, a strong and important connection point to the heart of Navarra, and his perverted mind's a lot like the park.

We walk past some fishermen.

"They catch catfish here, bigger than you," Miguel tells me.

"Yeah, right."

"What's the biggest one you caught?" Miguel asks the fisherman.

"Cien kilogramos," the portly fisherman replies.

Miguel hikes his grey eyebrows.

No way. I look it up on my phone, and sure enough, they regularly catch two-hundred-pound monster catfish in the Ebro river. We drop the dog off and go out with Miguel's pretty wife and visit every bar in Lodosa, twice. Miguel's son Mikel works at one of the bars; he's thin and athletic and wears his hair in the Basque mullet. Mikel's turning into quite an impressive runner. (The Basque from Miguel's parents' generation grew up under Franco, who banned the Basque language and forced them to name their children Spanish names. Since Franco's death, the Euskera language has returned; Miguel's generation has brought back the Basque names to their children, so in a way Miguel named his son Mikel after himself.) We walk to a bar in the main square and order *pimiento de piquillo*, the local red pepper breaded and fried with a buttery cheese inside, prepared sort of like a miniature Mexican-style *chile relleno*, but they serve it as a tapa on a toothpick. I take a bite into the buttery tender dough.

"Man, we gotta get another."

Miguel grins and shouts for more.

They take me to see a beautiful bull mount near the curve that I ran that day. The family invites us in. The black bull hangs boldly on the wall with the big lump of muscle in the back of its neck all swollen up.

We climb up to Miguel's apartment, and from his balcony I see a large beautiful white cliff run behind the town with caves lining it. A huge aerial photo of Lodosa hangs on Miguel's wall. It shows the white cliffs running along the back of the town and the cathedral and town hall. I gaze into that image while Miguel and his wife cook up a tasty meal. *That's it, it's official. I'm in love with you, Lodosa.* We eat a nice meal of sausage and rice with vegetables. They go up to their room for a siesta and give me their comfortable couch to nap on. I lie back on the couch with a full stomach. *Now this is hospitality!* I doze like a bull escaping the midday heat under the shade of a tree.

♉

Later we run vaca in the streets. Some kids watching from the window of the house with the bull mount stick their heads out of the window; they giggle and point at me.

"Where are you from?" the chubby boy with the box cut asks.

"Chicago, USA," I say as the vaca approaches. "Are you from Lodosa?"

"Yes, this is my grandpa's house."

"Nice," I say.

I turn and run the vaca around the corner, then come back.

"Why are you here?" the chubby boy asks.

I shrug. "I'm here to run with the vaca." Their parents laugh. And the chunky boy giggles excitedly.

"Do you like bulls?" he asks.

"Yes, very much," I reply. "Do you like bulls?"

"Yes, I like them a lot. We have a bull mount here." He points to the bull mount behind him.

"I know, I saw it earlier today. It's a good one!" The parents chuckle and the little boy looks very surprised and proud of his grandpa's bull mount.

It's getting late. I wave goodbye to the kids, thank Miguel, climb through the barricades, and shoot off for Mendiroz.

♉

The next morning the Toro Passion Ranch comes to Lodosa. Toro Passion is a big ranch in El Faro just outside of Navarra; they've purchased bulls from a variety of different esteemed ranches like Jandilla, Miura, and others.

I get on the course and bump into Miguel Angel Perez. He wears a white Toro Passion shirt and grips a pastore's willow cane. Miguel Leza stands with him, chatting.

I greet Miguel Angel Perez with a handshake.

"You're a pastore, too?!"

Miguel Angel nods with a grin and walks off to prepare.

"He owns a big part of Toro Passion, you didn't know that?" Leza asks.

"No, that's great!"

Raul Lasierra jogs past with his white Toro Passion uniform.

"Raul's a pastore too!?"

"Yes, Raul's the mayoral of Toro Passion, I think."

Fuck man, the mayoral, that's big! He's like the manager of the whole ranch! What a cool project. Man, Miguel Angel Perez is a legend. Images of him saving Xabier Salillas from Vaporoso in 2005 flash in my mind.

"Miguel Angel Perez is an incredible runner."

"Yes, but he's a recortador too, you didn't know? Bill, you have a lot to learn."

"I know, Miguel, that's why I need friends like you."

"Aye, *tres encierros, hoy,*" Leza tells me sternly.

"What?"

"Three runs today. One"—he points toward the bullring—"then back"—he points back toward the corrals—"then back again"—he points at the ring.

"*Depende en los animals,*" a runner passing by chimes in.

"Yes, yes, there might be more runs or less, depending on if the bulls get tired."

"Wait, are you serious?"

Miguel Leza sighs and walks off to get ready. I can never tell when he's joking or serious. I bounce on my toes as Aitor and his friends warm up way down the long straightaway before the final bends into the arena. *Could there really be three bull runs in one day? Naw, Miguel's just messing with me.*

The big beautiful bulls approach in a nice herd with Aitor leading them. I run with them around the first bend. I sprint beside the first bulls but they take the second turn wide and close me off, so I stop and let them go. But then a lone bull approaches and I run with him into the callejon and the plaza with a couple other runners.

Afterward the runners remain tensely in the street. They tell me "*Dos mas encierros!*" Two more runs. *Fuck, Leza wasn't kidding! Where are the next bulls coming from?!* Aitor walks into the tunnel to the arena and looks into the ring. I go over and stand beside him. He peers tensely into the open tunnel with the chest-high wall of the ring closed. They release the bulls from the pens. The bulls and steers ramble around in big circles in the ring. The coloration differences strike me: two black bulls, a white bull, a brown one, and a grey- and black-speckled bull trailing the pack. Then the doormen unlatch the doors to the ring and swing them open. Aitor bounces on his toes, dressed in all white with his grandfather's face on the chest of his shirt, his eyes in a deep taurine trance. The entire herd appears at the mouth of the tunnel. The animals roar aggressively; a big brown bull bounds toward us digging his horns low, the big mound of muscle swelling behind his head like a majestic pulsing furry mountain. The pack streams through the tunnel at Aitor and me. *What the fuck are we doing!* I give ground as they fly out incredibly fast. Aitor stands still in the tunnel. *Aitor, RUN!* I pause, expecting them to blast through my friend. Aitor waits. As the animals encounter him, it's like he's protected by a force field. The lead brown bull nearly stops at his feet like an obedient dog. The rest of the bulls bunch up and spread out at his brown hindquarters. Then, like a wizard with a rolled newspaper as his wand, Aitor entrances the lead bull with a wide swipe at his snout. It's as if a message spreads from the lead bull to the others behind him and they all bunch up into a wide glob of contorting fur. They accept Aitor as their leader. Aitor dashes before them in a wide curve out of the tunnel, and through the street into a hard left turn. *How the fuck is he doing this?!?!* All the other excellent Navarrese runners give fifteen yards of distance between the herd and themselves and watch, as shocked as me, as Aitor holds his newspaper wand inches from the lead bull's snout the entire dash. It's the most incredible thing I've ever seen. Aitor disappears into the rambling herd. *They'd have killed anyone else who tried that stunt.*

The herd soars past me as I watch, befuddled by Aitor's magic with the animals as he leads them around the second turn. Suddenly a black bull stumbles on the curb and falls right in front of me. A sorrowful bellow spills from his lips. *He's yours, man.* I pause before him and attract his attention with my paper as he rises—seething angrily. A big shiny line of drool dangles from his snout. *Let's go, my friend.* He shoots into deep gallop as I lead him with two other runners for forty yards up the street and through the next bend before I hit the fence.

In the last encierro back toward the arena, a brown bull separates near me and I help lead him into the arena. My heart pulses. I grip the red wooden bullring. I can't believe it. *This was incredible! But wait, where's Aitor?* A commotion approaches the tunnel from the street. I look as Aitor enters the ring with the grey- and black-speckled bull's horns hooking at his back. *He's superhuman.* Aitor cuts to the side as the bull crosses the ring, the final beast in one hell of a morning of runs.

Afterward all the runners mill around outside the bullring just shaking their heads, breathing hard, and grinning. Some of the young guys sit on the side of buildings exhausted, sipping a big bottle of water. *Three runs, three great encierros in less than thirty minutes. You were part of it, Bill. How lucky are you?* Everyone seemed to have gotten a piece. They all bask in their slice of glory, their connection with the animal. *We became a unit, like the Blackfoot nation at the Head-Smashed-In Buffalo Jump. A few dozen hunters, not blood but one tribe, and the hunt was a great success and now all there is to do is celebrate, share the stories, and feast.*

A muscled, blond-haired Basque runner greets me with a grin and offers me a sip from his big water bottle. I take it.

"Thanks!"

"Come on, let's go see the *capea*."

Aitor and the gang start off toward the main square. I bet they're going for breakfast.

"Thank you," I tell the blond guy and his friends, "but I gotta go do something."

"OK," he says, shrugging.

"I'll see you around."

I follow Aitor and the guys. *This is my chance, I'll sneak up and buy their breakfast while they're not on guard.* They laugh and point at a young gigantic handsome Navarran runner as four beautiful teenage girls, Red Cross volunteers, motheringly clean his bumps and scrapes from his fall.

"He's faking..." Xabi roasts him as he giggles, trying to pretend he isn't enjoying the attention.

I trail twenty yards behind Aitor, Xabi, and the guys. The old men of Lodosa continually greet Aitor with joyful tears in their eyes. An old man in a black cap hobbles up with his cane and takes Aitor's face in his hands. "Incredible," he says as tears tremble in his old blue eyes; he's seen seventy years of bull runs. Aitor sheepishly grins and humbly nods, and then they continue.

"This fucking guy, he makes all the old men cry with his running," Xabi says as they all giggle.

They go into the nearest bar and order sandwiches. I come up and order a water. I take a fifty and give it to the waitress.

"Por todo," I tell her and motion to the sandwiches.

"No!" Xabi says. "Cabrone, no!"

"Si!" I tell him. "It's already done!"

She gives me my change and I go out to sit with the guys. Xabi tells Aitor and Aitor's eyes bug out.

"No, Bill, no!"

"I already did it!"

"No." Aitor sighs.

"It's *solo bocadillos! Es un regalo!*"

They reluctantly let it go and feast on their sandwiches. *Haha I knew I'd get you guys back.* I spark a cigar, not very hungry myself.

"You buy us sandwiches, then you smoke right next to us while we eat them!" Xabi complains. *"Eres un Cabrone!"*

"Ha!" I laugh and squelch the cigar.

"Cristian!" they said and nod toward a *gigante* parade making its way through the square. We go over to see. They walk up to one of the *gigantes* then nod at me, hiking their eyebrows up. The guy in the big tall *gigante* suit flips it open.

"Como estas, Bill!" Cristian, their big strong friend, says as his grinning face appears in the opening.

"Cristian! You're a gigante! Cabrone!" I pat him on the back.

I head back on the long ride home to Pamplona gripping the steering wheel. *Jesus, this morning, it was so special. Not just because of the three runs in a row with sueltos and drama. It's the way the different generations worked together seamlessly.* I curve through the sandy hills. *From runners in their fifties to runners in their teens, and a pretty equal amount of each.* My mind summons memories of Miguel Leza dashing before the horns of a bull. *Aitor isn't the only one who got a great run, dozens of them did.* Adrenaline courses through my shoulders. *Then afterward, all that joy and respect flowing between all the runners. Man, I'll never forget it.* I charge up a hill like a galloping bull gaining momentum.

Back in Pamplona, I walk around the old section and suddenly a Middle-Eastern kid with short black curly hair rides right up to me on his bike and stops.

"Bill! Como estas?!" he says breathlessly.

It takes a second but I recognize him. It's Samir Fadil; we ran that suelto together this morning in Lodosa.

"Como estas, Samir?"

"What a run this morning!" His eyes bug out excitedly as he sits tall in his BMX's seat.

"It was incredible!" I shake my head.

"I gotta go," he says, his eyes lit with all the thrill of the morning. "I'm late for work!"

He pedals off quickly. I watch him go. *Man, something's changed, for a kid I hardly know to come up to me like that. Well, we shared a special morning together.* I walk into the wide expanse of Plaza del Castillo with the bright sky above. *Now we're bonded forever. A tiny piece of us'll never leave this morning in Lodosa. That's the life of a mozo, I guess.*

♉

Relaxing, I sit over at my office, the little café next to Bar Windsor called Café Lorek. Estella's next. Images of when JuanPe took me there after my goring roll through my mind: a chapel high on a hill with four distinct mountain ranges encircling the horizon; one round and green, another with huge white cliffs, a third dark and pointy and bursting up through the clouds. It's one of the most beautiful towns I'd ever been to. I was still walking with a cane, and before the run, JuanPe had pulled me aside.

"If you want to stand on the course, I'll protect you."

I thought about it. What if I get him hurt trying to protect me? I reluctantly declined and watched him run the horns of the vaca past a pretty stone corridor overhang.

And now JuanPe has started a new career driving buses in Pamplona, driving during all the fiestas of Navarra when they need extra buses. It's sad not having him with me, but family comes first. Either way, he's laid down a great foundation for me in the pueblos of Navarra. I check my email and find a message from JuanPe reminding me about Estella. I reply with a heartfelt thanks. I wonder if Gowen's around.

A heavy door shuts behind me and I glance back. Gowen smirks in the shade of the corridor, standing in front of his red door. He sits down next to me. We both laugh at our luck.

Gowen is one of the greatest American bull runners ever. There's plenty of debate over who was greater back in the seventies, Gowen or another young American, both the young disciples of Matt Carney. Gowen is also a decorated Vietnam War veteran, though he insists that after two medals in his first two battles, during his third battle they found him in a hole eating rations. "I guess I got hungry."

Before his tour was over, a large-caliber bullet struck and nearly killed Gowen. He spent around a year in the hospital enduring several surgeries. Sometime afterwards, Harry Hubert, a historic personality in Pamplona's fiesta, brought Gowen to San Fermin and introduced him to Matt Carney. Carney brought Gowen out to run two days in a row, and on the third, told him, "You know what you're doing. Now you're on your own, kid."

Gowen was running in the Telefonica section when a lone bull dug his horn into Gowen's shoe and threw him way up over the barricades to the other side where they used to set up bleachers. The crowd in the bleachers caught him and threw him all back onto the course. Gowen then ran with the rest of the herd into the plaza.

Gowen's girlfriend Maria comes out of the red door and scolds him.

"Tom, I'm hungry. We are late, let's go!"

Gowen laughs and introduces me. Maria is nice and warm-spirited. The two bicker playfully.

Gowen asks the waiter how much for his drink and my coffee, and I interrupt.

"Naw Tom, let me get it."

Gowen looks at me mischievously. "I'll play ya for it."

"What's it called again?"

"Chino. Haven't we played Chino yet?"

"Yeah, but we didn't finish the game."

"Your first game of Chino." He grins. "It's still going."

We stand up, get our coins figured out, and on the second call, I say, "One."

He looks me in the eyes, his white eyebrows hike up. "Good call, kid." He opens his palm, showing nothing. I open mine: one golden euro sits across my lifeline.

"You won Chino in your first game, kid." He laughs and pats me on my heart.

"Beginner's luck," I say.

Gowen starts across the plaza. "Naw kid, I don't lose Chino too often."

"See ya around, Tom."

"Call me, kid."

I check my email and find a message from Stephanie telling me they're having a party at their house tonight. Maybe Tom and Maria would want to go. I call and Tom answers.

"Want to go to a party tonight?"

"Yes."

A couple hours later we meet up and walk out to where I parked. But my rental car isn't there.

"La Grua!" Maria says.

"What?"

"You got towed, kid."

"No way."

We look on the ground and there it is, my neon orange ticket.

"They don't just write tickets here, pal. They just tow ya."

"I can't believe it."

We take a cab to the subterranean parking garage. The woman behind the glass booth laughs wickedly.

"One hundred and thirty euros," she says.

My eyes bug out. Ah, fuck it. I pay.

"Well, join the club, kid. You ain't a real Pamplonese until La Grua gets you."

We arrive at the party. Kiliki is getting the fire started but has to run off, so Gowen takes over fire preparations. He builds the kindling in a triangle.

"That's not how you do it, Tom," Maria scolds him.

"She thinks she can make a better fire than me." He winks at me.

They bicker hilariously over the best way to build a fire as people crowd around to laugh at their exuberant arguments. Kiliki roasts up a bunch of chicken and beef and lamb. We feast. Afterward, Tom and I sit in the chairs on the back porch.

"Tom, you want to go to Estella with me day after tomorrow?"

"Me? Go to Estella with you?"

"Yeah, come on, it'll be a blast."

"Alright, I'll go."

The little boys gather around us as we talk bull running. One of the neighbor's kids is really interested.

"Can you make a living running with the bulls?"

"Hahaha, no! There's no money in bull running."

"But you, your life is all bull running."

"I saved a lot of money to do this. I just do it because I love it."

"I want to try it!"

Gowen grins at me.

"You should, but it's dangerous. You gotta be serious about it."

"Maybe when I'm fifteen."

"Good thinking."

"Who knows, maybe you'll end up the next Aitor."

"Who is Aitor?"

I start showing them pictures of all the great Basque runners—Aitor, Dani, Sergio Colas, JuanPe, Julen. They guffaw at many of the shots. We pull up videos and they *ohhh* and *ahhh* at Aitor's and JuanPe's runs. They all agree they'll run with the bulls one day.

"Your mothers will be so happy," I giggle.

Stephanie comes over.

"If they want to run, they can run, but you have to teach them and keep them safe."

"Oh man, Tas, Oli, please don't run with the bulls."

"Come on, what about with the vaca? It'll be fun, hundred percent," Oli tells me.

"Ahaha OK." I try to change the subject as I roll my shoulders nervously. Man, I hope they don't run! Stephanie will kill me if they get hurt!

♉

I head over to Tom's place the next day. It's a palace of an apartment; it stretches long, with balconies overlooking Plaza del Castillo and the first stretch of Estafeta for the bull run. It's a four-bedroom apartment with dozens of framed photos of the encierro lining the walls, dating back to the fifties and through all the ages.

Gowen gives me the tour, pointing out historic run photos. One is a sequence of photos of James Michener running at the beginning of Santo Domingo; they were published in a big *Esquire* article Michener wrote.

"Carney told Michener, 'Run Santo Domingo, nothing ever happens there.'"

In the photos Michener stands against a drainpipe along the wall across from where they put the saint in the morning. A bull dislodges from the pack and scrapes the wall. It severely gores two men as it approaches Michener, who has nowhere to escape.

"San Fermin's capote was the only thing that could save old Jimmy."

For no apparent reason, the bull turns his head slightly away as he passes Michener, then goes back to scraping the wall.

"That's why you never talk encierro in broad terms, kid. Anything can and will happen in a bull run... And this, this is my proudest photo in the whole room." Gowen stands before a big photo of the curve with Tom Turley having a good run, the animals spilling out of the curve.

"My son, Kevin." He points at a young teenaged blond-haired boy running the curve.

"At sixteen he'd been studying the curve every morning from the balcony, I didn't know what he was doing. I thought he was just watching the run. Naw, he was making a plan. He snuck onto the course and I'm up here looking down and there he goes flying through the curve right alongside the bulls. The Basque paper interviewed me. I was so proud of him and scared for him. They published the story the next day, and I'm walking around, and the people, they kept coming up to me and telling me, 'Now you understand, now you're one of us,'" Tom says, tears welling in his blue eyes.

"The experiences you have here, the runs, the fun, that's just the surface, kid. The real gift of Navarra are the people. They're priceless. The friends you make in this town, they're friends for life, kid," Tom says, looking me in the eyes, his weathered face stern and serious and warm.

☿

We get up early the next morning and head out to Estella. It's a town of nearly fourteen thousand people. The Ega y Ebro flow through it. The mountains of Montejurra, Peñquda, Cruz de los Castillos, Santa Barbara, and Belastegui surround Estella like a crown.

"I ran Estella back in the seventies. We were going around the pueblos in a camper van, and I woke up after a night on the booze, and here come the vaca, running right down the street we're parked on. So I jumped up and ran with 'em. That beats a morning coffee any day of the week, kid."

We park by a river and walk right onto the course. The bull-run course goes over an ornamental purplish-blue marble path. My feet slip on the marble as we walk.

After a bit of a hike up the surreal street, we find the wide courtyard section of the course with the overhang corridor. As we prepare to run, we see an English runner we know on the course, one who wrote his own book about the run. He immediately begins to give me his dissertation on Estella.

"You missed the first run, what will happen is they'll come run this direction then the teenagers will form a wall over there and the vaca will come running back our way," he says, as if he's talking with himself.

I roll my eyes at Gowen. *Jeez buddy, I didn't ask for your advice!* Gowen and I walk off to get a drink while he's still trying to explain Estella to me.

"I hate that guy."

"Yeah, he can get a little annoying."

"He's part of that whole snobby asshole foreign runner group. He's one of the worst ones."

"What can I say, kid? Some people run a few years and get full of themselves."

"Yeah, I can't stand that shit. Ruins the whole thing for me."

A little Peña clubhouse sits along the overhang corridor behind the arched pillars. The Peña set up their own big wooden shield like in Puente la Reina. Gowen makes friends with the old men behind the shield. They invite him in and Gowen comes back with a glass of water for me and a cup of Patxaran for himself. We prepare to run next to the pillars.

The rocket pops and the vaca fly up the narrow marble street toward us. I miss the first batch, then run and find a little spot near a reddish-colored vaca. She throws her horns at my back and even gives Gowen a head fake before I run her horns a short distance as she hooks wildly for me. Suddenly at the end of the corridor the English runner steps out into the street and smashes his shoulder into me. I halt and glare at him. *Are you fucking nuts?* I want to punch him right in his stomach.

"They're coming back!" he barks at me. "Get ready!"

They don't come back. *Fucking idiot.*

I walk off to find Gowen as the Englishman follows, explaining, "Usually they come back and…" I just keep walking.

I find Gowen by the Peña clubhouse, grinning at me.

"That's my boy!" The old men behind the shield grin at me and raise their drinks toward me. "They're happy with your running. You started a little slow, but you got in there."

The Englishman walks up with some more know-it-all crap about some other pueblo. It just sounds like he's masturbating with his mouth. *This fucking guy wants to be my teacher. What the fuck do I need a teacher like him for when I got Gowen around? Not to mention my friends are some of the greatest bull runners in history.* Gowen finally lays into him.

"Who the hell do you think you are?" Gowen asks.

The Englishman abruptly stops talking and looks at Gowen like a frightened puppet.

"You think you know it all 'cause you wrote that crummy book?" Gowen goes on. "You wrote a book about the run after your first year in San Fermin? It's crap. It's a joke. You're an arrogant prick."

My jaw drops. Holy fuck, this is priceless! Then Gowen glares at him and motions to me.

"Shake his hand!" he shouts, nodding toward me. "Maybe a little bit of the humility will rub off."

I fight back laughter. I don't consider myself the greatest example of humility, but I try. I can't miss out on this shit! I reach my hand out and the Englishman reluctantly shakes it. I grin at him, embarrassed.

As we drive home through the mountains I confess that what he'd done to the Englishman was one of the greatest things I'd ever had the pleasure of experiencing.

"I hate the snobby crap," Gowen says, like he is taking the words right out of my mouth.

As we banter I can genuinely feel his spirit shielding me from the lingering depression.

"So how many runs you got so far?"

I do some quick math.

"Five in Puente la Reina, six in Lodosa, and one today makes twelve... Fifty-two," I say.

"More than halfway there, not bad."

"Yeah, I don't know if I'll make it to a hundred and one, but I'm gonna try."

"Ya know kid it ain't the number that matters, right? It's the path, the journey. You gotta stop being so hard on yourself and just enjoy the damned ride," he says, motioning to the view outside our windshield.

I grin as we flow through the epic Navarran countryside. Big lumpy green hills encircle us as rocky cliffs loom in the distance. *Sitting here with a true legend, probably the closest thing you could get to Matt Carney in spirit. Two American knuckleheads looking for that pure magic of Navarra.*

"When you're right, you're right, Tom."

"Alright. Cheers to that," he says, and takes a sip of his cocktail.

We make some more plans for later in the summer before I drop him off. I thank him and head for the train back to Cuellar.

Chapter 8

Iscar

As my train soars back toward Cuellar, my spirits lift to new heights. Less books and more energy: I feel like a bull that's been out in the wild a bit and lost some of the blubber he'd gained on the ranch. *Man, I wonder how good you can run in Iscar.* The train car jostles along the tracks as we shoot through a small pueblo. *This will be epic.*

I arrive at the hostel that night and walk smack dab into the middle of a party for blind teenagers. I slip through their dancing bodies unnoticed because of the loud music. They sing pop songs well into night, long after I turn in. "And I...eeigh! Will always love you-ooo-uuuuuuu!" I squeeze my pillow against my ears. *Please, God, stop this.* I giggle. I probably can't sleep anyway. *Man, I can't wait to run Iscar.*

I rise early and jump in the car with Dyango and get on the road.

"Cuellar is positioned exactly between Valladolid and Segovia," Dyango explains. "Because of this, they built the main highway through Cuellar. Cuellar's castle is much larger, and historically Cuellar has more influence on the area. Cuellar is the second-biggest city in its province, and Iscar is just over the border in Valladolid, where Iscar is a small town by comparison to their many big cities. But Iscar is a manufacturing hub, and it is growing fast."

"Iscar's like Cuellar's younger brother who's trying to prove himself with hard work."

"Más o menos." Dyango nods.

The bullring comes into view at the entrance of town next to a big dusty field. The structure is very modern but strikingly beautiful when you get up close. Rose-colored bricks create the first level, yellow bricks form the second, and red make the third. Tall tinted-glass arched windows line the exterior. Curved blue steel beams shape the roof with dozens of clear-glass windows spread between them. Metal sheeting forms the dome.

"It's a beautiful bullring."

"Yes, look." Dyango points up high on a hill. "The Castle."

The white stone castle of Iscar stands high above town on a cliff.

"It has a brewery and the Museum de Mariemma. It is the only museum completely dedicated to dance in all of Spain."

"Interesting."

"Mariemma was a great Spanish dancer from Iscar. The museum holds many dance costumes from various eras."

"Well, now we go dance with the bulls in the street."

"But not too close, eh!" Dyango and I chuckle.

On our way in we stop at the tent of the clothing line Al Limite. Epic photographic images of Spanish fighting bulls are splayed across the colorful shirts. The owner-operator, a spikey-haired guy, grins and greets us jovially. He points to a stack of my books that sit on sale on one of the shelves. He wishes us good luck and we head to the bull-run course.

A large, bulb-shaped arch sits above the big yellow-and-red metal doors with a series of red Xs laid over the yellow. *X marks the spot, I guess.* We walk away from the plaza along the course. Electronic dance music thumps from a big nightclub as a couple hundred hungover EDM heads bob in the street. We weave through them.

"Do they know bulls are about the rampage through here?" I ask Dyango.

"No, no, Bill. They break the bull run into two parts. First the *embudo* with the horses in the fields, then they pen those bulls, and later they run another group to the bullring," Dyango explains as we hurry across town.

We pass a makeshift pen at an intersection with bulls already in it. We take a peek through one of the holes in the wooden wall. Several nice fully grown bulls lounge lazily in their big bed of hay.

"An hour after the embudo, they will run these bulls to the bullring."

I peer in at the regal bulls that sit in meditation. *Them EDM heads'll be sleeping off their ecstasy hangovers by then.* "The dancers should be gone by then, and not trying to dance with the bulls."

"Yes," Dyango giggles. "It would be bad if they tried that."

Thousands of people line the fencing at the edge of town. One fence runs out two hundred yards alongside a gravel road.

A big brick barn stands at the very edge of town; beside it, a harvested wheat field rises over a big hill.

Dyango introduces me to a sharp athletic guy wearing a ball cap.

"Bill, este es Diego Alcalde," he says, and explains that Diego is one of the best runners in Iscar.

Diego looks sick with nerves. He shakes my hand. "Welcome to Iscar," he says, then goes off to prepare.

"This embudo is different from Cuellar. The hill in Cuellar lets you see everything from a distance. Here all you can see is the dust," Dyango says, pointing to the horizon.

A thick dust cone rises up to the sky and slowly snakes toward us from behind the little hill. As the first animals crest the field surrounded by horsemen, I choose to stay back with Dyango near the fence. The horsemen kick the pack into a gallop and they ramble through the dusty field toward us.

Diego Alcalde waits for the first bull of the *feria* at the edge of the field as all the other fifty runners retreat. He peers into the animal with the curved brim of his blue baseball cap pulled low across his brow. At the last possible moment, a black bull shoots out into the lead directly in Alcalde's path. *He'll kill him!* Alcalde stares the beast down; he links with the animal, turns, and runs impossibly close to the snout of the bull. *My god, he's like Aitor!* Alcalde's short chopping steps slow the animal into the embudo as the other animals and horsemen follow in a fanned-out calamitous stampede with a magnificent dust cloud lifting up off of them like the smoke from a thundering locomotive.

Dyango and I filter in and run, but the pack blasts past. Several unruly bulls tear off along the adjacent fields followed by horsemen; their dust trail sails through the hills and slowly vanishes on the horizon. After some tense waiting, the runners and spectators give up.

"Come on," Dyango says, and I follow him into town for the second part of the run.

Back near the arena, I position myself on the straightaway about a hundred yards from the tunnel. Dyango chooses a wide section near the middle of the course. I bounce on my toes as the animals approach. The Iscar runners run the horns in several groups. *Try for the first set.* I start jogging, looking back as the herd closes in. Three runners come into view leading a bull and a few steers. The runner closest to the lead bull barks orders at the others, and they adjust their positions accordingly. A spot opens in front of the bull as the runners rearrange. I move into place when the one closest to the bulls shouts to another and he closes me off, running tight on the horns. I give him space. As we run into the tunnel, the boss gives more orders. When we enter the domed arena he puts his arm around me.

"If you want to run with us you have to start earlier on the course," he says, along with some other stuff I don't catch.

"Thanks," I reply as the rest of the herd pours into the ring. I shrug. *You better not push too hard in Iscar.*

I head back out the tunnel to find Dyango. It's the first time I've seen runners working together so well, and I really want to run with them. I find Dyango on the course.

"That was fun, Dyango, thanks!"

"It's not over, in an hour, two sueltos!"

"Really?" I shake my head. *How many runs are there in Iscar?*

In the later run I use my rolled newspaper and help lure a steadily trotting suelto through the tunnel and into the arena with one of the three guys I'd run with earlier. He pats me on the back as he peels off inside the ring. Sweat beads down my neck as I stand on the sand in the cool shaded arena. The open windows in the dome allow a swirling breeze in. As I gaze upward into the rectangle-shaped openings to the blue heavens I fall deeply into the bull trance of Iscar. *This is truly a runner's fiesta.* The animals flow rhythmically through its avenues like seductive dancers continually calling you back into the street. You sit exhausted but energized by the wonder of it, and as the beasts approach yet again you rise for another chance to dance into the arena with the bull's horns gouging at your back.

♉

The next morning, I run the two runs, then ride home with my friend Miguelin, a nice father in his forties with spikey salt-and-pepper hair who is also running a whole bunch of runs all over Spain this summer—I've been bumping into him everywhere. I thank Miguelin as he drops me off in the heart of Cuellar. I climb the hill in the weaving streets toward my hostel. *Man, there's been so many runs in Iscar, they're all blurring together!* Images flash: horns, a suelto, the arena dome overhead, smiles, high-fives, joyful laughter, repeat.

I nap until Ernes Fernandez, a big, portly and gregarious Cuellarano, picks me up with his nice girlfriend. He is a big part of Eh Toro, the organization which gave me an award back in 2013. We drive into Iscar in the middle of the night. As we approach in the pitch black, the small castle sits high above town on a dark cliff. Crisp white lights illuminate its stone walls. Below it the enormous bullring glows like a beautiful alien spacecraft landed for an invasion. *I guess there is an invasion underway.* I giggle. *An invasion of galloping bulls.* I peer at both as we zoom toward the course. It's such a big contrast: the ancient and the modern.

Fernandez and his girlfriend brought along a tasty meal, and we eat with the Al Limite guys amidst the lively party.

"Toro Passion tonight," Ernes says, and chomps on a piece of bread soaked in stew.

"Two runs or more..." the Al Limite guy pipes in.

"I ran with them in Lodosa! It was great!"

"But be careful, OK, Bill? Don't let your guard down, *Boxeador!*" Ernes says.

Loosening up, I prepare to run near the bullring and Ernes sets up to photograph near me. I look down the long course and bounce on my toes as the run is about to start. All the runners turn to face me. *Why are they looking this way?*

"They're coming out of the plaza first!" Ernes shouts from the barricades.

"No way!" I laugh.

Well, maybe you can lead them out of the tunnel like Aitor did. Ha, not as close of course! But with that same idea anyway. I walk into the gorgeous tunnel with the domed ceiling of the bullring all lit up bright. They release the herd from the corrals. The bulls and steers round the sandy ring several times, sending tense murmurs through the arena and the street. Then the pack turns into the tunnel. The pack hugs one side of the tunnel. Several of the animals smash into the ring doors as they make the turn into the alley. Time slows as the herd crawls over itself trying to make it into the tunnel. *The herd'll break!* I prepare to run. Miraculously the pack sticks together—surging forward in one undulating mass. The bright lights of the bullring splay their horned shadows at my feet. I bounce on my toes in the tunnel as they trot along the concrete tunnel wall toward me—a silver sheen glowing along their hides. *Go for it!* Sprinting hard, I run them out of the tunnel and around the bend, then dive to the fence as they crackle past.

"Did you see that!?" I shout to Ernes.

"Yes!" He guffaws from the barricades. "Incredible!"

"Wow..." I pace around, the adrenaline shooting up explosively through my shoulders. It bubbles in my stomach and I nearly vomit.

About fifteen minutes later, they run them back in. As I round the final turn into the arena, I manage to fall over two runners that trip in front of me. I slap the blacktop hard. The lead bull's large white horn passes over me as I lie still.

Pain singes my elbows and knees. A line of blood trickles down to my wrist. *Here you are again, fucked up on the pavement in Spain.* I wince and scowl near the barricades, holding my knees to my chest while a final suelto rumbles up. *It ain't nothing to fall, that'll happen out here, mozo. It's about what you do when you hit the street hard.* I take a deep breath and stand, then wait in the inside of the bend as the mozos slowly bring him toward me. He emerges slowly around the bend, a Colorado (reddish-brown bull) with black spots along his back. *Hello there, my friend.* He huffs heavily, trotting slowly as us mozos stay at the edge of his vision. His savvy eyes tell me: just relax for one second and I'll charge hard and gore you.

I stand in the front line, waving my rolled newspaper in his plane of vision. He takes a deep breath and charges hard as several dozen of us sprint ahead of him, through the tunnel and into the arena.

We watch the *capea* for a few hours as the excellent recortadores put on a great show with the bulls we'd run.

"Look at this." Ernes shows me a video on his phone of my run with the suelto. "Good job, Bill." He pats me on the back. His girlfriend smiles and squeezes my shoulder.

We head home, and just a few hours later in the early morning, Ernes picks me up again and we shoot back to Iscar.

"Same thing today with Toro Passion. They run them out of the tunnel maybe twice," Ernes says and picks his nice camera up out of the center console. "I have my camera today, Bill. This time we get photos of your run for the website!"

"Ehtoroeh.com?"

"*Exacto.*"

Ernes sets up in a good spot as I stand in the tunnel waiting. Another runner stands beside me. He's stoutly built like me, with short thin hair and soft eyes. Didn't we run together last night?

"Hello, my name is Pablo."

"Hi Pablo, I'm Bill." We shake hands. "We ran last night together, didn't we?"

"Yes. Wow the animals were spectacular, no?"

"Yeah, I've never seen anything like it!"

"Today *mas.*" He grins and hikes his eyebrows up.

"*Exactamente.*"

The bulls shoot out of the ring into the tunnel much faster this time. Everyone clears out as the bulls approach except for

Pablo and me. We wait and as they get close, we sprint ahead of them and lead them out of the shady tunnel onto the bright sunlit street shoulder-to-shoulder. *Rock and roll, my friend!*

I glance back and slow as the animals enter the bright street. Suddenly, the pack begins crawling all over each other again as they gallop. The animals' bodies merge, with no way to tell where one ends and the next begins. Horns crack into each other. The pack ejects one white steer; he pops up and rolls over the backs of the other animals and flops hard on the pavement but climbs right up galloping with the pack. *How the fuck?!* A lead black bull with dark-brown patches between his wide horns surges ahead of the pack. *Oh damn, you're a beauty!* I dig in, sprinting. We lead him around the bend into the straightaway and dive out onto the fence as they roar past.

Fifteen minutes later we run the bulls back to the plaza and I get in the thick of it. Ernes calls me over to him.

"They're going to run them again!" he tells me.

"Another run?!" I can't believe my luck. *Every damn time you think it's over in Iscar there's another run or two left. It never ends.* My new friend Pablo and I position ourselves in the tunnel again.

"Bill, be careful my friend," he says in English as he pats me on the back.

"You speak good English and I speak OK Spanish. This is good!"

"My English is bad. Your Spanish is good."

"Haha...no way." *Pablo, this might be the start of a beautiful friendship.*

"Did you see the *cabestro* flip over the others?!" he asks excitedly.

"I've never seen anything like it!" I guffaw.

Pablo and I do pretty much the same thing, leading the pack out of the tunnel, except this time we run them much further down the street. I help lead the last suelto into the plaza on the final run. We cruise home through the pine forest.

"Man, I feel like I've gotten ten years of experience in the past three days."

"Yes, in Pamplona you only run one time per day. In Iscar you can run sometimes ten times in one day!" Ernes says.

"This is how the Spanish and Basque runners get so good. They run bulls hundreds of times a year." I marvel at the wide difference between foreign and homegrown runners.

"The more you run, the better you get, Bill. Look at the photos." He hands me the camera.

I flip through them. Pablo and me dashing before the horns out the tunnel with that pack undulating, falling and rising in split seconds.

"How do they move like that! Every time I think I've seen it all they go and do something that blows my entire understanding of them."

Ernes grins and squeezes my shoulder.

♉

Diego de Diego picks me up and brings me back to Iscar in the afternoon. Diego's father Jose Luis is the great bull-run photographer of Cuellar; everyone knows him as Bias. Bias is old and thin with long white hair and a full beard with a kind, fatherly spirit. Diego is a jovial guy with this humble yet royal presence.

"We've put together a huge exhibition for my father's photos in a few weeks. You have to come, Bill!"

"I wouldn't miss it, Diego."

"Pictures from the fifties and sixties, all the way until today."

"I can't wait to see them."

"Today they release five bulls in Iscar one at a time."

"Interesting." I hike my eyebrows up. "No steers?"

"No, today just five bulls."

We go down to the end of the course where the truck full of bulls pulls up to an opening in the fencing. *What the hell's gonna happen here?*

"Can we stay and watch the first bull released?"

"Ah, OK," Diego reluctantly agrees.

The first bull explodes down the truck ramp and blazes through the street. With a hundred-yard lead on the animal, we sprint as fast as we can but only make it to near the halfway point of the course when the bull surges up behind us and we cut out to the fence. *Bad fucking idea!*

"Sorry Diego, I didn't know the bull would be so fast!" I say; we jog behind as the bull shoots ahead and quickly disappears into the plaza.

"It's OK, Bill." Diego stops to run with his friends about three hundred yards from the bullring. "I'm going to run here. Suerte."

"Thanks, suerte!" I keep running to get close to the bullring. As I get near the final quarter of the course, the next bull blazes up. *Fuck, I'm too tired!* I dive out through the fence.

The third bull approaches. I take a deep breath. *OK, now let's get it on.* I run the bull's horns with several local runners. As we approach the final curve into the ring, I run along the outside of the curve. The bull accelerates, and I dive out onto the barricades as he thunders past. An excellent local runner with blond hair takes over, leading the bull with short choppy steps in the center of the street all the way into the arena.

Raul Lasierra stomps up in his Toro Passion gear with his willow cane. He glares at me, flustered.

"Bill, this is your *tramo*," he says, meaning it's my section of the course. "We've talked about it and this is your *tramo*, but running the outside of the curve like that is very bad! It is very dangerous. You should run the inside of the curve."

"Sorry Raul, you're right..." I pat him on the shoulder.

Raul jogs off to work the fourth bull. *What the heck does he mean I have a tramo in Iscar? Maybe they're impressed with my running.* Then I reconsider. *Probably not, you goof.* I shrug. *Man, I ain't never gonna run the outside of a curve again.*

With some luck, I help lead the fourth bull into the arena, but I can't get back out in time for the fifth bull. *Let him go.* I put my elbows up on the ring wall ledge and watch as he gallops into the ring with the excellent Iscar runners just a foot before his horns.

On the way out of town I buy an outfit from the friendly guys at Al Limite and plan to wear it in my next bull run. That night in Cuellar, I go over to my favorite establishment in Spain, Hotel Restaurante San Francisco, and eat my favorite meal in the world, *Rabo de Toro en Vino Tinto* (bull tail stew in a wine sauce) in the outdoor seating. The rich beefy scent hits my nostrils. *My god, this smells fantastic.* I take my fork and tap the tail vertebra and the hunk of juicy dark red meat falls clean of the bone. *It's perfect.* As I chomp on the tender *rabo,* I marvel at the images flashing in my mind of racing up the street with the bulls in Iscar. I can't even remember all of them. It's a fucking blur of dancing bulls. I check my notes. *You managed to run nineteen runs in the three days, and it could have been frickin' twenty if you didn't miss that last bull! Seventy-one runs this summer, with so much time left.* I'm gonna make it to a hundred and one. I feel free like a suelto out in the fields, believing I could run wild forever.

I hang around Cuellar haunting the bars in town, chatting with friends and writing my *Chicago Tribune* blog, which will later turn into this book. Gratitude fills my heart as I climb up the hill toward Bar San Francisco in the twilight. *How lucky am I? Walking around my favorite little pueblo in the whole world. I didn't make the bestseller list, but who gives a shit!* I make it to the top of the hill and cross the street into the park. I sit on a bench near a life-sized iron bust of a bull and a man in an ancient dance. I scribble in my notebook. *In life you can't control whether or not you're rich or successful. All you can really do is strive for happiness. You're here in Cuellar. You're living your dream. You're happy. You don't write because you want to be a Nobel Prize–winning millionaire. You write because it brings you joy.* I sigh. I fucking love my life.

A couple walks past arm-in-arm in the light broken by the leaves of the trees lining the courtyard. I miss Enid. I see her round smiling face in my mind. My *chilanga,* a girl from a poor neighborhood in Mexico City. Our love throbs very alive in my heart. *She's living her dream too, in the Peace Corps in Panama. How lucky are you to have a wife who'll let you do this—a whole summer of bulls? She is the luckiest thing that's ever happened in your life.*

My mind is leveling out as I cruise deeper into this summer in the pueblos. But as my three days off from the bulls comes to an end, my mind, body, and spirit begin to ache for another run with the bulls.

Chapter 9

Toros in Ribera de Duero

Taking a deep breath, I bend down and grip the big, new metal trailer in Dyango's warehouse in Valladolid and push as Dyango guides it into an open space in back. "August 15th is the most popular day for bull festivals in Spain," Dyango says as we ease it into position. "There are hundreds of bull runs tomorrow. But tonight we go to Tudela de Duero."

"There's two Tudelas with bull runs!?" I straighten up and wipe sweat from my forehead.

"Yes, Tudela in Navarra and Tudela de Duero in Castilla y Leon," Dyango says as he walks over to maneuver another trailer. "It's an important run, very old, almost as old as Cuellar. Their oldest document of the run is from 1509."

I follow him, trying to keep up. *Fuck, how the hell did I not know about this shit?* I bend down to move the next grey trailer. *Guess you don't know as much as you thought you did.* I push the next trailer as Dyango steers.

Dyango closes up shop then we stop off for a late-night McDonald's meal. The McDonald's is nice and fancy and you order through a series of electronic portals. We sit down to eat; it's a big hangout for the teenagers, and they chat along the benches as I chomp on my chicken nuggets.

"Tudela de Duero, the Joyful Tear of the Duero. The Duero river, the river, it is famous because it fertilizes the land around it to create incredible soil for asparagus and wine grapes. Many of the finest wineries in the world are along the Duero."

Man, I wish I could still drink. I take a slug of my water bottle.

"Tudela de Duero is a fascinating place. Branches of the Duero river encircle the town. Humans have lived there since the Lower Paleolithic because of the rich vegetation. Many archeologists go there to excavate, they're always finding new things."

"That's cool! How big of a town is it?"

"About eight thousand, it's pretty big. It's close, it's only fifteen minutes away from Valladolid. The run is at midnight."

"This is gonna be fun!"

"Tonight is the beginning of the Fiestas de Nuestra Señora de la Asunción and San Roque. Then many runs happen in the next few days. But you have to go back to Navarra, right?"

"Yeah, I wish I could stay, but there's Falces and Tafalla. I wish I could be in both places at the same time."

"And then you're right back for the Medieval Fair in Cuellar?"

"Then Madrid for Sanse, then back for Cuellar, and then Medina del Campo, then back to Pamplona!"

"You're like a pinball, bouncing all over Spain!"

"*Exacto!*"

ŏ

Dyango and I arrive in town about an hour before the bull run begins. We walk through the clean, newly paved streets toward the pens. *Man, this town is breathtaking.* Elaborate decorative lights depicting bulls and bull runners string overhead across the narrow street full of balconies. We pass a main square with an enormous beautiful cathedral and a pretty town hall. A large music stage fills the courtyard. We walk until we find a bend that leads to a big stone bridge over the main branch of the Duero river.

We cross it and walk through a few turns and into a wide street that is modern and less beautiful and leads to a field. The makeshift red bullring stands in the dark field with bright stadium lights hovering above.

"Where do you want to run?" Dyango asks.

"The bridge?" I shrug.

"Let's do it." Dyango nods and we head back to the pretty bridge. The bridge holds a two-lane road with rounded waist-high concrete walls lining either side and streetlamps hovering above. There's no escape on the hundred-yard bridge. The big deep river flows slowly thirty feet below to a dam on the other side of the bridge just downstream. If things go wrong on the bridge and you go over, you're gonna have to navigate the fucking dam. I peer down at the water flowing over the dam.

"*Es peligroso.*" Dyango reads my mind.

"Where should we start running from?"

"Maybe halfway across?"

I nod.

"Four bulls tonight without steers."

"That makes it even more dangerous."

Dyango shrugs in agreement. *Damn, the bulls'll be more likely to hook and zigzag.*

Mozos enter the avenue and limber up. Tense murmurs fill the street as the thousands of onlookers line the metal fencing before and after the bridge. The rocket pops in the distance.

"Suerte," Dyango says and shakes my hand.

"Suerte," I reply.

The bulls rumble into view around the bend about a hundred yards before the bridge, then disappear behind the spectators. Four young athletic young mozos position themselves to run the entire bridge. They rocket into view in front of the bulls as Dyango and I wait. The four black bulls gallop serenely along the new blacktop. We begin to run as they close in on us. The bridge stands empty before us. The black bulls run shoulder-to-shoulder in a near perfect line. Their mouths hang open as if entranced by the brave runners dashing before them. Dyango and I give the four young runners plenty of space. *Man, this is my only chance to run here, fuck it.* Toward the end of the bridge I slow and get in beside the foursome. I lead one of the bulls for fifteen yards before I shoot out at the end of the bridge to a small opening along the side.

Dyango and I high-five afterward. *Fuck that was a little crazy.* My heart pumps hard as I peek out from behind the wall.

A bull falls up on the path, then rises and shoots out of sight into the darkness. *Fuck it, you had to at least get a little action.*

♉

The next morning Dyango picks me up and we head toward Peñafiel.

"Peñafiel means loyal rock. It is the capital of the Ribera de Duero wine country," Dyango tells me as the spectacular castle in Peñafiel comes into view on the horizon. It sits high atop the narrow rocky cliff, mimicking the cliff's long, thin shape.

"Inside the castle, they have the wine museum of Valladolid. Beneath the castle, inside the gigantic rock cliff, the people of Peñafiel dug many tunnels. Some of them measuring over two hundred yards," Dyango tells me. "They use the caves to store the fermenting wine. There are chimney vents from the caves to ventilate the gases produced by the fermenting. You see the chimneys?"

I see them dotting the landscape throughout Peñafiel, with the castle looming above. "The castle, I've been thinking about it since you brought me a few weeks ago. At night, it's like a great white ship floating in a sea of dark wine."

"Ahh...exacto, Bill."

We park out by the corrals and walk into town. The streets bustle with runners and spectators.

"Be careful today. Two things, the tunnel into Plaza del Coso is very dangerous, a man was killed last year near the tunnel. The bull turned around and gored him in a doorway," Dyango tells me as we walk the long straightaway. "The other thing to remember is during the *capea*, they release one bull inside the ring and one bull outside the ring to run all through the square. They have an announcer, he will yell, *'Toro dentro! Y Toro Afueda!'''* Dyango giggles excitedly as excitement bubbles in my chest.

"This is gonna be nuts! I can't wait!"

We walk into town along the big wide straightaway.

"It's August 15th' Bill! The most important day for bulls in Spain!"

As we enter the last bend into the center of town, thousands of runners and spectators and partiers mill the street. A band plays before a memorial for the young runner who died near the tunnel the year before. I pay respects with a silent prayer. The photo shows a young man in his twenties. Had his whole life in front of him. *Rest in peace, mozo.*

Every single runner I meet that morning warns me not to run the tunnel, that it is very dangerous, and I agree, but deep down I know that if it opens up for me I'll go for it. I giggle, thinking of my older sisters telling me I couldn't do something, and how that meant I had to do it. I've always been a suelto at heart. I glance down the street at the opening in the façade and sigh. *When is enough enough, Bill? Why you always gotta be the super-badass?* But maybe it's not that…when I have a vision in my mind, I can't stop until I live it.

Dyango goes off to run the big straightaway and I hang back at the turn before the final straightaway and the tunnel into Plaza del Coso.

The bulls come, and I hug the inside of the final turn and drift toward the tunnel. The lead pack thunders past, snug along the far wall. Many excellent runners battle it out to run their horns. *Screw that.* I hang back. An opening forms in the street behind the initial pack as two beautiful bulls gallop alone in the avenue. I ease my way in front of them and run their horns for twenty yards as we near the tunnel. *No, don't, Bill!* I cut out. But the bulls slow and make the turn into the tunnel easily. *Fuck it!* I cut back in alongside the second animal and place my hand softly on his back. His taut fur contracts. I run through a memory, my vision. I see myself in action beside the beast in the short forbidden tunnel. I dash through it with the bull, and then into the bright sunlight as the crowd erupts. I throw my head back in elation. A voice whispers: *Didn't I show you this, kid?* The ship-like castle floats high above Plaza del Coso. *Hell fucking yeah!* I let the bull gallop on alone into the wooden ring.

Afterward Dyango and I find each other and greet each other happily, and hurry to find a good place to watch the capea. They've set up vertical metal barricades at each of the corner entrances of the big sandy Plaza del Coso. Metal bars stand in front of the doorways of the homes that open onto the plaza. Big bleachers line the upstairs of a makeshift balcony along the side of the plaza where the tunnel entrance is. Below the balcony, vertical metal bars wall off a place to stand and watch. The entire plaza, the bleachers and balconies, crawl with spectators.

Our friend Miguelin runs out into the center of the plaza with several others and waves a big protest flag, protesting the news of the banning of Toro de la Vega in Tordesillas. Dyango and I clap as the whole Plaza del Coso erupts in cheers.

"It's terrible, they banned Toro de la Vega. There will be a big unrest later in September in Tordesillas," Dyango says.

"I want to see that."

The garage-style doors that line the bullring open, and a big brown bull tears into the ring, kicking up sand. Then they open the ring gate and he explodes into the plaza, and they slam the ring door shut behind him. We scamper quickly through the vertical bars under the big makeshift balcony that hold the bleachers above. The bull dashes toward us and plows into the metal bars. They strain and threaten to break. Then someone distracts him, and he vanishes in a dusty white cloud. They release another bull into the bullring. The announcer comes over the loud speaker.

"Toro dentro!!! Y Toro Fuera!!!"

Sand flies in swirling sprays as the animals sweep through the plaza, a primeval spectacle with the castle basking proudly above the living history unfolding below. *How does a fucking place like this exist in this world?* Dyango and I dive into a doorway, evading the brown bull. We giggle and guffaw as an old man scolds us for bumping him and knocking his drink out of his hand. *Sorry old fella, we were just trying to keep from being stabbed to death by a bull's horns.* The old man angrily takes his position back, gripping the bars of the doorway as the bull's tail whips past. *A billion people sitting on their couches checking their Facebook feed on their fancy tablets all over the planet, that's normal life today. This is Spain, man. One of the few places on this earth that's still truly alive.*

Dyango and I walk around the square to see the capea from another angle. We end up in a home that opens onto the plaza. A drunken man in a neon cowboy hat offers me a shot of red wine from his leather sack. My parched mouth aches for a sip. *Don't do it. No way.* I grin and shake my head. *Sobriety is the key to your life's dreams coming true.* I close my eyes. Then open them in the ancient home, looking out the doorway as the brown bull blazes past, eyeing us. *I get drunk on bulls and life now, and that's it.* The brown bull bashes his horns against the yellow metal bars across the plaza.

With a handshake and a hug, I thank Dyango and jump a bus to Valladolid to rent a car and head towards Navarra for the bull runs at Tafalla and Falces. *What a great couple fiestas. You had no idea they had this much going on around Cuellar, did you? Dyango, what a great friend he is. He orchestrated all of those people to help you. You couldn't have done it without them, and especially Dyango. He is a warrior for his culture, and a true ambassador. Jeez, Iscar, Tudela de Duero, Peñafiel, Fuentesaúco, Novallas, Navas de Oro. Shit, what the hell else are you gonna find out here in the wild, you crazy suelto?*

PART II

Encerrar

Chapter 10

El Pilón

Falces is a pueblo in central Navarra, nestled at the base of a long, tall, rocky cliff. A steep, sandy path winds up the cliff to an immaculate chapel. A rickety old metal corral named El Pilón (The Pylon) sits midway up the dusty path. Ancient Egyptians used the term Pylon to signify a spiritual passageway. The bull run in Falces is named El Pilón.

The bloodline of Navarran cattle produces incredible vaca. They are particularly ferocious, large, and agile, with tall beautiful horns. The Falcesinos run vaca from El Pilón down the winding mountainside path to corrals at the edge of town. It's a chaotic scramble. Sometimes the vaca veer off the narrow path and climb up the mountainside, other times they plunge off the ledge and descend into the deep gully.

In 2014, JuanPe brought me to visit Falces for El Pilón, a month after Brevito gored and nearly killed me in Pamplona. I still needed a cane to walk. JuanPe and I sat on an adjacent cliff; he would have been running but he dislocated his shoulder the day before. Thousands of villagers lined the many nearby cliffs and listened to the band below playing soft traditional music. The rocket shot into the sky and popped high above, signaling the release of the vaca from the corrals. The animals cut through the switchbacks and disappeared behind a bend. Then they emerged into view, entering a hard banking turn. The lead animal didn't see the ledge. She dipped her head, gored a photographer, and scooped him up. With the photographer clinging to her horns, she leapt clear off the cliff. Her legs and hooves crashed into two other cowering spectators. All four of them plummeted thirty feet down, collapsed onto a steep grassy plain then tumbled and disappeared into the ravine.

Miraculously, they all survived.

El Pilón is an absurdity in the already absurd world of bull running. Its majestic beauty is intoxicating, and its outrageous danger sends shivers through every runner's spine. Yet it is also deeply spiritual. Mountains—and the lure of ascent—have always drawn adventurous souls. In El Pilón the aim is to descend, to ride the chaotic avalanche of horned bovines all the way to the base.

The history of El Pilón is deep and blurred, like all bull-running history, but sometime before 1751, they began running three- to four-year-old bulls down El Pilón. Then early in the 20th century something happened, and in 1915 they switched to vaca.

Falces has an interesting relationship with a nearby town of Tafalla. Tafalla's bull run takes place one hour before Falces. Tafalla is a beloved run for the Navarrese because it is a beautiful and wealthy town and they run huge full-grown bulls in their prime from the most prestigious ranches in Spain.

The trick is to run in Tafalla, then hop in your car and drive to Falces and run again. There's only a fifteen-minute window if anything unexpected happens on the road; there's plenty of folklore about car crashes, runners who narrowly made it, or even ones who missed Falces. Some say the road between Falces and Tafalla is more dangerous than the runs themselves.

♉

Tom Gowen invites me to stay in his apartment in Pamplona overlooking Plaza del Castillo. I've become very fond of his girlfriend Maria. She is like a favorite aunt who won't hesitate to set you straight about any silly ideas you might have on just about any topic, but at the same time is mothering and can throw together a very good and tasty meal for you in ten minutes flat. Maria buzzes me up.

"Did you hear?" she asks as I put my bags in my room. "A woman fell to her death today in Falces. That's where you're going, isn't it?"

"Yeah," I reply from the other room.

"You are so crazy. You and Tom, crazy, crazy."

"True," I giggle as I walk on the creaky wood floor into the TV room.

"She wasn't even running, she was watching with her son and husband. Here it is." She turns the volume up as I sit down beside her on the couch to watch the news footage of the accident.

"There was a problem with one of the vaquilla. It fell off the mountain and she got scared and she fell too."

I watch the blurry cell phone footage on the screen.

"The news is out that she is dead. So, good luck tomorrow!" Maria says with a jolly ironic ring.

☿

Groggy, I leave early the next morning, but Google Maps goes bonkers and sends me off the highway, driving through wheat fields. *I'm gonna be late!* I floor it back to the main highway and speed through the edge of Tafalla. Thick oak barricades span the street in the distance. I quickly park and glance at the clock. 7:57. *Fuck, I got three minutes!* I jump out and sprint the three blocks to the course, then step through the barricades. Everyone on the course faces me, staring at me tensely. The metal doors of the corrals stand tall to my left. The bells around the nervous steers' necks jostle inside.

I sigh. *Fuck, I want to run near the bullring!* I approach my friend Miguel Leza. He squeezes my hand and pats me softly on the back of my neck. I take a deep breath and start jogging down the clean street on the same path the bulls will follow in a few moments. *I hope I fucking make it in time!* My chest patters as I jog through the precious town. Further up the course I see Miguel's son, Mikel. I hadn't recognized him a few weeks before and saw that it hurt his feelings, so I make it a point to stop, grab his shoulders, look him in the eyes, and tell him, "Suerte, Mikel." He looks away shyly, then looks back and smiles. I continue into a big straightaway lined with hundreds of spectators. A powerful silence falls upon the streets as I pass through them. I flow into the staring faces of the runners. They gaze past me to toward the corrals, meditative and fearful, trying to see their fate. The rocket soars up behind me and the corral doors bang open. The rocket pops high above.

I run and as I approach Aitor and the crew; their eyes gaze deeply past me, through me, searching for the first glimpse of horns. Aitor's brow flexes on his stoic narrow face; he stands taller than the rest, with the handsome image of his grandfather on the chest of his white long-sleeved shirt. Then Aitor recognizes me and grins as he bobs on his toes. Xabi stands beside him, shorter and stout with his black spikey hair, sick with nerves. Xabi sees me, winks, and mouths "Suerte," as I close my eyes and give them a heartfelt nod.

Well you made it. I jog up a little past them as the thunder of the bulls builds behind me. The roaring chaos disorients me. *Hold off man! You got two more days.* I cut to the fence. The bulls gallop past, with Xabi and Aitor leading them. The enormous white horns of the lead animals bob just a foot behind their backs. And they disappear into the many running bodies flowing toward the arena.

Checking on my friends, I find Xabi. His chest swells and his eyes glow below his black spikey hair. Everyone greets him and congratulates him. *Look at him. All the runners love him. How could you not? Humble, friendly, excitable, hilarious. He's a leader all right. And a special one.*

"*Impresionante, cabrone!*" I tell him.

I jump in my car. Man, I hope I have better luck in Falces.

I arrive at the base of the mountain. The monstrous cliffs rise above the snaking brown trail. Thousands of spectators and runners mill up and down the sandy path. A horn band plays a somber melody a few feet up the route. I ascend the mountain and bump into one of my favorite guys from Aitor's crew, his other best friend and the copilot of his rally car, Mikel Izco. He's a tall guy with spikey hair, warm eyes, and a heartfelt demeanor. He greets me excitedly.

"Bill! Be careful, El Pilón isn't like any encierro you've ever run. The first vaca is very aggressive, she leads and she fights."

"OK, thanks, Mikel. Suerte." I continue up the mountain and find Aitor facing a grassy mound, kneeling in prayer. I tell him "Suerte," and he turns and grins, then goes back to praying.

I think of his grandfather. I wonder if he's watching from above. I pray to Aitor's grandfather. *I hope you are resting in peace, and I hope you can watch your grandson and the magic runs he is running for you.* I continue up the steep path. A voice comes to me from somewhere, my mind, or only God knows: *Doesn't he know that all of us from all the centuries are here to watch them?!*

I feel a thousand eyes watching us. I fear looking up into the green mountains. I fear I will see their ghosts.

Shaking the thoughts from my mind, I bump into my friend Jose Antonio on the course. He guffaws and arranges his black-framed glasses and a powder-blue bandana tied around his head. He's a great runner, which is remarkable because he's also deaf and mute. We greet each other with a big hug. He's very kind and an excellent communicator. Then his portly brother Pedro shows up. Pedro is also deaf and mute, but he is very loud, and a little ornery at times. Pedro screams indecipherable phrases while pointing and gesturing and trying to communicate how to run El Pilón. Some of the young drunken spectators nestled in the green hillsides start mimicking Pedro as he gives me his eager advice. Jose Antonio just shakes his head and rolls his eyes at his brother.

After thanking them, I head up. As I climb higher on the path, the sand ends and the path turns into dark jagged solid rock. As the path transfers to grey rock it also swings in a wide bend. The cliff that lines the bend drops completely out of sight. *You better not try this spot your first time.* I crane my neck trying to see where I'll land if I fall off: nothing, just an endless fall. Dizziness grips me and I stumble back from the cliff. *Dat don't look like a fun ride down.* The path turns to a grassy trail leading fifty yards to the corrals. I climb back down to run the sandy last quarter of the course.

The rocket pops and the vaca rumble down the way toward us. A stampede of runners floods down the path. Suddenly Aitor appears, directly in front of the lead vaca's twisted horns. He swiftly glides down the steep terrain, his arms out and flapping like a mountain condor swooping away from a bobcat. I run down the hill as others push and cut out. A runner falls next to me and grabs a fistful of my red running shirt. *Aye, I just bought this thing!* As he falls gripping the material, it elasticates. He twists and falls flat on his back and finally releases his grip; my shirt shoots back to normal.

The thunder picks up behind me. *Don't look back!* I just step sure-footed through the tangle of fallen bodies and make it to the bottom of the mountain and keep running. The hooves of the vaca ring on the pavement like bells behind me. *Shit they're here!* The crowd roars. At the last curve I cut and leap up on the barricades as the vaca shoot past me. My foot lands badly. A jolt of pain stabs my sole.

No one photographs the end of my run because Aitor is busy doing some incredible things behind me. All the photographers turn their cameras to see him in the middle of the pack of vaca; they hook for him as they pass him. He swings his hips side-to-side, evading their horns by inches like he's dancing with all of them as they dart around him.

Afterwards I buddy up with Aitor and Xabi and Mikel Izco and the gang. We walk up to a shop that printed up and posted photos from the runs on a board.

Forty photos hang on the board, and every single one of them is of Aitor running. He's leading the vaca down the mountain as everyone else scrambles and falls around him.

"Aitor look, all your photos!" I chide him. Some of the guys giggle. "He looks like a bird flying down the mountain," I guffaw, and Aitor scowls.

We move on to the big beautiful main courtyard of Falces. I run into Jose Antonio and peel off to chat with him as Aitor and the guys continue around town.

♉

Afterward, I head to the town of Lerin, which has a reses bravas run scheduled for later that day. I follow the Google Maps directions as I drive through the winding roads. I know nothing about Lerin; it's just a dot on a frickin' map. I round a tree-lined field and come to the base of an incredibly high, white-rock cliff with a pueblo on the very top of it. It looks like one of those anime cities floating in the clouds. I zoom up the road. The entire town of Lerin sits on a steep tilt. I climb the tilted streets to a big, wide lookout point that sits high above the cliff. You can see for miles into the Navarran countryside with the green mounds of the Pyrenees in the distance. I take a nap on a nearby bench.

I wake as they set up for the reses bravas. They've built a nice wooden bull square beside a tall white cathedral. The big gates break the streets in two. One section leads uphill toward the lookout point. The other runs downhill to the main drag. They release two vaca into the streets, one for both sections.

I run the vaca on both sides as they pinball back and forth on the narrow streets. An athletic teenage girl begins running with the vaca; she shows plenty of grit running their horns as her long black ponytail whips side-to-side and the brown vaca give her chase. The teenage boys run with plenty of pep too. They release the second batch of vaca. I lead one, then I dive out onto the wall of a chapel; a sharp pain stabs my foot as I land. *My stupid foot still hurts from hitting that damn fence in Falces.* I watch the girl take the vaca on another forty-yard dash, her black ponytail bouncing in the air behind her. *I'm calling it for the day.* I get behind a wall and let the vaca pass. Then I run for the far fence; as the teenage girl meets my pace, we look back at the vaca galloping behind us. I hit the far fence and she stays in the street as the vaca turns and runs back toward the cathedral.

"You're a good runner!" I shout to her. She smiles bashfully as I head to my car.

Then I'm following my Google Maps path back to Pamplona when the fences of a bull run block my way. I sigh, looking at the wooden barricades. *You're exhausted, your foot hurts, but come on, look at this!* The teenage boys of the town eagerly climb through the barricades. *You can't pass up this opportunity.*

I park, get out like a tired, weary suelto, and climb in the course next to a big metal industrial barn. I walk away from the barn along a nice stretch of streets as the locals take up their spots to watch along the porches and fences. The street curves left along a stone chapel, then runs alongside the chapel and turns uphill into a temporary wooden bull square full of sand.

Suddenly, they open the gates to the square and six small, black vaca shoot past. I leap up on a fence. *Jeez, that was abrupt.* I am about to jump back down when a big fat black bull runs down out of the square, tries to make the turn, falls on his side, and slides for ten yards. He moans dramatically before he gets up and chases after the vaca. *What the hell happens now?* I go and look in the bull square; it's empty. I'm starting back toward the metal barn when four little boys appear at the turn, bouncing and looking up the street. *Oh man, here they come.* I cautiously approach the frightened young mozos and look around the corner. A new younger bull is wreaking havoc on the street— banging into the fencing with his horns. I run with the little boys, leading that bull back into the square. *Where did he come from?* I head back to the barn and the doors of the barn open and three vaca shoot out. I run several times as the teenage boys try to impress the girls along the barricades running the animals' horns. One teenager cuts a nice circle with a brown bull as his friends look on. *Alright, they're all yours, boys. Enjoy!* I climb out and take off for home.

I round a curve along a mountainside toward home in Pamplona. *Fuck, I never asked what the name of the town was!* I laugh. I like that, though. Kinda poetic, I got stopped on the way home from a bull run by another bull run. That's just life in the pueblos in the middle of August.

♉

The next morning I make it to Tafalla with plenty of time to spare. I walk along a river path, which is quiet and pretty and peaceful. Suddenly the loud greeting of Jose Antonio's brother Pedro explodes at my side. Pedro wears a big backpack and communicates that he's stopped in Tafalla for a run. *It's nice to see you, Pedro.* Three pretty girls walk past us, and Pedro starts catcalling in loud indecipherable grunts and crude gesticulations. *No Pedro stop!* I giggle, embarrassed. The girls actually like it and turn, smile, and laugh. Pedro gives me a grin and hikes his eyebrows up, nudging me. *You sly dog, you!* We walk the long river path and Pedro suddenly turns toward the course before I want to. I turn with him. We are walking together when a young drunk guy sees him and runs up to him. I pause. *I ain't gonna let nobody mess with Pedro, because he's my friend.* But the drunk is nice and playful; Pedro scolds him and motions him to be quiet because we're preparing for the bull run. *Hmm, I guess Pedro is more popular than I thought.* I giggle. Pedro and I part ways with a wave.

After getting on the course, I warm up and feel right. The bulls approach as I run, and I realize I'll miss the first batch because there's a thick flock of runners crowded near the horns, with Aitor closest. As I approach the open entrance of the exterior wall that leads toward the tunnel into the bullring, a bull and steer approach. Several runners veer off from their path. I see the opening and accelerate. Mikel Izco shouts behind me, *"Ir, Bill!"* just as the animals pass through the gate. I lead the bull and steer through the twenty-yard dirt path and into the tunnel and then the arena.

Back out on the course a lot of the runners pat me on the back and congratulate me. A photographer nearby is looking through his shots and tells me to do the same. I do, and the photo of me is pretty good but then he flips to the previous shot and an astounding image of Aitor leading near the horns fills the small screen. We laugh and shake our heads.

I glance at Aitor smiling and greeting his friends.

"Espectaculo!" I yell to him, and point the guy's camera.

I head back along the stream to my car alone. Birds swoop over the water as fish splash, taking bugs off the surface. It's a nice thing to always have Aitor's runs in my mind; they put everything in perspective. *I'm a pretty good foreign runner who gets lucky and has excellent runs sometimes but Aitor...he's historic. All the exhilaration of running on the horns in a competitive and difficult bull run like Tafalla—it's beautiful, but with Aitor around I can't get carried away thinking I'm a big shot.* A tall white stork stands frozen hunting fish in the shallows. He's a constant check on my ego, but at the same time and much more importantly, Aitor is living history, he is unfolding history, every step another sentence, every astounding run another moment of him striving to fulfill his destiny and be one of the greatest runners of all time. The stork leaps up and flaps his wide white wings, then swoops away downstream. *Watching the magic he creates on the street with my own eyes is an honor. Seeing his humble shrug and the huge grin on his face after the run is just perfect; it's the tradition in its highest form.* As strange as it might sound, it's as exciting to watch Aitor running the horns as it is to do it myself.

On my way back to Falces, Google Maps goes haywire and sends me onto a goat trail through the mountains. *Oh, I'm fucked now, I'll never make it in time.* About ten minutes into my bumpy off-road trek I finally pass another human being: a construction worker working on some kind of a meter in the ground, with a big 4X4 truck beside him. He looks at me like: What the fuck are you doing here with that Audi rental?! *Come on didn't you know Audis are great off-road?* I giggle as I bobble around on the bumpy road like a cantering bull until I rejoin civilization at the edge of Falces.

I double-park about two hundred yards from the base of El Pilón. The clock reads 9:03. *I ain't heard no rocket!* I jump out and run toward the course. As I get within a hundred yards of the course, the rocket goes off. *FUCK! Well, don't quit now!* I sprint harder. A bunch of old ladies on a balcony see me running, point at me and start clapping and laughing and cheering me on. I sprint up to the barricades and step through. Everyone looks up the mountain waiting for the animals to arrive. I run up the hill and made it about forty yards up when the black vaca begin avalanching down with Aitor out front. Aitor swooshes past me with the lead vaca on his ass. *Go!* I try to cut in. The second vaca dips her twisted horns and swings them at me. I dive back into the rocky cliff as the pack blisters past in a white cloud.

♉

Afterward I go for breakfast in a nice little restaurant. I'm finishing up eating when I feel someone sneak up on me. I look up and Julen Madina stands before me with his big shaved head and small hoop earrings, smiling his bright vibrant smile. *He looks like he was never hurt at all!* I stand up and we hug. I marvel at him in his crisp white shirt with his clean red penuelo around his neck. It's been less than a month since I visited him in the hospital in Tudela.

"Maestro, I can't believe how good you look!" I guffaw.

The nasty foreign contingent has been spreading lies that I was in Tudela running with Julen and somehow got him hurt. Then they said that I took my book, put it on Julen's chest while he was barely conscious, and took a photo just to promote it: another disgusting lie. But no good deed goes unpunished by bad people.

Julen's warm vibrant smile washes away any worry that my visit or the photo that I took with him had done him any harm; we take a new photo together, this time with Julen looking happy and fine and completely recovered.

All the annoying nonsense makes me sad. *How could people get together out of spite and jealousy and come after me so harshly like they did?* Julen's warm presence pushes all the nonsense aside. It solidifies for me that that group of snobby egomaniacal foreign runners is a gang I want absolutely nothing to do with. Julen and I wish each other well. He grins and pats my face softly.

And that's it. That's the last time I'll see my friend and maestro.

♉

That night I hang out on the balcony with Maria as the Pamplona Choir practices. Every few minutes their heavenly voices flow out of the windows of their practice room across Plaza del Castillo in divine harmony as Maria and I chat. *How lucky are you? All these new doors have opened, and here you are on a balcony in Plaza del Castillo in August with a new Basque friend. This place is magic.*

My final morning, I run poorly in Tafalla. I just don't feel it. There's a big shout from near the curve, and two dozen runners fall simultaneously. I come back to help guys up. Luckily no one is seriously injured. Two of the fallen runners bicker angrily. I get between them and rub both of their shoulders. *Guys can't we all just be happy we're still alive and not headed to the damn hospital right now?* Their faces finally soften and they walk off, trying to untie the taut grimaces on their faces.

I arrive in Falces with plenty of time and bump into Juan Antonio Garaikoetxea, a talented local photographer. He calls me over and tells me he has photos of me from two days before. I thank him as he sets up to shoot the middle section of the mountain path.

I climb further up the trail; I figure I'll run the top today. There's hardly any runners up there. Just a few old men in these long button-up shirts. I walk along the jagged rocky curve. I want to run this with the vaca. In the videos, the vaca come through here slowly, I could pace with them. I peer off the sixty-foot drop. *If I go off this cliff...* I lean over the ledge and still can't see where I'll land. *Well, that's certain fucking death.*

I practice my run a few times, hugging the mountain side of the rocky curve, and soon I feel kind of confident. As the seconds close in, I position myself at the beginning of the curve. The old men line up closer to the corrals in their long open white- and blue-checkered button-up shirts. They glare at me and shout, "Are you going to run?!" I nod yes and they agree that is OK. The rocket goes off and the old men come running toward me. I look behind them for the vaca; they seem to be hesitating at the gate. The old men shove me down the path. I jog before them as I look back, still trying to see the vaca. *I ain't even seen them yet!*

The old men usher me around the rocky bend. *What the hell, old man?! Stop pushing me! Fine.* I dive to the side as I get to the beginning of the sandy path. They rush past, looking back, talking and jostling each other. Once they pass, hooves crackle and skid on the uneven stone of the rocky curve. *Showtime.* I reenter the path. The tall twisted horns of the lead vaca appear around the bend. *Holy shit!* I pause on the dirt path for her to close in, as her sisters trail in a fat and frightened pack. She transitions to the dirt and accelerates. I turn and run. The lead vaca rockets up behind me. Her sister's hooves pound the dirt. The mountain vibrates beneath my sneakers. *What the fuck did you get yourself into now?!* I run as fast as I can down the hill, my arms flapping wildly for balance as they close in on me. *Exit! Find an exit!* I glance left and see a grassy cliff ledge, with green tree branches sprouting up from far below. Twenty yards ahead, the flat grassy patch Aitor prays in sits vacant. I sprint up beside it, plant my foot, and belly-flop into soft damp grass. The lead vaca locks eyes with me and bows her head, pointing her twisted horns at me as I crawl to the side. The others echo her acknowledgment of me, but they choose to stay together and thunder past in a dusty pack. Their tails whip in the white cloud.

After they disappear, Juan Antonio yells at me excitedly and waves me over as he climbs down from his perch high on the cliff.

"LOOK AT THIS!!!" he says, and shows me what might be the most spectacular photo I've ever been part of in a bull run. The whole herd of brownish-red vaca are in perfect view. They are bunched up. I am the first person they've encountered closely, and they all seem to be arching their heads up to get a better look. They are very beautiful girls with narrow elegant faces; the lead vaca is bathed in morning light, bringing the silky red out of her face, while her sisters loom in the shade behind. She is fierce, the most dangerous of the gang—ready for battle and yet pretty in the same moment. I love them and cherish the moment, but if they had the chance, they would have torn me up.

Later on I send the photo (which will become the cover of this book) to Tom Gowen, and he writes this poem about it.

Hill–Man
Well named this boy,
for this, this day,
this downtown dance
manada Colorado
twisted horns
twisted man ahead
the cloud of fortune's dust behind.
To have that gang chasing you
with those weapons
does put CHI
in perspective.

The old men in the checkered shirts are very pleased with me; they come up to greet me and pat me on the back.

"You must run with us tomorrow! So we can show you how to do it right!"

"I'm sorry I can't, I have to leave. But maybe next year."

The oldest one, a bald-headed man with a grey stubbly beard, eagerly grabs me by the face and grins widely. Tears sparkle in his eyes.

"You will run with us next year!"

♉

Afterward, I soar through the Pyrenees toward Valladolid, head high like a proud lone bull. *What a gorgeous image. How lucky of a photo! Naw, luck is a mixture of opportunity and preparation. You earned this. It's your destiny.* The sun peeks out from behind a dark green peak as I career down the winding hill.

I drop the car off and head by bus to Cuellar. I tally my runs in my notebook. *OK, seventy-one going into Tudela de Duero, plus Peñafiel, seventy-three, six between Tafalla and Falces, seventy-nine, seven in Lerin and that town I never knew the name of. Eighty-six total.* Damn, I might hit one hundred and one by the end of Cuellar or Medina del Campo. *You crazy fucker Bill, you're going to do it.* I grin as we roll into the bus station in Cuellar. It's nice to be back.

The Medieval Fair starts up. My friend Diana who's from Cuellar gets dressed up with me, her as a maiden, me as a knight. She escorts me during the parade into the fairgrounds. I spend three days dressed up as a knight in a tent, and sell and sign a ton of books, and see a lot of cool stuff at the fair with Ernes, Diana, Craig, Reme, Bethany, Diego, and Dyango. All of Cuellar seems to come up to greet me, and it makes me feel very special.

Late on the last night, a witch street-performance group approaches my tent. A tall black witch on stilts chases a bunch of the kids from Craig's summer camp. One of the little girls runs over and grabs my shirt and hides behind my legs as we giggle. *Damn, this place feels like home.*

Chapter 11

Sanse

I spend a couple nights in Cuellar at Hotel San Francisco, enjoying my time off from the run.

When I walk into the hotel's bar for breakfast, I see Brevito hanging on the wall by the main entrance. *Oh! There you are, old fella.* I walk under the beautiful black bull and gaze up. Brevito's mount is incredible, a handsome broad face and girthy neck with two of the most beautiful wide and tall whitish horns I've ever seen.

"Is he a Miura?" an old man asks from the bar.

"He looks like one, doesn't he?" I reply.

"Yes, a very strong animal."

"He's a Victoriano del Rio," Mariano, the owner of Hotel San Francisco, says from behind the bar. Mariano's big round bald head beams as he approaches me.

"Thanks, Mariano. He looks great!"

Mariano grins proudly.

I inspect his immaculate fur; he's in great condition. *Mariano's been taking good care of you, Brevito.* I reach up and pet his silky fur. *I missed you, old friend. We went through a lot together, you and me. I will always keep you in a special place, my friend, where you'll be loved and taken care of. I wish I could bring you home with me, but my wife wouldn't like it. She just doesn't understand us. But you and I...* I look up at the right horn tip, the one that passed deep into my body; I remember all my weight hanging from it. Then the second puncture: his grace, his choice to let me live. *Thank you, Brevito.* My mind filters through the long lineage of men gored by bovines. I see them in Spain: Julen, Matt Carney, and then further. The Blackfoot Tribe, in the Head-Smashed-In Buffalo Jump, how many of them took a horn? Even *Homo erectus* must have taken a goring or two back in the Olduvai Gorge... I rub my big scar where some of the meat has vanished—a sacred wound.

I pull out my phone and make a silly little video of Brevito and post it on Facebook, saying, "Look who came to join me for breakfast! Brevito!"

Within an hour, extremely long and bizarre emails begin to pour in from the handful of stuck-up foreign runners. I read through them and guffaw.

"This is an attack on all that is holy in the world of the bulls!"

"Take that bull mount off that wall! You should be ashamed of yourself!"

"You've finally completely destroyed your reputation in the world of the bulls! You'll never sell another book in Spain!"

I love it when a snobby, spoiled, rich kid from England thinks he speaks for the entire country of Spain. Imbecile! The emails make me laugh, but also hurt and enrage me. I reread a few of them. I can't believe I used to be close with these people. If we were running together and something happened, I would have gladly given my life trying to save them. And now here they are, attacking me out of petty jealousy. *Hey, it's not my fault your writing career sucks! Lectures on purity sound ridiculous coming from a snobby egomaniac like you!* I see my fist crashing into their smug faces.

I glare at their words on my computer screen as the sun shifts lights the surface, and suddenly all I can see is my reflection in the screen. I remember the very first suelto I ran in Pamplona back in 2010. Tramposo. When I first encountered him, he was looking into his reflection in a glass window preparing to charge. I convinced him otherwise. My hands tremble above the keyboard like the tips of a bull's horns, ready to tear into them with the same bitterness they gored me with. *Don't. You'll only hurt yourself. Just leave them behind. They're a sad bizarre piece of your past. These are the same guys who claimed you somehow did something wrong to Julen by visiting him in the hospital.* Julen's smiling beaming face flashes in my mind from when he'd snuck up on me the week before in Falces. *Julen loves you. These guys, they're sick. They're just sad, sick people.* I close my computer as Craig walks in the bar.

"Bill, how's it going?"

"Not so good, Craig."

"What?" He sits down at my table.

"These guys are going after me online."

"About what?"

"Brevito being here." I motion to Brevito on the wall. "I don't know."

"Come on Bill, don't let them get you down." Craig squeezes my shoulder. "Did I see on Facebook, your birthday is coming up?"

"Yeah, it's tomorrow."

"Well how about Reme, Bethany, and I take you out for a steak lunch?"

"Sounds good!"

"Deal, see you at the steak place tomorrow at three p.m.?"

"Great!" I giggle as he walks off.

Well, I guess sometimes you gotta lose friends to gain better ones. I sip my cortado.

♉

That afternoon I sit with Dyango at his favorite bar, Paralex, as he tries to brighten my spirits.

"Bill, you have good things going. Your book is doing good in Spain, you're on all the TV shows and in the newspapers. It's not about Brevito on the wall in Bar San Francisco. It's just jealousy."

"I guess."

"It's a problem for successful people. But come on, you're here in Spain. Sanse is in a few days, we have a big event scheduled for you there! Then Cuellar, Medina, Tordesillas, there is a lot to be happy about!"

"I know, I'm just afraid if I see some of them, I'll punch them."

"Haha…maybe they deserve a punch."

"Yeah, I just don't want to. What if I go to jail?"

"This is true, do not punch anyone." Dyango giggles. "Be strong Bill. Come on." He pats me on the back.

I shrug my tense shoulders.

"You're right, Dyango."

Later I go up on the white stone castle wall and look out at the big wide expanse of farmland. *Those guys lashing out at you aren't bad people...they're great. One of 'em, he's the foremost expert journalist on the bullfight in the English language. He's written for and given expert commentary on the culture for the biggest outlets in the world. He's a brilliant guy and an excellent writer. You loved his fucking book, and his work to defend the culture. You guys were so close. Maybe he couldn't handle your sudden rise to his level?* I peer down at the immaculate town with its cathedral spires sprinkled throughout that seem to climb up the hill to the castle. *Is it the drinking? Does he do this stuff when he's hungover?* It's not just him though, there's another one, an old great runner, I look up to him and respect his accomplishments as a runner; he's had hundreds of great runs over the past fifty years, and his photos are marvels. But he seems obsessed with preserving his legacy as the greatest foreign runner since Matt Carney. *Am I really a threat to that? I wish I could have been there, but the 70s are long gone. Carney is long gone. The streets will never be that open again. I don't care about legacy. I am what I am. I had a few good years; legacy on that level is just meaningless to me. Why? So I can shove it in the face of people down at Bar Txoko after the run that I'm a greater runner than them, and make them miserable? You only need eyes to see who runs good, there's no need to debate it. And being a big fish in a little pond in this world just has no worth to me. I am interested in them: the bulls, the people, the pueblos. I guess some people just want to use whatever power they have to control things. Well, sorry guys, there's no controlling me. I'm a fucking suelto. I'm going to do what I gotta do to fulfill my own destiny and I don't care what or how the herd feels about it.*

The sun falls slowly on the horizon sending a soft pinkish-purple through the clouds. *Don't we all want the same thing, guys? To defend and explore and tell the truth of this culture? Guys, there are only so many defenders of this culture outside of Spain. We need to help each other, not hurt each other. When we fight over petty crap like this, this culture we love loses. I didn't put Brevito on that wall, Mariano did! What the hell are you supposed to do with a bull mount but display it!? What do you want me to do, keep it locked away in a basement? Would that make you feel all cozy and safe? I visited Julen because I love him. When people asked how he was, I posted that he was in a little pain and a little sad because he needed his friends and you all weren't there.* I grip the stone wall before me; my hands tremble. *Maybe that's what it is. I am here in the trenches and they are at home, and it is driving them crazy. I know the feeling, I've felt it before. Just don't feed it. You can't fight with someone who refuses to strike back. You can't kill a bull that won't charge.*

ᛟ

The next day Reme, Bethany, Craig, and I have lunch in a nice restaurant in the heart of town. They cook the big juicy steak perfectly. I chomp it down and sip a *sin* beer. Bethany goes off to play with a few little boys in an adjacent courtyard.

"You're looking better, Bill."

"I feel a lot better, Craig. Thank you guys so much."

"Just let it go, Bill. This is a special time for you. Enjoy it. You're in Spain, you're running good again. The book is doing well."

"You're right, Craig, and I'm surrounded by great people like you, Reme..."

"Cheers to that Bill, and happy birthday!"

We all clink glasses.

Bethany runs up to the table crying. Her blonde hair sways in tangles across her reddened face.

"What happened?" Craig demands, standing up.

"Those boys hit me!"

Craig storms over like a wrathful bull. I follow like a brotherly suelto having his back. We round the corner into the courtyard. Craig stomps up to the oldest of a group of Middle Eastern boys; he looks several years older than Bethany.

"Did you hit my daughter?" Craig looms over the little boy.

"She hit me too!"

"Did you hit him?" he asks Bethany.

"Yes, I punched him back," she says and scowls at the boy.

"You hit her first?"

"Yes," the little boy reluctantly admits.

"How old are you?"

"Eleven."

"She's nine years old. A nine-year-old little girl. Where are your parents?" The boys recoil. "I know your father. I'm going to have a talk with him. Do you have anything to say to my daughter while you have the chance?"

"I'm sorry," the boys all say, and reach their little hands out to shake Bethany's. Bethany stubbornly folds her hands over her chest.

"She doesn't have to accept your apology, you know," Craig says.

Bethany finally gives in and shakes each of the boys' hands.

We walk back to our table. Craig and Bethany fume.

"Wow you two are fighters!" I grin and they start to ease up. "You're very tough, Bethany!" I say. "Very strong!" She raises her fists like the horns of a vaquilla and gives me an adorable grimace.

Well if even the pretty little nine-year-old girls gotta fight in this world, then I guess I gotta fight sometimes too. I puff a mini cigar. *Best way to fight these assholes is to kill it running Sanse and sell a bunch of books.*

♉

As I pack up to head to Madrid, my mind drifts to Sanse. *So many great runners, Miguel Angel Castander, Piwi, Jose Manuel, and now Pablo Bolo…and in my opinion the greatest bull runner of all, David Rodriguez.* I can see him now, in all white with the big green patches across his chest. I throw my green pack over my shoulder and head down to the bar on my way out. *There's a lot of great runners out there, Dani, Sergio Colas, JuanPe, even now Aitor, but in these recent years no one has given more or risked more than David Rodriguez. He's an excellent runner on Estafeta, leading the pack long distances, and sometimes leading bulls from mid-Estafeta all the way into the arena.* I drop my key at the shadowed bar and say goodbye to Mariano. *But David truly separates himself from the rest when the most dangerous situation occurs in the run, a suelto, and he's paid the price by being gored several times.* I pause at the door and look up at Brevito. *You remember David, don't you? He was there with me. I'll tell him hi for you.* "Adios my friend," I say, and step out to the street.

I hop in my rental car and pull off, headed south. Arguably David Rodriguez's greatest moment was back in 2009 with Ermitaño. *Oh god, what a great bull.* A Miura black- and white-speckled bull, with the ankles solid white like a Clydesdale. Some bulls, they slip all over street but others, they find purchase in the stones, and can twist and accelerate quicker than you. *Ermitaño was the quickest suelto you ever seen, and he had true menace in his heart. He wanted war and mayhem, and he delivered it.* I accelerate onto the highway as the images of that day flood my mind.

Ermitaño slipped at La Curva and spun around as an American runner, Rick Musica, loped behind him. Musica stopped, petrified, as Ermitaño locked on to him and charged. Rick backpedaled as Ermitaño surged, when suddenly my deaf friend from Falces, José Antonio, appeared, and he called to Ermitaño. The bull swung with him and followed José Antonio through the curve and up Estafeta. Later at Telefónica, David Rodríguez engaged Ermitaño and started working him up the way. The man and bull danced in a circular fury. It was like San Fermín possessed David, compelling him to exorcise the hellish fury from Ermitaño, and for a moment David quelled the beast, leading him steadily toward the arena, but Ermitaño escaped David's spell and accelerated toward the tunnel. A forty-four-year-old veteran runner named Pello Torreblanca dashed before Ermitaño's horns. Ermitaño bellowed and lunged in an extraordinary leaping dive. His long muscular legs with the white ankles and hooves extended airborne. In midair, Ermitaño gored Torreblanca in the thigh and flung him upward. Many runners rushed to Torreblanca's aid. David Rodríguez grabbed hold of Ermitaño's tail. Ermitaño next inserted his horn in the center of Torreblanca's chest and lifted him high off his feet and pinned him to the inner wall of the tunnel. He looked like a man impaled on a tall spear. Dark blood spewed from Torreblanca's mouth. When Torreblanca finally came off the horn, Ermitaño bellowed savagely. In the chaos the others released their grip on Ermitaño's tail, but Rodríguez held tight. Ermitaño dragged Rodríguez while he undressed Torreblanca and split him open for all the world to see. Rodríguez still held that tail by himself. It was Torreblanca's only hope to survive. Finally Ermitaño relinquished his attack and tried to swing back at Rodríguez while the other mozos dragged Torreblanca to safety.

The images flicker through my mind like a movie as I cruise toward Valladolid. *See what I'm saying? He saved that man's life almost single-handedly.* There are great runners, and then there is David Rodriguez. The runner who would, and has, risked everything to save a fellow mozo's life. And when you see David running, you feel the sense that he is willing to die to do just that. Shivers run through my arms and back. No doubt, David is the greatest, the Muhammad Ali of bull running.

☿

Itching for some action, I get online and find a bull run just south of Madrid in the town of Añover de Tajo, in the Castilla-La Mancha region. I weave through the web of highways that encircle Madrid. *Man, I haven't even ever been to Castilla-La Mancha!* Don Quixote takes place there. The festival Añover de Tajo is in honor of San Bartolome. As I drive, I tune into a news radio show, and a review of my memoir comes on. "It's a very passionate book," the commentator says over the airwaves. Bizarre!

Castilla-La Mancha seems pretty flat, but Añover de Tajo is built high up on a tall hill. I drive through the sleepy town. *Everybody must be taking a siesta.* A passerby points toward the bullring on the other side of town. I drive over and see the vertical bars of the bull-run course. Then I park and head over.

Now there are thousands of people milling about, and I can see a beautiful but odd-looking red brick structure with arched windows butting up against the barricades. *Is it the corrals?* When I reach the corner, a beautiful entryway comes into view. A white structure with burnt orange borders lines the big bullring doors. Above the doors it reads Plaza de Toros Añover de Tajo. On either side of the door, two large frescos adorn the white walls, one of a bull run entering the ring, the other of bulls in a pasture. A black ornamental balcony stands above the doors, with the Spanish flag waving in the breeze above. I peer through the tunnel at the white seating of the ring and the brick arches lining the top of the arena walls. *Where the hell am I?* Well, walk the course, see what you got to work with.

They've filled the street with about three inches of sand. *I don't like this sand. What if you cut and slip? That'll be the last thing you do if a bull's on your ass.* The course takes a bend right, then another left into a four-hundred-yard straightaway, cutting through a nice neighborhood with trees lining the sidewalks. I head all the way to the pens and find a bunch of bulls inside them.

"How does the run work?" I ask an old man at the corrals.

"Four bulls with steers, then more bulls back and forth."

"Really? Wow."

"No, no," another old man argues. "There is the encierro, then it's recortes."

I leave them to continue their bickering and set up to try to run the last section of the course. I want to bring them into that beautiful bullring.

Chanting in my mind, I stand at the end of the straightaway. The rocket goes off and the bulls and steers shoot down the street in two packs. The lead pack looks good, four steers and one bull nestled inside them. One black bull lags back between the two packs; he zigzags the street, dipping his horns and gouging at the runners along the sidewalk. *I don't want none of that suelto.* I run with the first pack, leading the steers and bull into the arena. *Well, that kind of sucked.* I look back as the lone bull charges into the ring and barrels after several runners as they leap over the wall. *Good idea not to run with that fucker.* The crowd erupts. I look up into the packed stands. *There's got to be twice as many people in here than this place holds.*

The young mozos shoot out of the ring onto the course, and I follow excitedly. As we near the second bend, another bull approaches. Bulls and steers ramble in all directions. I cut out to the fence repeatedly, then come back. The young men in Añover de Tajo communicate brilliantly and keep us up-to-date on new animals. I lead three or four bulls into the arena as the crowd rejoices.

Then the mood shifts. The sun sizzles us. Sweat beads off my back and chest; it gets so bad I take my shirt off. Another bull approaches, and I run back out and around the bend. The big black suelto with wide horns comes charging around the second bend, stirring up a sandy cloud around him. I attract him using my white shirt like a matador's cape. We slow at the final bend. I entice his charge with my shirt, and lead him into the beautiful tunnel as the crowd's roar slowly builds. I watch the black bull's contorting neck muscles as he gallops head-down into the shady tunnel, charging after my dangling cape. He breathes heavily at my back as the roar rises ahead. When I enter the sunlight of sandy arena I cut to the side and whip my shirt up in the air over his horns. The big black bull hooks for my cape and leaps; his forelegs kick upward as he enters the bright light of the ring, his fur glistening in the sun. The roaring crowd rejoices in a joyful explosion as I dash to the side and he gallops out into the center of the ring. I grip the red wall of the bullring, breathing hard as my fellow mozos pat me on the back. *Who would have thought some town you never heard of would fuckin' rock and roll like this?* I look at the clock: *Shit, I gotta go, if I'm going to make the other event.*

With bulls still on the course, I climb out and shoot off toward Sanse. Fernando Corella published a beautiful illustrated children's book on the bullfight; he's having a book event with Chapu Apaolaza, and if I hurry, I might make the end of it. I speed the whole way.

I pull up in front of El Foro Real 52, my favorite bar in San Sebastián De Los Reyes. A big group of people mill around inside. *Yes! It's still going.* I park and rush over. I hurry in under the big chandelier into the back room, which has a high-pitched apex ceiling. *Man, it's packed!* My heart aches with disappointment. I could have been part of this event, and I screwed it up and miscommunicated with the event producers.

Man, I've made so many mistakes this summer with the book sales stuff. I always seem to zig when I shoulda zagged.

As I make my way through the thick crowd of people, Don Paco Foro emerges before me. He's a handsome guy with well-kempt salt-and-pepper hair and clear framed glasses. He's the owner of the El Foro, and was for many years the head pastore of Sanse. Don Paco looks at me with a stunned excitement, then he comes up to me slowly.

"He's here... He's here..." he says and hugs me and takes a photo with me. As we stand there talking, David Rodriguez walks up. I'd written about David's running with a lot of passion in my memoir. A vision of him holding Ermitaño's tail with Torreblanco impaled against the wall flashes in my mind. David greets me kindly, reaches out and shakes my hand.

"Your book is good. Thank you for the things you wrote. It means a lot to me."

My heart sinks in my chest. Man, I've been dreaming about this moment a long, long time. "Thank you, David, it's been an honor to witness your running."

He humbly shakes his head and pats me on the shoulder. "Una foto," David says, and Don Paco and David put their arms around my shoulders. *Look at you, sandwiched between two of the greatest spirits of this culture!* I thank them, and walk off with a giddy grin on my face. *Who cares if you weren't part of the event? In life, success isn't measured by the amount of sales or the money in your pocket. Life is measured by moments of deep and pure joy.* I mill around the event saying hi to people. *That moment with David Rodriguez and Paco Foro, it couldn't have been equaled by five thousand sales. That's it, man.* Images of JuanPe fighting back tears at my release event, and Javier

Solano telling me, "You are one of them." *It just doesn't get any better than that stuff: the friendship and the comradery, that's all that really matters.* I fight back joyful tears as I get in line to have Chapu sign my copy of his book.

Chapu's becoming a kind of guru for me, both as a writer and a runner. He smiles and chats with the people he's signing books for; he's shaven and looks a lot younger. He's got this warm, big-brother type of presence. *I gotta get to know him better.* We chat and I get to talk with Emilio Sánchez Mediavilla, Chapu's publisher; Libros del K.O., their publishing house, intrigues me. Their vision is very ambitious and vigorous, and they've cut out a strong position in the publishing world in Spain in a short period of time.

"I have to tell you, Bill, I like the title of the English version better. *Mozos,* ah! It's stronger than this running with Hemingway thing," Chapu tells me.

"Yeah, me too. I should have fought to keep the title the same," I say, and shrug. "You know how it goes, they come up with an idea, you don't want to make waves."

"For future prints keep it *Mozos*. It's better, more brotherly, you know, more in the spirit of the encierro."

"I will, Chapu, thank you," I say. "I'm heading out. Congrats, see you in the encierro?"

"Yes, I hope to run a few of the days in Sanse. And maybe Medina del Campo too."

"Great! I'll be there too!"

Outside, I walk along Calle Real, a main drag of the bull-run course. The town strung beautiful Christmas light decorations above the street, hung in the shape of mozos running in front of bulls. People stroll the street along the red bull–run barricades with festive excitement in their eyes. *The title's just another time where you zigged when you should have zagged. But fuck it Bill, it's done, just let go.* I grin, looking down the long straightaway of the nice clean blacktop. *You made mistakes, but look at all you've accomplished. Enjoy the now. Look at all you have to look forward to!* Images of Sanse's explosive encierro lit in my mind. The future is brightening.

♉

I crash out in my nice hotel room in the neighboring suburb of Alcobendas. The next morning I find a run online in the small town of Arbancón about an hour north of Madrid in Guadalajara. I take off and get lost in this beautiful brown stone canyon. I trot along on the bumpy road like a suelto that's lost his way. *Damn, this place reminds me of Colorado.* Finally, I find Arbancón about twenty minutes before the run is set to start. I park and hop out. *Man, Arbancón is by far the smallest town I ever ran in.* One-hundred fifty-six people, according to Wikipedia. I walk down winding streets way too narrow for a car to fit. *Man, I'm surprised even that many people live here.* I pass through a little diamond-shaped square with little trees and a garden. *Fucking beautiful, though.*

Baffled by the silence, I walk the winding streets for fifteen minutes. I haven't seen a soul. It's a ghost town. I check the time. There's no way there's a bull run in five minutes. I walk down a hill and find some city workers tightening bolts on some rusty metal barricades constructed of hollow metal pipes and rebar. I grab hold of one and give it a yank. *Pretty sturdy.* I follow the metal barricades to a turn as the town begins to wake up. Later the course turns into the steepest tunnel I've ever seen on a bull-run course. A concrete ramp leads down at what feels like a forty-five-degree angle to a dark tunnel that turns out of sight. I walk down it. The roof of the tunnel is less than six feet tall. *Man, if you come running down the ramp and you're looking back at a bull...bam! Hit your head on this tunnel roof, it'll knock you out cold!* I imagine lying unconscious in front of a bull in the steep tunnel. *Duck!* I follow the tunnel that turns ninety degrees and opens into a small square concrete bullring full of sand. *This place makes Navas de Oro look fancy! But man, I like it.* A truck with cattle in it shows up. *Right on time, guys!* It drives into the sandy square with the bulls' horns banging the metal sides. I drag my hoof in the sand looking at the box. *Let's roll.*

Locals fill the stadium and workers quickly stand up the fences as they transfer the animals into the pens underneath the concrete bleachers. *Maybe I can run them up the ramp into the street. Worth a shot.* They release the first bull into the ring, a three-year-old black bull with smallish horns. He rambles around the ring as a few teenagers and I wait in the tunnel for him. He comes barreling at us and we run him up the ramp. I cut out as he closes in on me.

The recortadores work him over in the street, turning fancy circles with him, and when he tires I lead him down the ramp with a tall local boy with a big loose white T-shirt and an earring sparkling in his ear. Both of us dash in front of either horn. Long frothy strands of drool dangle from his black mouth. *Don't forget the low roof!* As we near the tunnel we both duck as the shadowy tunnel envelops us. We lead the black bull onto the sand, and cut out as he trots into the pens.

As we lead animals in and out of the bullring, I begin to feel very comfortable with the steep ramp. The bulls slow to keep their footing, and I slow with them, and it is a nice smooth jog into the curved tunnel and the plaza.

I take off after some high-fives with the local kids. There's a bull stirring up chaos in the street, but I'm done. I shoot toward Sanse. *I'll call it four in Anover de Tajo, and three in Arbancon. That makes ninety-four for the whole summer! Shit where are you going to hit one hundred and one? Medina del Campo, probably.*

♉

San Sebastian de los Reyes is an industrial suburb of Madrid with a population of around ninety thousand. I walk the very urban town full of ten-story apartments and climb up the long hill to Calle Real and into the heart of town. I pass a poster for Sanse's festival of Holy Christ the Redeemer, and grin. *I could use some redemption myself.* I've always sucked running in Sanse. I just can't focus.

Images flash of my first run here: I approached the tunnel in between two packs of animals. Where it opened into the ring, a writhing waist-high pile of bodies completely blocked the passage. I decided to jump it, and cleared the entire pile. As I crawled onto the sand and looked back, the mountain of faces and arms and legs grew; they were all straining to escape. The rest of the herd crashed into the pile and struggled to trample through it; the horror of that image froze me in fear. A catastrophe was unfolding before me, and I felt helpless until several brave runners ran back to the pile and started prying people free. I finally dove in to help. As I got closer, the pile began to unravel; many mozos climbed to their feet. I filed through the escaping runners and saw one guy struggling to get up; I grabbed him by his buttocks and yanked him out and pushed him to safety. Finally I got to the core of the pile and crouched over it. A half dozen hands reached out to me. Horrified faces gawked—eyes urging and pleading for help. I reached my hand into the pile, not wanting to have to pick one, hoping one of the hands would grab mine and I would pull them out. Suddenly all the faces turned to my right, all the hands fell limply down. A large black bull plowed through the pile and swung our way. It stepped toward us ragefully. I reached my hand deeper into the pile. No one took it. The bull gathered, dropped its massive black head, and hooked into us. I dashed to the side as the animal drove its horns into the pile. His horns plucked several runners out by their abdomens; he lifted them and pinned them high against the bullring wall. A dark red-faced pastore named Miguel Angel Castander gripped the bull's tail. He whipped the bull with his cane and the animal swung out of the pile and spun for me. Miguel screamed at me in his deep, visceral Spanish, and I dashed away to the wall. He twisted the animal around, and the bull trotted into the center of the ring. The rest of the animals finally cleared the pile. I ran back in to help, and all I found were shoes, dozens of running shoes scattered atop the sand...

My shoulder bangs into a black metal light pole. *Man, that was a hell of a bad day-mare! I guess you're blocked. Mentally, that memory, it's keeping you from going for it in Sanse. Well, quit being a fucking wimp and face it down, man!* I giggle as I turn into Sanse's nice town hall square.

Sanse's town hall is a pretty, white structure in the plaza with a wide balcony. Families fill the square, and some rowdy Peñas crowd in, in front of town hall. The national TV station Antena3 is making a big video presentation on the main stage. Antena3 is broadcasting the Sanse bull runs live nationally for the first time this year. *That's great. They cancelled the run in Alcala de Henares, and that hurts, but them broadcasting Sanse's run is a big victory against the anti-taurinos.*

The mayor announces the opening of the ceremony; fireworks burst high above town hall as the crowd rejoices. The crowd pours out onto Calle Real, dancing and singing. I flow with them. A bunch of teenagers and children call to an apartment high above the street.

"La Agua!!! La Agua!!!" they sing.

I watch the kids' faces from under the overhang. One little boy with blond hair and blue eyes bounces on his toes hopefully, his hand clasped in prayer. Suddenly the mass of forty kids' eyes light up in unison. They squeal as a shower of water droplets sparkles in the streetlights, falling in a misty rain onto their heads and dousing their whole bodies. They bounce and celebrate, and then they look back up and plead for more. The people on the balconies shower down more buckets of water on the kids on both sides of the street as the kids cheer wildly. I'm alone, but I don't feel alone. *You're with the Spanish, observing and enjoying the celebrations...and they are alive and well!*

That night my friend Carlos Manriquez writes me.

"What has happened with Julen!?"

A series of terrible articles flood my feed. Julen was swimming at the beach in San Sebastian/Donostia up north in Basque Country, and he was caught in a wave. The wave rolled him violently and broke his neck on the hard bottom; they found him unconscious floating on the surface. Medics revived him and doctors placed him on life support. *No. It's impossible!* I feel a knife stab me in the heart. *His daughter, she's just a little girl!* I grip my head with both hands. *My god. Could it really be over? Julen...* An image of Julen's smiling healthy vibrant face flashes in my mind from the last time I saw him in Falces, just a week ago. I feel the strength he hugged me with. *You're one of the strongest people I've ever known, maestro! Fight!* If anyone can come back from this, it's Julen.

I hang my Gohonzon and pray for Julen and his daughter and his whole family well into the night. Finally I sleep lightly, waking with thoughts of my friend.

In the morning, I walk down Calle Real in a haze, still thinking about Julen. Jose Manuel, my dear friend, approaches me in his pastore uniform. Jose and I used to both wear blue-striped shirts; we'd run horns together dozens of times in Telefonica, and with Julen, too.

"Did you hear the news!? Julen!" He closes his eyes and shakes his head and we hug. I fight back some tears as he hurries off to work.

The pressure of running Sanse, and Julen's peril, both wrench my chest as I try to warm up.

You don't have to. Only do it if you feel it. The pressure evaporates as I take a deep breath. I'll run.

The rocket sails into the sky.

"Do it for Julen," I whisper as the rocket pops high above.

Thinking of Tudela, I climb up on the fence about thirty yards from the curve into Estafeta to get a look at the pack. As the bulls approach, three steers gallop out front. I wait until they parallel me. A set of bulls surges behind them, and I jump down and run along the barricades. I hug the inside of the curve as the first bull and steer pass. Everything slows and spreads. I run straight for the last steer's ass. As I do, runners push and pull me. I just focus on the steer's ass and something tells me: *follow them, the bull, follow their scent trail.* I run directly in the center of the street. The second bull zooms up behind me. The gravity of his presence and focus weighs down on me. *We're linked, Julen. You're with me.* The hooves of the beast thunder behind me in a steady rhythm, resonating my whole being. I run down the long downward-sloped street linked with the galloping beast, with Aitor and a few of the Sanse runners. Wind whips through my ears. *I can't believe I'm fast enough!* I enter the arena with the bull close behind, and I peel off to the side.

Afterward Aitor rushes up to me in the ring.

"Bill! Good run!" He hugs me.

I shrug.

"Thanks." It must have been even better than I'd imagined. I never looked back. Just felt him.

♉

Later I walk past Pernatel Bookstore at the corner where the course meets Calle Real. The photos of that day's run play in a slide show on several screens in the front window. *Wow.* I'm running in all white with my tan cap and red Air Jordans, directly before the snout of the big black bull with the white speckled chest. Runners at either side tug at my arms. My cap covers my eyes as I look downward at the center line of the street, emotionless and focused. Aitor runs beside the horns of the bull watching me, worried. *Five years. I've been trying run good in Sanse for five years. And finally today it happens?* My heart hangs heavy for Julen. *Maestro, this is for you.*

Onlookers congratulate me and I struggle to smile through my great sadness. *Bittersweet, so bittersweet.* I go inside the shop for the booksigning Luis Barbado set up for me through the help of Dyango Velasco. The owner and his family treat me very warmly and kind. Fernando Corella drew an awesome illustration of me, and they present it to me during the signing. They bring me into the other room to give red bullfighting capes to the little boys that had trained as matadors. One little boy is in a wheelchair, and I make a special effort to congratulate him; he smiles at me bashfully and whips his cape in the air. My heart swells with joy as we take pictures with the little boys. *The new generation!* I grin.

Dozens of people come to buy books. I sign for over an hour. Even the mayor of Sanse comes in to buy one. We take a photo with the mayor. *Oh, wait. Didn't one of those snobby foreign runners say I wouldn't sell another book in Spain ever? I guess the mayor of Sanse disagreed.* I giggle wickedly.

We finish up the signing and have a drink with Don Paco Foro at El Foro. Then I head back to my hotel for a siesta. I drive back toward the neighboring town weaving around the fiesta. I let out a long exhale, thinking of the guy who wrote that nasty bizarre thing about me never selling another book in Spain. *It's sad, he's just jealous of my writing and running.* But men are jealous creatures. Jealousy is a constant for men, and there're two kinds of men in the world: the ones who turn those feelings of jealousy into inspiration to strive harder to succeed, and the other ones who believe they are owed success, who lash out and try to sabotage the person making them jealous. The ones who continue to turn jealousy into inspiration eventually conquer the world. The other ones turn bitter and cold, and sneer at the world from the shadows of who they once were. *You're better than that shit, brother.* I drive into the bright sunlight of the Sanse streets, grinning. *I know what kind I am. I'll never stop striving. I'll keep galloping up that hill.*

♉

The next morning, I go down to the beginning of the course in Sanse to run with my friend Piwi. He stands thin and tall with his long black hair draped down over his shoulders. His weathered tough face grins as he greets me warmly.

Piwi has a really stylish and daring way to run the outside of the first curve in Sanse. As the herd approaches, he leads them into the curve, then weaves in and out of them as the pack thunders past. To the untrained eye he looks like a drunken man weaving obliviously with the pack, his hands and long hair whipping up wildly, but if you study the tape year after year you realize Piwi is a master runner.

As the time nears for the rocket to go off, a thousand-yard stare falls upon Piwi's face as he gazes towards the corrals ahead. He ceremoniously takes his red bandana from his chest pocket and ties it around his head tightly above his brow. *Rock and roll, Piwi.* I bounce on my toes.

The rocket bursts and the bulls pour out of the garage doors of the pens. They thunder toward us, four black bulls in the lead. I wait as Piwi takes off. As the pack nears twenty yards from me I turn and run, leading them into the inside of the curve. As I round the curve they are close, and I dive out to the fencing. I slip and another young mozo grabs my forearm to keep me from falling off the barricades.

"Thank you!" I say.

He looks me in the eyes and nods as the herd thunders past.

Stephanie Mutsaerts arrives in town, and I go to pick her up from the train station. We plan to head to Cuellar but choose to stay in Sanse one more night. Steve Ibarra, who is like the ambassador for Sanse, takes her out for a long night of fun. The next morning, I run through the curve onto Estafeta when Mikel Izco yells "Run Bill!" I sprint onto the horns of a black bull and take him twenty yards down the long hill.

"No! No! Bill!" Mikel shouts, I look back as the bull accelerates and dips his horns to gore me. I cut out to the side and he rambles past me. Afterward I grin as Aitor and his crew take photos: David Lerga, Xabi, Cristian, Mikel. Many of their parents made the trip to be with them, to watch them run from the big bleachers that line the course in Sanse. *Look at them, making memories. What a great group. Julen would be proud.* Something steals my breath from my lungs. *Ah maestro, please don't leave us. We need you.*

News comes that a bull gored an American kid named Gab on Calle Real. *Oh shit, I gave that kid advice a few nights ago!* I find the video online. Gab is running the inside of the curve at Calle Real. *Just exactly like I'd told him...* A bull peels off from the pack after the curve and cuts across the street, dips his horns, and hits Gab in the butt, flipping him high into the air. He comes down hard on his back. *Shit, that's exactly what I warned him about! Ah...there's nothing he coulda done. It was just his time.*

Stephanie and I head to the hospital on the way to Cuellar. After some struggling, Stephanie gets back to see him and does some translating for him with the doctors and nurses.

I go in to see Gab. The adrenaline's still flowing, and he is pretty gabby, laying there in the white bed with his curly short blond hair all messed up. His pale face glows red as he grins: high on morphine.

"I told you to be careful! They always cut across the street after the curve!"

"That's actually exactly what I was thinking while I was flying though the air: 'Man, that Bill guy really knows his stuff.'" Gab laughs.

"Don't sweat it kid, there was nothing you could do. It could have happened to any of us. Matter of fact, that's the exact same thing that happened to Steve Ibarra ten years ago. Almost the same exact spot!"

"Who is that lady that was just here?"

"That's Stephanie."

"Why…" He clears his throat. "Why was she so nice to me?"

"I don't know, man." I shrug. "She's just good people. She can't help but help people, man. She's just a kind person, I guess."

"I just still don't even know what happened."

"The bull cut across the street after the curve and gored you, man! Flipped you way up in the air."

"How do you know that?"

"There's a really crazy video of it."

"No way!" His blue eyes bug out. "I want to see it!"

"I got it here on my phone." I pull it up. Then I reconsider. "Are you sure you want to see this?"

"Yes I…I just want to know what happened."

I nod. I remember that feeling from when I got gored.

"OK." I shrug.

He watches the video on my phone. His eyes light up and then his face falls somberly.

"You OK?"

"Yeah." He shakes his head. "My mom is gonna kill me."

He starts to talk to me; I get the sense of a twenty-one-year-old kid growing up before my eyes.

"The horn was an inch away from changing my life forever. When it almost wrecks your life, it makes it different. Now it's more real. Well, my scrotum is bruised. It sounds like it will be very painful when the meds wear off. When they told me it was an inch away from my balls, I thought right away: Can I have kids?! I realized in that moment I want to have children." He stares up at the ceiling, thinking. "You know, I dropped out of college and came to Europe because I didn't want to have regrets. I came to Europe after Christmas last year, and I've been using Workaway to pay for everything. I've been in London, Italy, Spain, Portugal, Morocco. Now my grandfather is sick. And my brother's football season is starting. He's growing up, and I don't want to miss it. I don't want to live with regrets. That's why I left, and that's why I'm going home next week."

As we roll out of town toward Cuellar, Stephanie takes a nap to sleep off her Steve Ibarra–induced hangover. *Man, that was a beautiful little talk with Gab. What a great kid.* It reminds me of all the things that flashed through my mind the moment Brevito gored me: kids, my future, what's really important. *I'm happy for Gab. He's so young, and to have those kinds of big epiphanies at that age is a blessing.* I glance at Stephanie. *She's a great mom.* Her boys' smiling faces flash in my mind; they're really terrific kids, with awesome spirits and hearts. *I want to be a father...and time is starting to get tight. Enid wants kids too and maybe this summer is a blessing too. Maybe it's my last chance to really run a full summer. My last chance to live with that kind of abandon.* The summer memories I've made flash through my mind like a Rolodex: bulls, pueblos, friends, all melding into a joyful blur. *Jeez…you only have a few precious weeks left. Ninety-seven runs, you'll hit one hundred in Cuellar. God damn, that's a lot of bull runs!* I soar onto the highway like a bull galloping into an open wheat field.

Chapter 12

Cuellar

Stephanie and I arrive in Cuellar with the fiesta of Nuestra Señora del Rosario in full swing. We unload our gear in our rooms at Hotel San Francisco. Then we cross the street to Bar San Francisco's patio in the stone parkway where we drink and eat at the chrome tables as the rest of our group arrives.

The locals mill past on the parkway as our three tables fill up with foreigners. *Man, look at this. Twenty foreigners, and it all goes back to 2010, when Dyango friended me on Facebook and started posting videos of the run in Cuellar that I obsessed over.* Images of the videos of Cuellar's run roll on a loop through my mind. It was such a quest for me back then. Cuellar, the mystical town where the bulls gallop down the big hillside surrounded by hundreds of horsemen. *The oldest known bull run in Spain. The origin, maybe. Fuck, who knows.* The history of the run is as blurry and mysterious as that dust cloud that engulfs the bulls as they ramble down the hillside into town. By 2012 I had convinced the *Chicago Tribune* Travel section to let me do a piece on the town. *Wow. My destiny running and writing have always been so intertwined.* I take a sip from my *agua con gas*.

It's like they helped each other, pulling me forward deeper into both. And now I've talked and written about Cuellar for some of the biggest outlets in the world. *It's such a special town. It's like home.* Diana walks past with some friends, she smiles and waves to me. I wave back with a grin. *I've got so many friends here, now. Five years in Cuellar and counting. Hell, I pretty much lived here half this summer. Look at all these guys.* I scan through the faces of the many foreigners, Gus's big muscular brow, Mike Webster's round grin, Mikael Anderson's long blond hair and pointy nose, and all of them staying at Hotel San Francisco. Elisa and Mariano have been so good to me. *They must be thrilled. They really deserve it.*

An argument sprouts up with some of the foreigners. They shout and bicker over some petty shit across the way. One gets up and storms off; another follows him, trying to quell the argument. I roll my eyes. *Why can't they just relax and enjoy it without the drama?*

Later in the evening, we drink at an Irish bar around the corner. This big rich pompous asshole with spikey hair and clear-framed glasses begins to lecture me on what I should do with my writing career. I roll my tense shoulders. *Motherfucker, have you ever written anything in your whole stupid life?* He goes on and on. I lean in, looking him in his crazy eyes, and I'm just about to say SHUT THE FUCK UP when my dear friend Mikael Anderson's voice shoots over the nonsense.

"Bill! Bill, come here!" He's calling from a few tables over.

I get up and head over as the pompous asshole continues his speech to my empty chair.

Mikael is a tall handsome dark-skinned Swedish guy with long blond hair. Even though he's in his early fifties, he's still very athletic and runs excellently. He was a legend in the eighties, and is incredibly humble about it. He came to visit me almost every day in the hospital after my goring. One of those days, he walked into my room limping and said his leg hurt. He went down to the ER to get it checked out. An hour later he walked back into my room in shock.

"I have to go home on the next flight. I have a blood clot, they might have to do surgery," he said, trembling at the foot of my bed.

Later that summer we were in Alcala de Henares for their run. Mikael limped up to the course; he looked like he was in worse shape than me, so I offered him my cane. He declined, climbed onto the course of one of the fastest runs in Spain, and ran the horns of two bulls right before my shocked eyes as I sat on the barricades. Mikael Anderson is a very special bull runner.

And now Mikael introduces me to a young awkward Swedish kid with long blond hair and glasses.

"I read some of your articles about Cuellar," the new kid says.

"Really? Nice."

"I had to come see it for myself."

"I hope you enjoy it," I tell him.

"A young Swedish kid," Mikael says proudly. "The new generation!"

Mikael starts telling stories about the old days when he and his young Swedish pals rambled around San Fermin. I grin at them. *Look at Mikael, he's a true pillar of the Swedish contingent. He's brought two of his friends along with him this year and this kid shows up out of the blue.* Mikael grins broadly and answers the eager Swedish kid's questions. *Look at him pouring his joy for the tradition into a new runner. Fucking Mikael Anderson, that's what it's all about. He's the real thing humble, open-minded, loyal. A genuine maestro.* I glare back at the bickering foreigners who are already poking fun at the awkward new Swedish kid. *Fucking assholes like them ruin the whole thing.*

Mikael turns to talk to me. "Julen. I can't believe it."

"I know, me neither, Mikael. All we can do is pray."

We shake hands and hug with strength.

"It could have been me too…" Mikael says, tears beading in his blue eyes.

"I know, brother. I know."

Mikael's been battling cancer over the past three years, and I've been trying my best to encourage him through it. We make plans to go to the suelta (the release of the bulls at the pens outside of town) the next morning with him and his wacky Swedish tribe.

With gratitude swelling in my heart, I walk off through the raucous fiesta night. A purple- and yellow-clad Peña group waves to me as I pass. Their purple-shirted children giggle and play along the nearby old stone walls. An elderly couple with white penuelos tied around their necks slowly walk through the party arm-in-arm, grinning. *In this life, nothing is guaranteed. Every fiesta could be your last, every conversation with a dear friend, the final one. Fuck it, I'm going to cherish my time with Mikael and just ignore the nonsense.* A drunken old man in a white top hat dances into the street all by himself—smiling into the wild fiesta night of Cuellar.

Exhausted, I head back to my favorite room in Hotel San Francisco. It's a gorgeous and simple room with cream-colored walls and dark oak trim and furniture and two big glass-paned doors that lead out onto a little balcony. The old, red-tiled rooftops of Cuellar fan out to the horizon. Peppy horns flare up as the deep bass drum of a Peña marching band bangs a steady beat. Other bands and music acts overlap each other faintly in the distance throughout town. I push the beds together and move the desk and chair to the balcony. *This is such a place of solace.* I sit in the chair and look out over the rooftops and tap the wooden desk surface. I've come to terms with the death of dear friends and written some of my best writing right here.

♉

Before sunrise, we pack into my small rental car: Stephanie, Mikael, his two giggling Swedish friends, and the new Swedish kid, all headed toward the suelta. As we weave through town, several horsemen trot along the street toward the corrals far outside of town. At a gas station near the highway, horse boxes line the lots and side streets. A man in a white button-up shirt pulls at the reins of an upset black Spanish stallion who rears back on his hind legs and unleashes an angry neigh. His mane, knotted in an elaborate braid, whips above his head in the bluish morning haze.

We shoot out along the highway, park on the access road, and walk in the cool, damp, and crisp morning.

"Guys, I'd be doing you a major injustice if I didn't tell you the suelta is really dangerous," I say to our group. "People get gored all the time, so be on your guard."

"Well, thanks for inviting us, Mikael!" one of the Swedish friends chimes in merrily as we all giggle. "Such a great pal!"

We arrive at the squat white corrals. Hundreds of Cuellaranos stand around the big green corral doors, sipping steaming cups of *caldo* and chatting. Horsemen slowly trot in from all directions as the morning haze rises off the sandy field and glows in the rising orange sunlight that peeks through the pine forest.

"Where should we watch from?" Stephanie asks.

I scratch my chin.

"I mean, there's really no good place. I've seen them peel off to both sides of the field." I point to the dozens of cars parked across the way. "I saw a bull go in through the cars and gore a woman in the stomach." I point beside us, toward a grassy bank with a pine tree. "A bull came over there my first year and gored an old man seven times. Threw him around like a rag doll."

"Well, what do you think?" she pleads.

Several people climb a big electrical structure behind us that looks like a big metal erector set.

"Why don't you get up there and watch?"

"Really?"

"Yeah, Steph, it's not safe. I'll come and get you when it's over."

"OK." She climbs up and finds a good comfortable position to watch from, her curly blonde hair shining in the morning light.

"Don't come down until I come and get you. No matter what anyone says, OK? There might be a bull you can't see that looped around and is knifing through the cars and trees."

"OK," she says.

The rest of us set up to watch near the tree where the old man was gored. Meanwhile the hundreds of horsemen fill up the big dusty meadow. One horseman on a white steed comes trotting up through a trail beside us. The man is fat and drunk, and as soon as his horse sees the meadow full of people and horsemen, he neighs fearfully, and rears up violently on his hind legs. The man flies up and flops onto the dirt beside us with a heavy thud. He gets up angrily and grabs the reins of the horse and slowly walks him back from where he'd come as the locals laugh and call after him: "Where you going? It's almost time!"

"He's taking that horse right back to the barn," Mikael's bald friend pipes in with his heavy Swedish accent as we giggle. "When a day starts that bad, you don't drag it out."

"Right back to bed," Mikael's other portly friend chimes in.

A few minutes later the corral doors bang open. A flock of twenty brave runners bob on their toes at the opening, calling to the frightened pack inside the corrals. The steers stand emboldened before the passageway. Then the herd gallops out, and the flock of runners disintegrates. One mighty lead black bull charges ahead through the sandy field, throwing his horns as the pack of horsemen swallow the herd. Then they all evaporate in the big golden hazy dust cloud, heading into the shadowy pine forest. Suddenly one bull materializes near the cars across the way. The spectators scream and retreat between the vehicles. Out of nowhere, a horseman appears on a beautiful dark-brown mount and kicks into a gallop. He takes his long staff and drags it behind the horse's hindquarters and lures the bull along the front bumpers of the cars and trucks lining that side of the meadow. The bull snugs his nose close to the horse's hindquarters as they shoot along the front bumpers of the cars. Dusty sand flies as the spectators scramble for cover and the horseman leads the bull toward his brothers in the pine forest.

We pick up Stephanie and take off for the car and drive down to the embudo. I position Stephanie on a log fence that runs alongside the funnel into the streets.

"OK, sometimes a bull will come over here, they can break this fence." I shake the rounded plank of the fence.

"OK."

"So if a lone bull comes here, just run back to that rooftop." I point to a nearby factory roof. "And climb up. He won't follow you there."

"OK, I will."

"If it goes bad, I'll come running as soon as I can. Good luck." We hug.

I wait tensely with a hundred mozos at the base of the long sloping hill. A dusty trail snakes up the hill. Spectators line the nearby bank. An image of last year swirls in my mind, when two bulls shot right up through that bank. *There ain't no place safe in Cuellar. Cuellar is fucking wild!* I gaze up along the adjacent hilltops. Trucks full of spectators roll to a stop atop them. There's a thick strand of yellow caution tape that extends from the fence line that Stephanie sat on to a small patch of pine trees, and along one ridge. *What do they think that caution tape is gonna do?!* I giggle. *That oughta keep the bull out!*

The dust cloud of the initial herd crests the hillside. First I see the poles of the horsemen, and then the hundreds of horsemen flood over, with the herd nestled in the center. Dust kicks up around the horsemen as they break into a hard charge. As they descend, I can only see three bulls in the pack. *Did they lose some bulls in the fields?!* I wait at the base of the hill as the thunderous cacophony avalanches toward us. A lead horseman gallops on his black stallion, his face looking back at the herd as he drags his long pole behind him. The pack morphs into a dusty haze with a thorny crown of horns. The dust billows up around them as if they are emerging out of a dream. *My god, it's beautiful.* As the horsemen peel out of the lead, three big steers gallop out in front of the bulls. The other runners clear out, and I stand alone at the edge of the field bouncing on my toes. Just as they approach us on the dirt, one bull swings out my way beside the pack. I turn into sprint, leading the bull for twenty yards before he melds back into the herd behind a steer. I run down the steep road to the main street and cut out through the fencing.

"Three bulls!" The other runners echo the call as the herd rambles up the street and around the bend.

Fuck, three are still out there?! I run back to the base of the hill and look for any sign of them, and I check for Stephanie; she sits on the fence looking up into the hills.

A black bull materializes over an adjacent hill with three horsemen trying to guide him toward us, dragging their long poles behind them. The bull refuses to go toward the embudo into the street. He crosses the field near where Stephanie sits atop the wooden fence.

"Stephanie!" I yell, and she climbs down and retreats to the factory roof. *Good job!*

The black bull winds around, sniffing the air for his brothers' scent track. Then he huffs off toward the patch of pine trees. He looks at the yellow caution tape flapping in the morning breeze, pauses to read it, then dips his head and horns under it and trots into the patch of trees. The crowd erupts in a bout of laughter. *Well, I guess he can't read! They're gonna have to fine him.*

I walk over to Stephanie. She sits frightened on the roof.

"Thanks for listening."

"What do you think? Is he going to come over here?"

"I don't know. Hard to say, but just stay up there a minute."

"OK."

After some waiting, I slowly creep into the trees. *I bet I can lure him out here.* The branches of the pine trees hang low. I crouch and step into the shady wood. The black bull sits exhausted, his tall horns reaching upward into the low hanging branches. Fear and frustration tremble in his black eyes as his torso heaves. *He's hiding.* He sits content in the small calm oasis, safe from the blustering morning. Several drunken locals have climbed the trees; they cling to the branches, laughing and calling to the bull.

"Go to sleep, lazy!"

"You fatso, you're supposed to go with your brothers into town, not into the trees!"

I slowly creep toward him. As I enter his space, he sees me and stands, ten yards away. *My footing's gonna suck on these pine needles. Maybe I can use the trees to cut fast circles.* He digs his front hoof into the pine needles and drags it several times. *I know...I know you're tough. You can fight.* I creep around a tree. *If he gets me, my only hope is these goofy drunk guys. He'll kill me.* I move into his plane of vision and wave my paper. His eye follows my paper and he steps my way steadily, curiously sniffing the air. *I've got him.* I lure him slowly in the direction of the field. A horseman trots at the other edge of the wood near the small cliff. The horseman shouts at him and he turns, confused. *That's it...I've lost him.*

"If you don't come with me, they're gonna dart you and drag you away," I whisper to him. His ear flicks open and seems aimed at me. "Come on...let's go see your brothers."

He spins, looking towards another horseman that's cantering at the edge of the trees. I sigh. *He ain't interested.* He sits down again, stubborn and proud, and looks at me as if to say: I'm not going out there, I'm just going to stay here where it's nice and quiet.

I agree, and bed down with him until the truck comes in to dart him. He drops his head in the pine needles and dozes. "Sweet dreams," I sigh.

ర

I drop Stephanie at the train back home to Pamplona and thank her for everything. She thanks me for the fun weekend.

Then I start back toward Cuellar. I remember Dyango picking me up there, way back at the beginning of the summer. *What a great friend. I miss him. Cuellar ain't the same without you, Dyango.* I cruise toward the highway. I hope he's having a nice time out in Castellón with his family and that the deal for the big bronze bull sculpture he's going to make for them goes well. But still, I do wish he was here. He's part of what Cuellar means to me. He has a lot of the same mood swings as me. Sometimes dark and brooding, other times jovial and excitable, with his goofy chuckle and big smile. His passion for his town's fiesta is absolutely contagious; he's a devoted servant to his culture, and a hell of a runner.

I pull onto the highway. Even though I don't like running the curve at San Francisco, I miss running it with him. It's his favorite place to run, even though he got gored there! I chuckle. *Ain't that ironic? Bull runners, man. When it grips you, even a bad goring can't keep you away. Shit, I'm gonna hit ninety-nine runs tomorrow! Wow. I got there way quicker than I imagined.*

I zoom home toward Cuellar, the curly tail of my hair flowing in the breeze.

♉

When I get back to town I am heading through Bar San Francisco on my way up to my room when a voice calls to me from the packed bar.

"Bill!" Diego stands in his royal high-chinned posture as he waves me over. I join him and his pretty, sandy-blonde-haired girlfriend Nathalia.

"Are you going to the suelta tomorrow?"

"Yeah, I think so."

"Will you come with us?!" Diego's and Nathalia's eyes lit up eagerly.

"Sure!"

"Alright! We'll pick you up right here on our way out."

"Great." I head up to sleep. *Dyango ain't here, but I still got a lot of Cuellaranos to hang out with.*

The suelta is fun and beautiful; as usual the pack breaks out nice and clean, with no issues. Afterward we drive around to where the bulls cross the road outside of town. The massive white dust cloud blisters across the road hundreds of feet into the sky.

"We're late!" Diego yells as we park.

We run toward the massive cloud. *Are the bulls past? Are they still here?* We pass under the highway bridge into a white nebula. It's like another universe. The sun burns through the white cloud, giving it a golden aura. A horse neighs fearfully. *It's so close!* We stop running as a deep slurping inhale fills an enormous lung near us. The shadow of a great beast materializes five yards in front of us. Massive horns that span wide and curve upward to two sharp points. The girthy neck, the boulder-like shoulders. We glance at each other and freeze. Diego takes Nathalia's hand. *If he charges, we'll have to protect her.* The dusty haze thins as a chalk-white Jabonero stands there, his eye scanning us calmly—taking us in.

"Don't move," Diego whispers.

The dank scent of him swirls in in my nostrils. *He knows he could kill us.* A low grumble hums in his massive chest, followed by a kind of light clicking. Then he snorts explosively. A string of snot spurts from his big nostril and lands on the pavement just a couple feet from my red shoe. Three other bulls appear in the haze near him, their cloven hooves clattering on the pavement. He looks us over as if to say: I see you. *We see you too, my friend.* His long tail flicks up high above his back. Then he slowly steps away like a dinosaur. His hairy hooves *ca-clap* the pavement as the entire herd and all the horsemen emerge ahead of him from the cloud as they climb the slowly sloping hill.

Diego turns to Nathalia, grabs her in his arms, picks her up and kisses her. She melds around him. I watch them kiss. *Enid. She'd never understand a moment like this. Such a pure moment with the animal. Look at them.* They kiss deeply in that way that only young lovers can. They're a beautiful couple, so in love with each other and this animal and their traditions. They stop kissing and look into each other's eyes as he still holds her in his arms with her legs wrapped around his waist.

"Are we dreaming, Bill?" he says, still looking into Nathalia's eyes. "Or did this just happen?"

"It happened, Diego, and we're dreaming…"

"This is Cuellar, my friend."

"Yes it is."

♉

Diego takes us up on the highway and around the back way to the bullring and parks. We hop out and walk into the busy fiesta morning. *Man, we just beat a half hour's worth of traffic.* We sit down at one of the chrome tables out front of Bar Paralex sipping coffee. The steam sifts up off our cups as we gaze out through the barricade and into the final bend into the big yellow bullring. We chat, giddy with the moment we shared with that incredible Jabonero in the fog.

"This was the ultimate, Bill!" Diego grabs my shoulder and squeezes it. "In all my life going to the suelta, I've never been this close to an animal in this beautiful of a moment."

"Nunca, nunca!" Nathalia echoes.

"And he didn't charge us!" Diego's eyes bug out.

"He wanted peace, I guess…" I grin and sip my cortado.

"Exacto!" He looks Nathalia in the eyes, they clasp and squeeze each other's hands.

I watch them, the joy in their eyes matches the surging warmth in my heart. *What would it be like to have a woman who understood this? Hell, one who understood and felt it more than you?* My mind drifts to all the beautiful Pamplonicas I'd ever fallen in love with walking down Estafeta street in San Fermin. *In another life maybe I'd marry one of you and have little half-Navarrese babies, with your beautiful face and hair and my blue eyes.* Then: *Naw, Bill. Stop it. You have the love of your life already. Without Enid, you wouldn't even be here.*

We climb onto the course near the big stone chapel about two hundred yards from the bullring as thousands of spectators fill the metal barricades. My friend Luis Vicente appears with his tall frame and shaved head, grinning.

"Bill! You ready to run?!"

"Yeah, I'm gonna run on the horns of a bull from here all the way into the arena."

He cracks up.

"No, I am!" He chides me.

"OK, well, we will run with you in front of one horn and me in front of the other horn, all the way to the plaza. If we're lucky."

"That's it." He grins, shakes my hand, and we hug, giggling.

The bulls approach in a wave of chaotic roars and frantic mozos. I climb up on the barricades to get a look at them: the bulls and steers are galloping out front in a wide pack. I hop down and run with the excellent runners of Cuellar. The excellent blond-haired runner and a few others run the three bulls; I glance back, running five yards ahead of the blond. *Fuck, how'm I gonna get in? These guys are kicking ass! Just keep going, I guess.* I keep running, and the blond finally tires and cuts out, and I run the horns of the white bull for twenty yards. *Fuck, I'm so tired.* My legs burn from the long sprint. At the final curve I cut out. The bulls swing wide. The white bull gasps heavily; froth speckles his snout. *Fuck, he's tired too!* I echo their turn and let them pass, following them into the arena. *Stupid ass, you could have taken them all the way in.* Luis Vicente picks up another white bull behind the first pack and runs him a hundred and fifty yards into the plaza with no one around him. I look back as he leads the bull into the arena, his shaved head glowing in the morning light as the white bull charges behind him, hooking for him. Luis Vicente peels off and bumps into me on the sand.

"Bill! Where were you?!" he scolds me. "I was with a bull the whole way, you could have been with me!" He flails his arms, exasperated. "You could have been right here!" He motions beside himself.

"Ah." I shrug. "Sorry Luis, I got carried away."

"It's OK," he says and pats my chest. "Mañana…"

I nod. I blew it, but it was still fun. Shouts and yells fill the ring from the street.

"Another bull!"

"A suelto!" Luis agrees.

Fuck it. I take a deep breath and dash back out to the street. A black suelto spins and twists in the street, sending runners dashing away. The willow canes of the pastores poke above the mass of runners. I close in and see Kiké Bayon Brandi, a thin white-clad pastore with long pointy sideburns, mastering the animal and progressing him up the street. Another younger pastore engages the bull and cuts a tight fast circle with him. The bull twists but can't make the turn. His hooves scrape on the pavement, his hindquarters buckle, and he collapses. Sometimes a suelto finds good purchase and needs tight circles to control them. Other times they need a slow steady lead.

I step into the front line with the other mozos. The bull climbs to his hooves, panting. His mouth hangs open; slime dangles down from his lips. His torso swells violently with each deep breath. *He needs a slow steady hand.* I let him close on me. He trots into the tunnel. As he passes through the shadow of the tunnel into the bright sunshine of the ring I pause, just three yards before his horns. He stalls, peering into the great expansive arena. *Come on, big fella.* I twist back with my paper and waggle it in his vision. And he trots after me onto the sand at almost a walking pace.

Afterward I chat and walk around with Diego and Nathalia. Don Bias appears; his long curly grey hair encircles his wrinkled smiling face. He snaps a shot of us, and we giggle and greet him.

"Bill, have you seen the exhibit?"

"Not yet!"

"Let us be your guide, my friend."

We head into the old chapel that they'd converted into a cultural center. The exhibit's pretty black-and-white photos span the decades. They show the old great runners from the past. I find an image of a street I didn't recognize, with bulls galloping up the way and the horsemen encircling them.

"Where is this?" I ask.

"This is the old embudo," Don Bias tells me.

"Wait, they didn't always run them down the hill?!"

"No," Diego pipes in. "They changed the route in the sixties."

"No way!"

"Yes, it was very different back then," Don Bias says, tapping the photo with his long thin fingertip.

"Who changed it?"

"I don't know, the mayor or someone."

"Man, I want to shake that guy's hand. The embudo is the most incredible spectacle."

"He might still be around," Don Bias says, the history of his Cuellar swirling in his brown eyes.

We head out into the bright light in the busy street.

"This was a spectacular morning, Bill!"

"It was, Diego! Thank you so much for sharing your fiesta with me."

"Bill, it is a joy! It's a joy to share it with you."

"I gotta go lay down for a little," I apologize. "I'm a little overwhelmed."

With a lot of gratitude, I hug them all and head back toward the hotel. Diego is really becoming more than just a friendly local guy. He can't replace Dyango, but he's bringing a new spirit to my fiesta in Cuellar. *You got a new friend.* I grin and head up for a nap.

I fall to my hands and knees and lie down slowly, like a tired achy bull. My mind flicks through it all like a Rolodex of luxurious taurine images. *All that in one morning? It's no wonder you love Cuellar so much.*

℧

I wake with the buzz of the good morning flowing through me. I head to the children's run with the vaca in the afternoon. *Well, you promised the kids at Craig's summer camp you'd run with em.* All the little boys stand nervously in the street. I walk around, shaking their hands and wishing them suerte. One little boy with Coke-bottle glasses and spikey hair shakes my hand and looks up at me, but when he tries to speak he gets choked up with the nerves. *Poor little guy is petrified.*

"It's OK to be afraid. I'm afraid too," I tell him, squeeze his shoulder, and continue greeting the young runners. Their precious fearful demeanor gets me excited about the run, and when they release the vaca I can't help it. I start running with the little boys. They zigzag in front me frantically. *Look at them, trying to run the center of the street!* One athletic little eleven-year-old boy with floppy brown hair leads a black vaca's horns for forty yards and dives out to the metal barricades, with all the daring panache of a young Kiké Bayon Brandi. A pretty little girl with huge long curly brown hair jumps up and down excitedly as the vaca come; she runs alongside them for a strong distance. *Not bad!*

Afterward I congratulate as many of them as I can. I run into the Coke-bottle-glasses kid and two other boys from Craig's camp.

"Mozos! I told you I'd run with you, remember?"

"Bill Hillmann!" one excitable little guy yells, and throws his fist up in the air triumphantly.

"And one day you'll come run with me in the full encierro, OK?"

"Si!"

"Exacto!"

"Adios amigos," I say, ruffle their hair, and head off with the tradition glowing in my heart. *Shit, that was my ninety-ninth run! I didn't expect that. I'll hit a hundred and one in Cuellar now. Great! How fucking great is that? I'll hit a hundred and one in the pueblo where it all started for me, the oldest and the greatest peublo of all, Cuellar.*

♉

In the dark of the morning, we go down to run the embudo. As the incredible stampede approaches, two bulls shoot out front. I wait as everyone leaves. When they get within twenty yards, I turn to run. One guy in a red shirt turns to run with me. *Damn, that's a brave motherfucker! Must be a Cuellarano.*

We dash down the hill shoulder-to-shoulder with the bulls at our backs. We lead them down the hill and around the bend onto the street. The bulls begin to zigzag, and I climb up on the fence as they blister past. I try to take the shortcut to the bullring, but the bulls beat me there.

Later the foreign runners chatter that a bull hit the other American kid from Utah named Anthony Fizer. I pull up the video. *Holy shit, that guy in the red shirt!* It says UTAH on it. *That's not a local! It's Gab's friend Anthony!* After I'd escaped to the fence, Anthony had run way up the street to the next bend. In the video, he seems to tire and tries to get out, but instead of cutting out quick, he feints one way, then cuts out the other as the black bull charges him. As Anthony cuts past the bull's face, the bull lunges his horn at him. The horn hits Anthony in the butt and catapults him fifteen yards sideways under the bottom barricade. In shock, Anthony pops up and walks off as the bull gets to his hooves. *Jesus, that kid is gonna get killed!*

I bump into Anthony and the guys at a bar on the course.

"My god, man! What a run!"

Anthony shrugs humbly.

"He didn't gore you?"

"No, he ripped a hole in my jeans though."

"Fuck, you're so lucky, man."

"I know."

"You almost ended up like this guy." I point to Gab, who's been limping around fiesta until he can catch his flight home.

"How many runs do you got?"

"That was my seventh."

I sigh. *He's gonna get killed if you don't help him. Too much bravery, too much athleticism.*

"Anthony man. If you're gonna run in the bull's space like that, you gotta keep your escape in your mind. Always! And save that last burst of energy to escape fast. Boom! Dive out."

He nods thoughtfully.

"Your out is your most important thing, kid." I pat him on the shoulder. "You like bulls, huh?"

"Yeah, I'm getting into it."

"Good. Have you seen the suelta?"

"No, not yet."

"Want to go with me tomorrow? I'm gonna walk the fields with them."

"Wow, you can do that?"

"Yeah. It's dangerous, but yeah, meet me out front of San Francisco at 6:30."

"All right!"

I sigh, and walk off. *The bulls got a strong hold on that kid. The kind of hold that can get him killed. When your passion and your knowledge don't match, man, it can be fucking deadly, and quick.*

♉

The next day I take Anthony out to the suelta, and later we park where the bulls cross the road and walk through the fields with the horsemen and bulls. As we crest the first hill, the horsemen spread, and twenty yards away a gorgeous brown bull walks tranquilly, eyeing us as we walk parallel to him about thirty yards away.

"These bulls they can kill you in a split second. You gotta know your out. Your escape is the most important part of the run. You gotta save that last burst of energy to escape the danger completely. You gotta get all the way out through the barricades."

Three bulls look at us curiously as they slowly step through the golden wheat field.

"They're beautiful, ain't they?"

"Yeah." Anthony sighs, watching them walk along.

"And don't ever feel like you have to run. If you feel like something is wrong, then don't do it. Just get off the street."

Two black bulls bob their heads following the horses. The brown one peers at us as we step calmly with him. Another black bull trots off track, battling with the horseman to escape. The animals continue, all in their various moods, as the morning haze lights the dust at their hooves.

"There's more to life than the bulls," I say, as we start to jog through a huge cylindrical metal-sheeted tunnel under the highway. *I don't know if I'm trying to convince him or myself.* I glance at Anthony, his eyes lit with excitement. *I guess it's both of us.* The thunder of the hooves of the horses and bulls reverberates loudly in the tunnel.

They bed the bulls down on the other side of the tunnel, and we choose to jog into town so we can meet them at the embudo.

We get down there to the embudo and just a few minutes later the first horsemen crest the hill.

"You gonna run?" I ask him.

"No, not today." He sighs.

"Good, it makes sense after a scare like you had yesterday."

Anthony wishes me luck and goes to the barricades. The first horses crest the top of the hill. *You don't have to.* I bounce on my toes and watch the horizon for the animals as the dust cloud smolders. Horns pierce the dust cloud at the crest of the hill. *This is it. My one hundred and first run of the summer. What a ridiculous fuckin' number. But look what it's given you.* The animals break into gallop down the hill as the thousands on the adjacent hillsides clamor excitedly. A lead light-brown bull shoots way out in front. *OK buddy, you and me.* He vanishes as two horsemen cut in front of him to slow him. As the horsemen approach the embudo, everyone clears out except me. The horsemen bail to either side as the brown bull charges toward me. I link with him, turn, and run fifteen yards before his white snout. The massive herd rambles behind him enveloped in a wall of white dust. One Spanish runner slightly ahead of me cuts out across me. *Fuck!* I pause, letting him escape. *I lost contact!* I linger in the center of the embudo trying to reset, looking back for him. I lose balance. *Get out!* I listen and follow the Spanish runner to the cinder-block wall as the lead bull and the rest of the herd roar past.

I pant as a hundred horsemen flood into the street. *Well, that's a nice place to leave off.* I ran pretty good in the embudo, but there's plenty of room for improvement. I've never been more fascinated with this mysterious beauty of the embudo in Cuellar. I can't wait to get back here next year.

News circulates through the street that Julen has passed away. A big black crack opens in the center of my chest. I walk up the streets of Cuellar, the mood falling with the final run of the year complete. I grip my chest. *Julen, what a life, what a spirit.* It doesn't make sense: all those moments of near-death in the streets with the bulls, only to be taken by a wave. True, he had been seriously injured by the bull a few weeks before. But to go that way: catching a wave, playing in the water. *He was just living his life, Bill. He lived it to the fullest till the end. We only have so much time. Why not take it to the limit?* I see Julen dashing into the ring with his shaven head glowing and his little hoop earrings dangling from his lobes, a massive brown Jandilla suelto chasing him into the sand as if connected to him by a magical golden chain. *Love the ones around you. Cherish them and the moments you have with them. The end is nearer than you think, for all of us.* I walk through the mozos who love Julen; we only have to see each others' faces to know the pain we share. *He touched so many of us.*

(If you loved that man, then you know the great void that was formed when he left us; it was cold and crippling and too much to carry.)

I crouch down on my hindquarters and put my back to the metal barricades. I see his little baby daughter, her curly hair bouncing around as she runs up to Julen with a big smile and he picks her up in his strong arms. Tears swirl in my eyes as I feel all the fatherly warmth of Julen around me. *Ah maestro...I'm so sorry...*

I will miss you.

Chapter 13

Medina del Campo

I take off toward Medina del Campo, my heart still aching over Julen. I curl through the streets of Cuellar. *Well Julen, I hope you know I'm doing this for runners like you. The local runners who love it and live it to the fullest. Matter of fact, I dedicate this whole summer to you, maestro.* Shivers run through my shoulders like falling raindrops. *And hopefully it will help spread the truth of your beautiful culture and help protect it so your great-great-grandkids can run with the bulls just like you.*

Zipping through the hills outside of town, I pass a sign that reads: Medina del Campo. *Man, all my Spanish and Basque friends always go on and on about how great Medina del Campo's fiesta is. Well, I got high expectations, Medina. The fiesta of San Antolin!* San Antolin is the coolest saint I've ever heard of. I giggle at the research I'd done the night before. The guide of hunters, he's almost always depicted with a knife going into his neck or shoulder. Legend has it he had an affair with the queen of Toulouse, and of course the king didn't like that, so he imprisoned San Antolin and then immersed him in a big cauldron of boiling oil. When that didn't kill him, they tied a humongous millstone around his neck and dropped him and the stone in the Garona River. The king figured that'd be the last time he'd see ol' San Antolin. But San Antolin miraculously survived, escaped, and returned to Toulouse to continue preaching. Finally the gobsmacked king captured him again. This time the king didn't play around with any bizarre torture methods; he told one of his mightiest soldiers to take a big sword and do it right. The soldier swung the sword up over his head and came down with it on San Antolin's collarbone. The sword cut San Antolin's torso in half; his head and left arm on one side, and the rest of his body on the other.

I giggle, shaking my head at the wild images as I pass a big green tractor bopping slowly along the road. *What a legend. Screws the king's wife, survives two torturous attempts to kill him, escapes, and just says "Heck, I'm going back Toulouse to see my girl!" Legendary. Man, if I was still drinking and he was still alive, San Antolin is definitely a guy I'd want to throw one back with.* A big black bull billboard up on a hill floats past my window.

As I drive into town a large, dark, fortress-like castle dominates the skyline. Castilla de la Mota, Castle of the Hill. The massive brown structure looms above the twenty-thousand–plus population city. I wonder if San Antolin's fiesta is gonna live up to his legend.

I find the main square Plaza Mayor de Hispanidad. It's large and beautiful. The Church of San Antolin sits at one end; its huge white stone wall and walkway dominate the plaza, with the bell tower looming above. Tall buildings line the rest of the square, with an overhanging walkway supported by thick oak beams. The center of the plaza is full of ornamental benches and light poles and small trees; it reminds me a little of Plaza del Castillo in Pamplona.

Dyango Velasco and Juan Pedro Lecuona both highly recommended I meet up with Juan Carlos Rebollo. But I'm weaving through the street lost, until finally Juan Carlos messages me to meet him at the bullring. I find the barricades of the bull-run course, park, and jump out, figuring the bullring can't be far.

"Excuse me sir," I ask an old man. "Where's the bullring?"

"It's way over on the other side of town." He points up the course.

"Really?!" I take a deep breath and gallop down the course. *Fuck, that's right. Medina del Campo's bull-run course is two kilometers long, twice as long as Pamplona's! Crap!* I can't keep Juan Carlos waiting. I sprint toward the bullring, down the long wide street with the metal fencing lining it.

I arrive at the big, red brick Plaza de Toros. Juan Carlos waves to me; he stands beside a bronze statue of a bull and a bull dodger. He's wearing black-rimmed spectacles, and his hair is short and well-kempt; he looks like a cool Spanish dad.

Juan Carlos greets me warmly. "You didn't have to run!"

"Sorry, I got lost."

"Welcome to Medina del Campo!" he says; he gives me a ticket and we head inside.

Juan Carlos brings me up to the packed stands where his family is waiting. Workers bring a big metal-sided truck into the ring. *Are the bulls in there?* The workers swiftly build a big ramp alongside the truck in front of the six doors. They release several steers that trot nervously into the ring from the corrals. Workers climb up on top of the truck and pull the first door up. A massive black bull squeezes his horns through the opening and leaps down. The crowd roars. The bull trots with his nose up toward the steers, who retreat from him. Then he bows his head and charges one big steer and picks him up with his horn tip. The steer scrambles off the horn and trots away as the bull charges another steer. *Wow!* They pull the next metal slot up, and an equally impressive bull leaps down the ramp and charges his brother. The two bulls lock horns with a cacophonous crack. Their horns rattle as they battle it out—their hooves kicking up tufts of sand.

Juan Carlos's three-year-old son Matias jumps around cheering the bulls. I put my hand up and he slaps me a high-five eagerly as Juan Carlos laughs.

We watch them unload five trucks of bulls; each animal looks stellar.

"We're running out of time," Juan Carlos says. "We have to go to your event!"

"OK." I stand looking at four bulls rambling around the ring battering the steers. They slide another door open. An epic brownish-red bull sticks his head out of the opening. Whitish rings encircle his eyes and snout as he blinks in the bright sunlight. He sees his brothers, bellows, and leaps down the ramp into the sand. He bows his head and dashes into the circling pack. *Man, I can't wait to run with you guys.*

We head to my book event, in a fancy courtroom in the town hall near Plaza Mayor. Juan Carlos put it together, and it goes great. A nice woman helps translate, and we go to a local bar for a few drinks and a chat afterward before I drive back to Cuellar to sleep one last night at Hotel San Francisco.

♉

The next morning, I get up early pack and drive in to Medina del Campo so I can be there when they release the bulls at nine a.m. My head aches. *Man, I ain't a morning person.* I already like Medina, though.

I park near the bullring and look down the street. Two blocks away stands a grey metal barricade. *Is that the embudo?* I hurry over. The fencing turns into a long wooden post the girth and length of electric poles laid on their sides. They stretch out a hundred yards into a field. *It's the embudo. My god, it's just two blocks from the tunnel into the bullring! Oh yeah, Dyango said you can run both sections in the same run. Run the embudo, then jump out and sprint to the bullring while the herd is making the two-kilometer loop through town, and then you can run the last section into the ring with the same bulls!* I guffaw. *It's like tits and ass! Embudo and tunnel, every morning.* The embudo fills with runners and spectators. Juan Carlos takes up his post on one of the long wooden barricades; I come over to say hi.

"We have twenty minutes maybe, Bill. It's hard to say. The bulls are in the fields with the horsemen now."

"Nice." I walk around mixing with the runners, some I vaguely recognize, when suddenly Pablo walks up and grins.

"Bill, you made it!"

"Pablo! It's great to see you!" We hug. "You live around here, right?"

"Yes...fifteen minutes away."

"We had so much fun in Iscar in the tunnel."

"With Toro Passion! Yes, it was good."

A small athletic-looking guy in a yellow shirt walks up; his black hair's slicked back, and the sides shaved.

"Hey, Pablo."

"Jose Rico, meet Bill Hillmann."

I shake his hand as he listens to an earpiece sending news of the bulls.

"The bulls, they come now," he says after listening to his radio. "Oh, no, not yet, they have a problem with one in the fields."

A restlessness builds in my chest as we wait. A big barn sits out about two hundred yards into the field. There's a metal barricade blocking another roadway across from it that connects to a long chain-link fence encircling an industrial farming plant. *Fuck it, I'll jog out and get warmed up and maybe see them coming.*

I head out there. About a hundred people stand near the barricades peering into the field. Harvested farm fields spread out as far as the eye can see. *Where are they gonna come from?* I squint at the heat waves on the horizon. Suddenly the waves begin to move erratically. Cars blaze across the fields. Then the poles of the horsemen appear in the trembling heat. The wavering dark spots in the distance form into hundreds of horsemen surrounding the herd as they gallop toward us. *Fuck, I gotta get back!* I run back to the embudo as hundreds of galloping horsemen fill the fields. The herd seems broken into several packs.

Pablo laughs as I run up, flustered by my bad decision.

"Bill! They're here!" he giggles.

"I noticed!" I say breathlessly.

The lead pack of a dozen black horses gallops slowly, with riders all around in their collared uniforms holding their long poles. As they near the edge of the wooden barricades, the horsemen peel open and a lead bull black emerges, snugly surrounded by horses. I stand on the road with a few runners, all of us bouncing on our toes. The pack approaches, clomps of mud flipping off their hooves. *Well, here we go again!* I turn and run in front of the bull's horns for about twenty yards, then cut off to the wooden barricades as the bull and horsemen pass. Several steers follow him into the street as the horsemen stop and curl, heading back toward the field. A minute later, another group of horsemen approaches, with another bull snug between them. I wait and run that bull's horns. I run directly in the animal's line of sight, wiggling my paper in his vision. His eye swells; he bellows and cuts hard toward me. I cut sideways as he chases me. I slide feet-first under the thick wooden barricades like a baserunner sliding into home. My thigh rolls over a big rock as the bull smashes into another guy who couldn't escape quickly enough. Then the bull rambles on.

Fuck! I get up and peer over the medics. *Is he OK?!* A big bruise rises on my thigh. *I'm outta here.* I cut across the street and run toward the bullring, and arrive at the ring breathless. *Did I beat them here?!* I look around. The gates to the ring stand open. Runners are preparing in the street, looking down the long straightaway for the bulls to come. *I beat 'em!*

Bending down, I step through the barricades a hundred yards from the ring as the first pack approaches. I run and look back and slow down. I let the other runners shoot past me and let the black bull close in on me until I link with him. I dash toward the tunnel with him close behind me, and enter the six-thousand-seat arena with the bull at my back, to the sound of the roaring spectators.

I shoot back out and find Anthony Fizer in his Utah shirt.

"Good one," he says.

"Thanks."

The second bull approaches. I glance back at the ring. The doors to the ring close.

"Let's sit this one out," I tell Anthony.

"OK." We sit atop the barricades and watch the bull ramble past with Jose Rico, who I'd just met in the embudo dashing before his horns.

"You see that guy in yellow?!"

"Yeah."

"Kick-ass runner!"

They open the tunnel doors as the pack approaches.

"Alright, we're good. But it's always best to err on the side of caution, especially in a new town."

"Yeah, good thinking."

A reluctant suelto approaches, spinning angry circles in the street. About fifty yards before the tunnel I enter the front line of mozos luring him up the course. In the tunnel I stand with a bald local runner with wire-rimmed glasses and a big white penuelo flapping in the breeze. We entice the bull to charge as he lingers outside a few feet away. The bull swings his horns in the sunlight before the tunnel as I urge him into the dark shade with my paper. He twists before me, froth hanging from his mouth. *I know, you're tired.* His nostrils slurp air. *Let's get you with your brothers.* The sunlight glows in the silky sheen of his fur. His tall coral-colored horns twist above his muscular head. Then he turns and charges us and we take him in as the other mozos scatter at the mouth of the tunnel.

"And the final bull of the morning in the encierro of Medina del Campo!" the announcer shouts over the loudspeaker as the band kicks up in the stands.

I walk back to find my car as my mind reels with images of the morning's run. I can't comprehend each moment. *Did that all really just happen?! My god, everybody was right, Medina is incredible.*

♉

I check into a youth hostel. It's a big new concrete facility, and all the official horsemen are staying on the floor below mine.

On my way into town I find a nice-looking bar; they've laid a big green rectangle of Astroturf on the street with new white tables and chairs on it and black metal fencing around it. A big red retractable overhang casts the tables in a nice shade. Lettering on the overhang reads *Bar Castellano* in white cursive.

What the hell, I'll give it a try. I sit down at a white table, hungry as a bull. A tall older man with thick black eyebrows comes out. His rich deep voice is equal parts tough and jovial.

"I saw this hat in the encierro this morning." He taps the brim of my hat.

I giggle.

"Yeah, I was out there."

He hands me the menu. "The eggs and sausage are good today." Then he darts back inside.

I glance over my shoulder into the bar and see him standing there in his white apron, watching that morning's encierro on a loop on the TV screens.

He laughs, turns, and comes back.

"You ran in the embudo and the callejon today. Aye, mozo." He pats me on the back. "I'm Antonio, what's your name."

"I'm Bill, nice to meet you, Antonio."

His son, a big portly guy, comes out. He looks at me and his eyes bug out. "You wrote the book on the bulls in San Fermin!"

Antonio gestures. "This is my son Chucky."

"Nice to meet you, Chucky."

"I bought your book!"

I giggle.

"Haha… what do you want to eat?"

"Eggs and sausage, señor, por favor."

"Very good, that's it?"

"Y un cortado."

"Un cortado." He hikes his eyebrows. *"Fuerte?"*

"Si! Muy fuerte, por favor."

Don Antonio brings out a plate of steaming eggs and sausage with a little hash browns and a damn strong cortado. I munch eagerly on the nice-looking plate. *I can't believe how good this is! Well, I guess you've found your spot in Medina.* I open my laptop and sure enough a Wi-Fi feed for Bar Castellano pops up. Chucky gives me the password and I open my email.

Josh Schollmeyer, my editor at *Playboy*, has written me out of the blue: *Bill, I started working for a new online magazine, we pay good, do you have any story pitches for me?*

Fucking-a right I do. I whip up some pitches and send them over. He gets right back with three yesses, $500 a pop. *Holy shit.* I start writing. *Man, I need a smoke.* I walk in to see if I could bum a cigar off one of the old men smoking inside. I look behind the counter. A pack of mini-cigars sits on sale.

"Don Antonio, how much for the pack of cigars?"

"Five, but you can buy one at a time, I don't care. Fifty cents for one."

I buy two and go back out to work, smoking like a chimney as the old men inside bicker and fight over their card games like old married couples. And Don Antonio tries to mend fences and hold in his laughter at their antics. *This place is a riot.* After several hours, a few cortados, a plate of calamari, and some sports drink that for some reason I can never remember the name of (Don Antonio laughs at my attempt to say it; it turns out it's called Aquarius), I'm finally ready to leave. When it comes time to pay, Don Antonio steps up and holds up eight fingers.

"Eight euros, that's it?!"

"Yes."

I give him a ten and head out.

"Keep the change, Don Antonio, gracias!"

♉

As I walk toward the embudo the next morning, this strange feeling takes hold of me. A heavy gravitational sensation like the bulls are drawing me. I push against it in my mind. *You don't have to run today. You went hard yesterday. Just take a day off. Your thigh is sore. Take it easy. You ran good yesterday, you've got nothing to prove.*

I bump into Chapu and his friend, TV presenter Juan Ramon Lucas; we greet each other nicely.

"So this afternoon the event should be good," Chapu says.

"Yeah, thanks for letting me be part of it," I reply.

"It will be a fun time."

"Man, I don't know if I'm gonna run today, my leg hurts," I say, stretching my quad.

"If you don't feel good, take a day off," Chapu says.

I nod, trying to convince myself.

The bulls and horsemen approach the embudo and a switch flips in my mind. Chapu and I run the horns of several bulls in the broken pack, Juan Ramon is in the action too. Then we dart through the back streets to the last stretch near the bullring. The first bulls approach, and I run slowly, letting the other runners filter past me, until I am in the front line with three mozos leading the bull into the tunnel. I glance at the runner beside me. *It's Pablo!* A big laugh bursts in my chest as I pat Pablo on the back.

"Aye Pablo, how's it going?" He looks at me urgently and keeps running. I lead the bull in with the same bald runner with the wire-rimmed glasses. After we enter the ring, there's commotion; another bull's approaching in the street. I sprint back into the tunnel, but the runners pouring in force me to the side. I step through vertical metal barricades to the hall of the bullring, and wait as the runners flood past, standing half in and out of the metal barricades. *Fuck, maybe I can cut in. No way, don't do it...* As the last runner passes, a five-yard space opens between the last runner and the bull's horns. *Don't do it... ah fuck it!* I dash into the gap with the bull's snout at my back. *Jesus, what the fuck are you thinking?* I sprint hard as his hooves crackle behind me. *I can't fucking help it!* I enter the bright sunlight of the arena with the bull at my back, the crowd explodes in a brilliant cheer. *I'm possessed!*

Heaving for breath, I lean against the bullring wall. *You shouldn't have done that!* But I love the spontaneity of it all; I keep pushing the limit, but it's because I can. I'm getting in this grove where I can bend the rules around my desires to link with the animal. *It's a compulsion, and it's growing.* I step along the sand toward the tunnel. *What if you go too far? What if you get gored out here in a tiny pueblo? It's not like Pamplona, it'll be a long trip to a trauma center and surgeon. You gotta stop this bullshit!* I giggle. *I fucking can't!* I walk out the tunnel into the bright morning light. *Take it to the limit, I guess that's what this is all about. Live every moment of life to the absolute fullest. Any moment can be your last, just look at Julen.* My heart aches as I walk through the smiling faces out on the long straightaway. *One day you won't be able to run bulls anymore. You'll be glad you took this chance today to do what you love—to connect with this amazing animal.*

☿

Afterward we head to Chapu's book event at a Peña clubhouse on the course. They call me up about halfway through, and we talk a little. This feeling surges in my chest; I want to say something, but the conversation is moving and flowing nicely. My book is interesting because it's about how the heart of the tradition of the encierro changed my life for the better. Chapu's book is great because it is the heart of the tradition. I'm grateful for Chapu's friendship; it's already changing me for the better. I want to say it, but I just get tongue-tied and don't jump in. Sometimes with epiphanies like this, you don't have to say them because the most important audience is yourself.

That night I meet up with Chapu and Juan Ramon in the packed Plaza Mayor de Hispanidad. Music and food fill the massive square. Ramon's beautiful wife's family is from Medina, and we all chat merrily.

"You know the runner who I admire the most? Not just because of his running, he is an excellent runner, but it is more for his spirit," Chapu says, grinning widely.

"Who?" I ask.

"It's Tom Turley."

"Yeah, Tom is like a guru."

"Yes, he is a guru with such a wise spirit."

"Exactly, he's like Gandhi of the bull runners."

Chapu laughs.

"Yeah, I look up to him so much," Chapu says and pats my back.

"Me too," I agree.

Chapu's a lot like Turley, himself. He's like a spiritual guru and leader of this generation. I take a sip from my water as the conversation flows. There's something special about him. *Well, I guess you went and made another Basque friend, Bill.*

♉

The next morning Chapu runs one last time in Medina before leaving. I do everything to convince myself not to run again, and again I run like mad—leading two sets of bulls into the ring. As I run with the second bull, two runners fall in the sand ahead. *Guys, stay down, please.* I lead the bull onto the sand and cut right as the fallen runner closest to me stands. The bull that I led in charges him and explodes upward with his horns, sending the man flying into the air; his shoe dislodges from his foot and flies thirty feet into the sky above the ring, flipping end over end. *Jesus, is he alright?* I look back as he crawls away and the bulls dash across the ring.

I invite Chapu for breakfast at Bar Castellano, and Chapu is pleased with the quality of the food. "This for only six euros?" he guffaws.

We finish up and say our goodbyes.

"I wish you the best, Chapu. It's been great getting to know you."

"Thanks Bill, I feel the same way."

Chapu heads off and I sit back down to write.

♉

In the cool morning air, I head through the modest neighborhood toward the course. I pass an abandoned prison yard with the strangest feeling hovering over me. The way I've been communing with the bulls, it's like nothing I've ever experienced before. My shoes clap atop the sidewalk like hooves. *I don't want it, I have no desire to run, I don't try to run close either. But when the animals close in, it's like they draw me to them, very close to lead them. I take absolutely no responsibility for it.* I pass Bar Castellano and Don Antonio waves, and I wave back as I turn toward the embudo. *Maybe that's how Atanasio, Carney, Julen, Rodriguez, Gowen, JuanPe, Turley, and Aitor felt and feel all the time, like the bulls are drawing them close.* I really don't know, because I'm not great, nor will I ever be great like those runners. But I'm here now, deep inside this dream, a very exotic, beautiful, nightmarish, and intoxicating taurine dream.

Waiting in the embudo with the rest of the mozos, we watch the horizon for movement. I don't know if I'll ever fall into this trance again, and I don't know if I want to. There's just more to life than bulls. Or at least, that's what I keep telling myself.

The bulls approach in a wide mass of horsemen and bovine. The animals never cease to amaze me. Their intellect, the variance in temperament and agility, and the complexity of each individual animal, how its mood can shift so dramatically in a split second, and how other times they can almost speak to you with their eyes and their faces, they can almost trust you. *I'm so fucking in love with this animal.* The bulls approach the embudo with the horsemen driving them hard—big clumps of mud fly up from their hooves. The nerves spike in my stomach. *Bill, you don't have to.* A bull charges squarely at me, and the monstrous force of him seems to grab hold of my whole being as if it is our destiny to be one being, a minotaur. The nerves evaporate. I bounce on my toes, waiting. The lead bull approaches, galloping fiercely, I turn and run, leading him toward the streets, his bellows and calls rumbling in my chest.

ʘ

That night I meet Juan Carlos and his family for the *cortes* championships of Medina del Campo. In Medina del Campo they don't call them *recortadores*, they call them *cortes*, but either way Medina del Campo produces the finest bull dodgers in all of Spain.

The spectacle thrills me. I recognize a lot of the *cortes* from places like Iscar and other nearby towns. In one of the semifinals, the bull gores and tosses a *corte*. I close my eyes. Every time I see a goring now, I hear it. The sound of a knife digging through thick Styrofoam. It's the sound of your heart rate spiking and cycling through your ears, or who fucking knows. I listen to the crowd's anguished roars and open my eyes to see every single *corte* in the competition, and others who weren't competing dashing in the animal's space, attracting him away from their fallen friend. They carry him to the infirmary; the bull inflicted two·major wounds, but he will survive. Later, another incredible *corte* makes an impossible dodge. When he arches his back, the bull leaps up toward him and smashes his head into the *corte*'s back. The collision breaks ribs and knocks him out of the competition, but the crowd really loves him for the spectacular display.

After they crown the cortes champion, they call all the old champions down from the crowd. They all wear street clothes, and they make cortes with the final bull; the capacity crowd in the big plaza de toros is rocking and rolling, full of the spirit of the cortes.

"This was a hell of a spectacle, Juan Carlos. Thank you so much."

"I'm glad you enjoyed it, Bill." Juan Carlos grins at me proudly.

♉

The runs in Medina del Campo continue to thrill me. I begin new a ritual that actually started back in Sanse. I tell myself, "You don't have to..." in the final moments before the run, as I dig my shoes in the sandy dirt and kick tufts behind me. For some reason, that clears all the pressure and all the bad feelings. I lead the bulls in the embudo and through the tunnel every day. They hold other runs scattered throughout the day, and the animals compel me to run close in the smaller runs too.

I deepen my friendship with Luis Rico and Pablo. Every morning in the embudo, Luis gives Pablo and I updates on the location and status of the animals while listening to the radio on his earbuds, then Luis leads the bulls two hundred yards on the straightaway in the middle of the course. Pablo and I run a lot more horns together. The local runners treat me warmly, and I am grateful for it. I see Juan Carlos every day. Everywhere I look in Medina del Campo, I see smiling friends.

The final morning, I am close to running the horns going into the tunnel, but another runner holds a better position, and I try to squeeze in next to him, but he pushes me a few times and I almost fall when we get to the ring. *Fuck, this is the first day I didn't lead a bull into the ring.* I sigh, my stomach churning with regret.

It gnaws at me throughout the day. I want to end San Antolin on a high note, not like that. My plan is to leave that day after the morning run. *Fuck it, I'll stay for the afternoon run.* I go to Bar Castellano and Don Antonio gives me a yellow Bar Castellano shirt as a gift.

"Wear it in San Fermin!"

"I will," I promise him.

Wearing my new shirt, I loosen up for the evening run. They plan to release one huge bull, and he will run the whole course by himself. *Kinda like me crisscrossing Spain by myself.* I prepare to run and bump into Juan Carlos on the fence near the tunnel; his family is with him, and a bunch of kids. They excitedly await the final bull of the *feria* to run into the ring.

Hold my ground about eighty yards from the tunnel, I watch the street for horns. Suddenly through the mass of moving bodies I see Chucky running in front of one horn of the bull, and then Jose Rico is there leading on the other horn. I turn to run looking back, letting the other runners filter past me. Forty yards from the tunnel at the final bend, Jose chooses to cut out hard, and as he does three of the other guys near the horns bail out, and Chucky dashes out to the other side. The street opens up. The massive bull approaches with his very wide horns, his head up, eyes looking for an ally, someone who knows the way. I slow before his face. *I will take you, my friend.* He sees me and bows his head; the force of his vision locks into my moving body. I slow and he slows with me. *It's just you and me, my friend. Let's go say hi to the arena, they're waiting for us.* I lead him through the tall arched brick tunnel. His shadow spreads before him and spills onto the ground at my feet, morphing with mine. I dash through his shadow into the immense red bullring as joy bubbles up in my chest. *It's like it was our destiny, you know? Do you believe?* I lead the final bull of feria onto the sand as the crowd erupts. I throw my head back and yell: "Viva San Antolin!"

The bull slowly trots into the corrals. *It's like Chucky and Jose cleared the course for me. One last gift from Medina del Campo.* I look up into the raucous stands. *Thank you.*

I leave the ring quickly, hoping to catch Juan Carlos and his family; I exchange excited high-fives with all the kids, and Matias too.

"You treated me so well, Juan Carlos. Thank you so much."

"It was a great pleasure, Bill. Thank you."

Giddy, I walk the streets as they slowly empty. *Medina is a gem. What a special place.* There's no way around it, this has been an incredible summer, but San Antolin is my favorite fiesta this summer. I came here with such high expectations; the people, the bulls, and the encierro, they've blown my mind. I think of San Antolin and his outlandish adventurous life. I look up to the bright sky. *San Antolin, your fiesta definitely lived up to your incredible legend. Gracias, Santo, it was an honor.*

Chapter 14

The Valladolid Circuit

I sit at Bar Castellano's patio writing in the afternoon heat. *Fuck, I'm in a flux. Don't know what to do...I hit a hundred and one runs, I'm up to almost a hundred and twenty now. I could go back to Cuellar and hit some runs, but this youth hostel here in Medina is so cheap and nice, and I've got Bar Castellano to hang in. I could also head back to Pamplona, I'm sure they've got some runs going. I wonder though, didn't Larry Belcher say there was a circuit of bull runs around Valladolid in September?* Suddenly Luis Antonio Prieto writes me on Facebook Messenger.

"Bill! Will you come run with me in my hometown tonight, Laguna de Duero?"

"Sure! I'll see you there!"

I check the map. Shit, that's just south of Valladolid. I wonder if this is part of the Valladolid Circuit...

Don Antonio comes out to the steps for a smoke.

"Hay encierros ahora cerca de Medina, Don Antonio?"

"Si, yes, yes, there are many runs now. You should go, a lot of them are at night."

I search feverishly online until I find a website called Callendario Taurino which focuses on bull events in Castilla y Leon. I scroll down the list of a dozen runs throughout the Valladolid region set for that night and over the next week. *Fucking unreal, Larry was right!* I pull up Google Maps and start compiling potential runs, calculating how much time it takes to drive between towns. Finally I work out a map that zigzags the Valladolid region from eight p.m. through to two a.m. *Fuck, I could run ten or twelve runs tonight! Medina is smack-dab in the middle of the whole circuit! How fucking lucky is this?! I could have headed back to Pamplona and missed the whole thing! Guess I'm staying in Medina...* I pack up and head out to Laguna de Duero.

☾

Laguna de Duero is a big town just south of Valladolid city. Expansion in industry spurred a population boom in the past twenty years; at twenty-one thousand people, it's now the second-biggest city in Valladolid. I roll into the main strip; eight-story apartment buildings line both sides of the street, and the bars and food tents are bustling with families and partiers.

After finding some parking near a big nature park and lagoon, I head down to the shores and take a look. A variety of birds swoop over the waters, and a big white stork stands in the shallows. *That's a hell of a lagoon.* The setting sun casts the water in a purplish haze.

I start in toward the heart of town to find Luis. The lively fiesta of Nuestra Señora del Villar spills through the streets. I find the bull-run course. A long string of a Peña marching band parades through the clean blacktop street. A tall man blows powerfully on his shiny trumpet as the drummers bang out a hard bass line. *Can't wait to see Luis. He's such a warm spirit. We've run together in Pamplona and Cuellar. About to add another town to the list, and it's his hometown!*

Luis materializes on the clean blacktop street about a hundred yards away. His big round shaved head gleams in the streetlights; his hoop earrings make me think of Julen. He walks up smiling: a quiet calm presence. We greet each other with a warm hug.

"So Bill, tonight there will be four young bulls. They will run from the arena..." (He points down the long straightaway that turns into the big arena.) "...through the street..." (He points the other direction, where the straightaway winds around a corner.) "...then back to the arena. They'll run them four to eight times. It all depends on how tired they get."

"Holy shit, I'm about to add, like, six runs to my count?! Crazy. And I got another three towns to hit tonight!"

"Yes, this is normal in Valladolid. Where do you want to run?"

"Here, I guess." I shrug.

"OK."

Luis and I limber up. A mother and her two grammar-school-aged daughters sit in their big window that opens onto the course.

"Are you two runners?" the mom asks.

"Yes," Luis replies.

"No, you aren't," she chides us.

"We are, he is from the United States. We run in Pamplona."

"Prove it," the mother says mischievously.

I pull up one of my best images on my phone and show her. Her eyes bug out. The little girls squeal "Wow!"

"OK, OK, you're runners, fine," the mom says.

"We'll put on a show for you guys," I say, grinning.

"It's dangerous, you know!" she replies.

"Yes, we know," Luis says as I giggle.

As the rocket pops in the sky, the course is completely clear. It is just Luis and I standing in the center of the street, the entire path vacant all the way to the bend into the arena. The four bulls come into view around a corner about three hundred yards away. We watch them swing and hook for a few spectators, cutting completely across the street. We wait there shoulder-to-shoulder, and as they close in to about fifteen yards, we start running. We lead the four black bulls, finding their pace and rocketing up the street with them. Their calm heavy breathing fills the silent street. I start to tire; I see a big open double door into a hotel and dive into it, pushing through the drunken spectators. Luis takes the bulls up another thirty yards before he hits the fence.

"Why'd you get out, Bill? Come on!" Luis chides me.

"You're in good shape, Luis! I got tired, man," I reply, winded. *Too many fucking cigars.*

A few minutes later the bulls come charging back, and Luis and I prepare to run them again. This time we wait until they are ten yards away to turn and sprint. *Man, this is so easy!* As we pass the mom and two girls, I look over at them, grin, and wave.

"Hola chicas!" I say merrily as they giggle and clap.

This time, we take them another hundred yards before one of the bulls starts closing in on me.

"Bill! Look!" I glance back just in time to cut out before the bull catches me. Luis takes them another twenty yards up the street.

"Thanks, Luis! That was close!"

"No problema, amigo Bill!"

We take off again on their horns. It's so quiet. The sound of bulls breathing and their hooves clapping echoes in the tight corridor of the street. We communicate with them and each other as we soar up the way. *Man, this is like magic. I've never run in a more peaceful place.* Luis dashes beside me, grinning. He reaches out and pats me on the shoulder. *Another great fucking friend.* I pat him back as we glide up the street, leading the animals as the hundreds of spectators lining the doorways and fencing cheer, and the cameras flash.

Afterward we do a little interview with the local paper in Laguna, and then I take off for Boicillo with a warm goodbye and a sincere thank you.

"Tomorrow?" Luis calls after me.

"Of course! *Hasta pronto, amigo!*"

♉

I dart toward the small town of Boicillo like a suelto trying escape the horsemen, with the adrenaline of the run pulsing through my body.

The origins of the name Boicillo are disputed. One legends claims that the town is named after a small ox who came to drink from the fountain in the main square every day. In Spanish *buey* is the word for ox, and a little ox would be *bueycito*, but who knows? I arrive at Boicillo's Fiesta de Virgin de Salve with about half an hour to spare.

I slip onto the course next to the corrals. The steers' bells ring sporadically inside. The corrals open onto a two-hundred-yard straightaway. The street is filled with sand, and metal barricades run along the curbs so you can watch from the sidewalk. Trees line the sidewalk and cast shadows on the course from the streetlamps hovering above as the locals mill around.

As I walk the sandy street, a drunk guy sitting on his front stairs waves to me.

"What's going to happen with the bull run?" I ask.

"Bull run? There isn't one."

A chubby old man with a grey cap on walks past. "Eight bulls, eight vaca, and ten cabestros… zoom!" He points toward the bend in the course. "Zoom!" He points back to the corrals.

"All at the same time?"

He shrugs and nods as he moves on. *Well, thanks for the info.*

I walk to where the course takes a hard bend. A small square full of bars sits behind the metal fencing. The sand thins until it's just a slippery dusting. *Great, make it harder, why don't you?* The brick street heads downward into a dark park and past a little amphitheater, with the vertical metal bars of the barricades lining the way. *Well, you can slip through these if it gets ugly.* I practice slipping through the bars. Then the course enters a brightly lit arena with vertical bars forming the ring walls, and half-moon-shaped bleachers above. *I ain't never seen nothing like this!* I walk back down by the corrals.

They shoot a rocket off and open the corrals; three vaca, a bull, and two steers careen out and zigzag the course. I run the horns of a vaca for twenty yards, and suddenly another bull comes flying around the corner ahead of me headed the other way. *Fuck they let bulls out of the ring too!?* I dive to the fences and the animals gallop past; the bull spins around and runs with the broken pack. *This is fucking nuts! They're releasing animals from both ends?! If I woulda took that vaca around the bend, that bull mighta killed me.*

The young boys urgently communicate from the corner, pointing and shouting "Toro! Vaca! Cabestro!" whenever they see something coming. I bounce around the course running animals. At one point, I take a big full-grown bull from near the corner down the shadowy hill; he breathes at my back as his hooves clatter down the dark slope. Then I lead him from the shadows into the bright light near the ring. Twelve animals stand in the center of the ring in a scared pack. The crowd sees us coming as a nervous cheer rises; I go to break left, but another bull is battering the fence along the left side. The crowd roars fearfully. I fake left and cut right; there's a steer trotting along that wall. The bull behind me sees the steer, dips his horns, and smashes the steer as I cut between it and the big pack of animals in the center. The crowd rejoices and laughs as I shake my head and throw my hands up, exasperated. The crowd roars laughing. I grin up into the stands. *Fuck, this is chaos! I love it!* The bull knocks the cabestro to the sand, and he struggles to get up. *Poor little bueycito!* I giggle.

I run bulls and vaca in the streets of Boicillo for an hour, communicating with the teenage runners at the curve and trying to avert calamity. If it wasn't for the excellent communicators, somebody would have surely been killed already. I check my clock. *Fuck, I gotta get to Simancas, or I'll miss their run!* After ten long runs on the horns I try to head out to my car, but there is a traffic jam of bulls and vaca blocking my path. *How can you leave a place where you're running the horns to go to some other town to try and run bulls!?* I run with the bulls and vaca, getting them far enough up the street to escape behind them so I can get on the road to Simancas.

♉

Simancas is about ten kilometers from Valladolid city. I take a wrong exit on the highway and double back, speeding recklessly. *Fuck, I'm ten minutes late! The run'll be fucking over!* I bang my fists on the steering wheel like a bull battering a metal barricade.

I speed off the highway into the extremely hilly town. I stop at an intersection, peer down a long hill, and see people milling around a wooden fence. *Barricades!* I park and run down to the barricades. People are perched along them. I dive in and rejoice. *I fucking made it in time!*

A very tall and steep hill with wooden barricades descends down into the big bullring beside me. *This thing's as steep as El Pilón!* I climb the cobblestone hill of the run course.

"Bill!" Chucky shouts from the barricades.

"Chucky! What's going on with the run?!"

"The bulls are stuck way back at the beginning. They can come any second!"

"Thanks." I limber. Nothing like knowing what to expect in a brand-new town! A bunch of the kids I was running with in

Boicillo shout to me and wave. I wave back with a grin. I want to run this hill into the ring; I'll just wait for them.

After forty-five minutes of waiting restlessly, I sigh. *I can't frickin' wait anymore. I gotta go see what's going on.* I walk the incredibly hilly and winding course of Simancas. The streets are dark, with only a few streetlamps casting beautiful shadows on the cobblestones. I pass below a family that sits atop a big stone fence in front of a house.

"Where are the bulls?"

"They're coming," the father sighs impatiently.

I arrive in a small diamond-shaped square full of spectators. The path goes down a steep hill and then ascends another hill about eighty yards away. Suddenly, three runners round a corner nervously, then disappear back around the bend shouting and waving their arms. *A suelto! Must be.* A few seconds later the five runners round the corner sprinting; a big black bull follows them around the bend headed toward us. *Fuck, I'll never get back to the hill in time!* I run as fast as I can up and down half of the hilly course, then finally arrive back at the top of the final hill.

"They're coming!" I shout to the teenagers lounging around on the barricades. They pop up, ready to go.

Runners round the final bend and the bull makes the turn, trotting fast. I turn and run with the teenagers; we descend the hill, and suddenly it's just me and a kid in black Adidas track pants, running down the steep hill shoulder-to-shoulder, with the big bull clattering down the stones behind us. We slowly lead him into the tunnel and dash off to the side in the brightly lit ring. We exit through the same slot in the ring and laugh heartily, then exchange a high-five before I head out to Navas del Rey.

♉

I speed into Navas del Rey. *I'm fucking late again, and I have no idea what to expect!* I round a corner and see the big bullring with the bright lights floating above. *Shit, the tunnel is open!* Runners dash around. I park illegally and sprint over and jump through the fence. The gates to the tunnel sit open, with the crowd inside cheering.

A teenage pastore stands ready in the street in his white uniform, holding his willow cane.

"What is it, bulls? Vaca?" I shout to him.

"Six vaquilla!" he shouts as he jogs past. Suddenly the vaquilla thunder out of the bullring tunnel. I run them with the local teenagers through the streets; they're full of bystanders, adults and kids standing right on the course. Then I cut off to the side as the very young vaquilla hooks for us. They run the vaquilla up the long straightaway that turns into what looks like a garage under a home at the end of the course. A big white chapel looms above the course beyond the last barricades. *You made it again! Four towns in one night! Unreal.*

The runners and partiers stay in the street, waiting. *Are they going to run them again?!* Sure enough, the garage doors open, and the little black vaca ramble out and gallop toward us. I run with the teenagers again, then cut out. *Fuck, I'm hungry as a bull that's been running encierros all damn day! I haven't had time to eat!* I slip through the fence and order a kebob with everything from a food truck next to the course. He hands me the kebob and I run back onto the course with it, trying to eat it before the next run. The vaquilla approach. *I still got half the kebob to eat!*

I bob on my toes. *I ain't tossing it!* I start running, and as I run on the horns of the six vaquilla, I take a bite of the kebob and chomp it a few times. *Too good to throw away.* I look back at the vaquilla. *Want a bite, guys?* I bail to the fence, giggling. They continue to run them back and forth. The local teenage boys run impossibly close to the vaquilla's horns, then make out with their girlfriends between runs, right on the course. It's 2:30 in the morning, and Nava del Rey is in full-blown fiesta mode. A toddler in blue footsie pajamas watches, cheers, and dances on a balcony above the street. An old man stands with his wooden cane, smoking in his doorway that opens onto the course. Teenage girls chitchat on the small porches right smack-dab on the course, ignoring the danger. *Damn, I love Spain.* I run eleven runs before they finally shut it down for the night.

I jump in the car and head home toward Medina around three a.m. *How many fucking runs did you do tonight!? Eight in Laguna, twelve in Boicillo, one in Simancas, and eleven in Navas del Rey. Thirty-two fucking runs in one night?! Unreal. You cleared a hundred and fifty runs for the summer. You're gonna have to try for two hundred, just to fucking keep it interesting.*

As I fall asleep in the youth hostel, my mind races through all the animals I ran with. *And it was still only a few of the runs in Valladolid tonight! Hundreds of animals ran through dozens of towns, like mice flying through mazes, except here there are mozos sprinting ahead of them, dodging their gouges, linking with them and soaring up the way in this ritual, erasing the divide between bull and man. Dozens of them enacting the same rite in the same moment miles apart, flowing a streaming memory stretching millions of years long.* It all bubbles up in my mind. I see tiny bulls and tiny men shooting down channels of one massive structure, the Valladolid circuit; it pulses before me as I drift to sleep.

♉

I return to Laguna de Duero the next night. This time Luis brought his friend and pretty girlfriend with him to watch us run. We run a different section this night, closer to the arena. There are a lot more runners, but Luis and I continue to run shoulder-to-shoulder on the bull's horns, just like the night before. I run into another one of my friends there, Javier Delgado in his green-and-white running shirt. He greets me excitedly between runs. Javier dashes some sensational runs, Luis and I hand the bulls off to him and he runs them all the way out of sight into the bullring.

Luis and I just keep laughing and high-five-ing in between runs. *This is so much fun. I can't believe how smooth it's going: no injuries, no problems.* Then after the runs end for the night, a fat drunk guy with long hair barges up to Luis.

"You two are hogging the bulls!"

We are not, you fat prick. We were transitioning on and off with the other runners the whole damn night. The big guy towers over Luis, complaining angrily. *You touch Luis, and I'm fucking you up, asshole. I'll drive a left hook right into your spleen.* Luis strongly but calmly listens to the guy.

"You're more than welcome to run with us anytime. If you think it's hard to run close to the bulls here, you should see how hard it is in Pamplona," Luis says.

The big guy shakes his head and walks off angrily. Luis's grace with the guy astonishes me.

"Good work, Luis. I really wanted to punch that guy."

"Bill, why? He's just drunk."

"You're right." I pat Luis's back as we all walk to the bullring for the capea.

♉

I return to Simancas and run a big suelto down the hilly course with the guy with the shaved head from the tunnel in Medina de Campo.

Then I shoot over to Arrabal de Portillo for their Santa Maria la Mayor de Portillo festival. Arrabal de Portillo, a suburb of the town of Portillo, sits high on a hill. Portillo holds a bull run in the morning with horses, sort of like Cuellar's and Medina del Campo's. I drive around looking for parking in Arrabal de Portillo. I hate the morning. I'll always choose a night run over a day run. I wake up feeling like hell most days, miserable and ornery. By about noon I feel human, and by night I feel good and full of energy.

I find the vertical bars of the course and climb in. A big truck full of bulls backs onto the course. The course comes out of where the truck parks and takes a right turn and shoots about three hundred yards to a big red metal makeshift bullring. Big apartment complexes line the course. *Looks like the 'burbs in Chicago. Imagine if they had a bull run in Schaumburg.* I giggle. *Oh wait, they had one in Cicero! At the racetrack, what a joke. Rodeo bulls afraid of the runners.* I choose to run down about a hundred yards from the bullring. They've spread sand out into the street near the ring. *That makes things a little more complicated.* I dig my hooves through the deep sand. *How's that gonna be at full sprint?*

They release the first bull, and he rockets back and forth through the streets. A teenage kid in a black tracksuit with short curly hair sprints with me in front of the bull; we lead him a hundred yards into the arena and cut out.

We come back out for the second bull and wait. The bull dodgers slow that bull down and make nice circles with him. The kid makes some flashy cortes with the second bull, then we run him another long eighty yards together into the ring.

As we wait for the next bull, the kid introduces himself as Juan.

"Are you a bull runner or a corte?"

"I like both!" He grins.

"Impressive, man, how old are you?"

"Sixteen!"

The next bull comes and Juan runs off, pulling nice circles with the bull in the street. *Fucking kid is like a young David Rodriguez.*

Exhausted, I hop in the car and drive home. *Well, you're on your way to two hundred runs.*

♉

I sleep in the next morning and go over to the Medina del Campo pool for a nice relaxing afternoon on the pretty green lawns and in the cold pool. Then I head over to Bar Castillo for dinner and check my email. There's one from Dyango:

"Bill there are big problems brewing in Tordesillas with the animalistas, you should go."

After some research I find out Tordesillas is real close. They have a run scheduled tonight. *Fuck, I can make it!* I pack up and head over.

Tordesillas is a town of almost ten thousand people. It's a transportation hub with an economy based in wheat and tourism. In 1494 Spain and Portugal signed the Treaty of Tordesillas, which split up much of the New World between the two colonial powers. I wind through some thick woods. *Seems like they need a new treaty between the people who value their traditions, and the people who believe an animal's rights are equal to a human being's rights. But see, my problem is plants have brains and thoughts and souls too, so they should put all the bulls in jail for mass murder of grass, and sentence them to death!* I giggle as I blaze through the wheat fields. Tordesillas is famous for its ancient festival of Toro de la Vega. This is the act of a single man engaging a fully grown bull on foot with only a spear. The bull of course has two spears (his horns), and more than a thousand pounds of muscle on the man. The man also engages the bull in his territory, in the woods in the dirt and grass, where the bull can spin on a dime, and the man might slip and fall. If the man is skilled and lucky, he kills the bull with the spear. Except this year: the regional government banned Toro de la Vega in Tordesillas.

Similar rituals are carried out all over the world: in Africa, tribesman kill lions; in North America, tribesman kill whales. Whether or not flimsy, modern-day Disney-inspired pop culture accepts these traditions isn't important. Hunting is an innately human right. Millions of years ago the transition from a plant-based diet to a meat-based diet triggered a rapid evolution; our stomachs shrank, and our brains grew. Hunting animals, especially large game, spurred technological advances in tools and weaponry, and brought people together in larger groups in order to take down larger game, forming early societies. In short, if *Homo erectus* stayed vegan, we never would have evolved into human beings. It seems absurd to try and change laws to take that away from us. *Meat and hunting gave you that brain to think up those silly ideas!* I make the exit onto a path toward Tordesillas. *Don't bite the hand that feeds your brain.*

The ban this year seems to me a terrible and tragic blow to human culture. The mayor of Tordesillas lashed out against the ruling, and the fight is far from over, but this year the regional government's forced the town to put on a bloodless version of the great tradition; this new version's called Toro de la Peña, and they're having it tomorrow.

I swerve around a big slow-moving truck full of hogs. The banning's become the heart of a huge global story on the tradition and the future of the taurine world in Spain; ten thousand animal rights activists are planning to attend Toro de la Peña. *I guess they want to rub it in the locals' faces that they won.* A group of boxers and MMA fighters (who are also animal rights activists) said they'll be there; they're threatening violence against the locals.

I accelerate up a long hill. *The leader's a washed-up boxer with a crappy record, trying to use his participation in the protest as a way to publicize a fight he wants with the Spanish champion.* I giggle. *The Spanish champ's actually a good boxer and would easily kick the leader's ass!* I always dreamt of going for a pro career as a boxer. *If I catch that motherfucker bullying or getting violent with the locals, I'm gonna knock his ass out cold, right in front of his little coward-ass followers. Gang followers always fold when their leader gets taken out. I can't wait to see them trying to pick him up off the ground, then scurrying off with their tails between their legs. That'll be about as close to a professional boxing career as I'll ever get, and the fucking right thing to do. No trained boxer should ever bully innocent people. Especially people who just want to enjoy their cultural heritage.*

I approach Tordesillas. It rises out of the horizon white and beautiful, high up on a hill. A long tall bridge crosses the Duoro river and rises upward to the base of the hill. *Epic pueblo.* I drive around a roundabout in the center; three humongous ancient-looking stones stand in the lawn, rectangular and tall. *Man, those things look like Stonehenge. What the heck are they?* Metal barricades run out into the fields and funnel the course toward the bridge. *Are they going to run them over this bridge?!* I roll over the bridge. I peer down over the railing; the bright sunlight flickers in the rippling river two hundred feet below. *I gotta run this bridge!* I drive into town and follow the course to a nice red bullring. I park in a parking space where the bridge ends in front of a few restaurants. People are milling around and heading down towards the Stonehenge roundabout. I walk down the bridge looking for exits; a few little spots offer shelter where the light poles sit. *Hopefully the bulls won't jump that curb. But don't count on it, buddy.*

They swing the gates shut and stop all traffic through the roundabout at the beginning of the bridge. I stand in the Stonehenge lawn. *I wonder if I can live-feed the run on Facebook?* I start playing with my phone trying to figure out how to do it when three ten-year-old boys walk up and start trying to climb one of the rocks to sit on it and watch during the encierro.

"*Amigos, necisitas ayuda?*"

"Yes, please!"

I give each of them a boost up on top of the ten-foot-tall rock.

"You're a fucking badass!" one of them says as I laugh.

"You're welcome. Don't fall off!"

"We won't." They giggle.

Man, I wonder if they'll do the live feed of it for me.

"Amigos, if I give you my phone, would you be willing to live feed the run?"

"Hell yeah, man, you helped us! We'll do it."

I hand it up already live feeding. They argue over who is going to film it, and how the phone works. *Them kids'll figure it out better than me in a few minutes.*

The horsemen and bulls appear off in the distance. I watch, trying to get a read on where the herd is. The horsemen struggle to lead a bull our way; they block my view of the animal as they clutter onto the circular lawn. I give ground until the first suelto emerges through the horses. I begin to run him up along the steep hill of the bridge. I run him about halfway and cut out over the curb near a light pole as he continues up the bridge. I fall back and down by Stonehenge as a second bull approaches.

Meanwhile my film crew are making a hilarious video that gains hundreds of live-feed followers on Facebook. They catch some footage of me running with the bull on the bridge.

"Oh no! Our friend is in danger!" one of them says dramatically.

They bicker and fight to hold the phone, and suddenly as the second bull approaches, they drop the phone down to the lawn. The black bull passes over the camera as he dashes between Stonehenge. The live-feed followers tune out by the hundreds.

Once the animal clears out, the boys ask a runner to pick up the phone, and he tosses it up to them. They cheer and thank him and continue filming.

I run the sueltos across the long bridge several times with the local runners, and at times all by myself. In the midst of the runs with sueltos, there are long pauses between animals coming through the embudo. At one point, I recognize a friendly face from Iscar as we run up near the top of the bridge. I turn to him.

"Amigo, como estas!"

"Bill!" He grins, looks at me, and reaches his hand out to shake it. The suelto gathers to charge a few feet from us.

"Oh no no! The bull!" We both reset and dash before his horns. He stalls again.

"Why are you talking near the bull?!" another runner scolds us angrily. "Are you crazy!"

We giggle and pat each other on the back. *I ain't Matt Carney, I better stop with this nonsense, or I'm going to get someone distracted and hurt.*

There is a long break between animals, and a friendly group of locals standing next to Stonehenge starts chatting with me. They wear Peña uniforms. A gregarious guy named Teo Diez Lopez really gets me laughing. The other guy is humongous, incredibly muscular with a shaved head—he looks like a World's Strongest Man champion. His name is Antonio Diez Posada, but as big and mean as he looks, he turns out to be nice and friendly. It turns out he's a trumpet player for the official band of Tordesillas. The two of them invite me for a meal at the Peña clubhouse, and I agree.

I help my young filmmakers down from the big rock and thank them heartily for their help. When I watch the feed, it turns out to be a pretty impressive work, and the drop was a nice splice of humor. They thank me for the help climbing.

The clubhouse is a nice little spot with a backyard and a big grill; my new friends' families show up and I drink a bunch of zero beer and eat some great meat while I listen to their stories. And then we get on the topic of Toro de la Vega. Teo seems especially upset about it, and calls tomorrow's event—the new version the politicians have forced on them—"Bull of the Shame."

"When we learned that there wouldn't be a Toro de la Vega, we had a mixture of feelings. Mainly a lot of anger. All the defenders of the Vega bull feel cheated by politicians when they presented the decree that there would be no tournament. The Toro de la Vega tournament is regulated so that the animal is in the same conditions as the lancers. Face to face, body to body. So the La Vega bull song says. It's much more than what they show on the TV, which they edit terribly."

Teo pulls up a video of last year's Toro de la Vega. The animal rights activists viciously yank and pull at the barricades in the fields that protect children and old people from the nearby bull.

"They should be arrested for attempted murder!" I guffaw.

Teo nods in agreement.

"It's crazy! It's attempted suicide too!" I say.

"They are sick in their brains," Teo says.

It's an attack on their culture and the people of Tordesillas, and potentially a suicide attack. I look around at the nice families eating merrily, living out the traditions they'd passed down for centuries. *How could you attack something so wholesome and beautiful? All because you grew up on Disney films and think animals can talk and have feelings?* It's pathetic and it's tragic. I promise my new friends I will return for Toro de la Peña the next day.

I go over to Cuellar to see Dyango that night. I get a little food poisoning, and as we're chilling out at the park playing fetch with his dog, suddenly the urge to vomit grips me. I puke three times and decide to head back to Medina to sleep. I drive back woozily.

♉

I wake sick and lie in bed naked with my stomach bubbling. What I thought was a fart turns into an explosive shart. I jump up and take the white sheets to the bathroom and wash the big brown stain in the shower. *Damn that must be what it's like to crap like a bull, the shit is just exploding out of there whenever!* I finish and shower up. *Fuck it, I gotta go to Toro de la Peña.*

I drive to Tordesillas; there are military police stand staked out everywhere. I park a mile outside town and start walking in. Suddenly, Antonio Diez Posada appears, stomping around angrily with a flag protesting the end of Toro de la Vega.

"Antonio!" I jog to catch up to him as he stomps into the forest. I get close and he stops, turns around, and gives me the meanest grimace I've ever seen. His whole body swells up like a comic book monster.

"It's me from last night," I stammer. "Remember? Your friend, Bill?"

He recognizes me and his grimace lifts.

"Come on!" he yells, and I follow him into woods.

Well, if we run into the gang of boxers and MMA fighter anti-taurinos, it's a good thing to be with the biggest baddest guy in all of Tordesillas. Hell, me and Antonio'd probably kick that whole gang's ass! I giggle as I follow him. *Antonio, just let me get the leader guy. You take the rest of 'em.*

As we stomp out of the forest into a wide field, a big cold wind rushes up. The sky darkens, and suddenly heavy rain pours down on us. I see a commotion near Stonehenge and head that way as Antonio stomps off into the woods again, his protest flag waving wildly in the gusts. I get to Stonehenge as the bull trots through a sea of mozos. A large group of animal rights activists obnoxiously chants in the rain behind one of the fences. A mass of police stands between them and the ancient culture they hope to crush completely. *Fucking bastards.*

A dark sadness hangs in the air as the bull scans and trots through the people in the rain. My soaked clothes cling to me as I tremble in the hard, cold wind. My stomach bubbles loudly as I consider trying to find the anti-taurino boxers and MMA guys in the group near the police. An image flashes in my mind of one of them punching me in my upset stomach and my bowels emptying through my shorts and onto the wet pavement. *Fuck it, I'm out of here. There ain't any point in making myself sicker than I already am, and the activists aren't hurting anyone.* I glare at them. *This bull trotting around here, it's not going to live happily ever after like in* Charlotte's Web*, you idiots. He'll die in a ring or a slaughterhouse like all cattle. Human beings will still eat him.*

No one is more heartbroken and angry than the locals. Especially Teo Diez Lopez.

"The day of the Toro de la Peña was very hard, because in addition of not having the tournament, the anti-bullfighting protesters were there to bother us, even without a tournament. And the worst is that they were just there to insult us, assault us, and to disturb, if not worse. I would tell to the animal rights activists to inform themselves before protesting. Toro de la Vega is much more than what they show on the TV."

I head out to my car, change into some dry clothes, and drive to the train station in Valladolid. *I hope this isn't the end of Toro de la Vega; I hope that the people can rise up and fight and win and protect their ancient culture.* I imagine the sorrow their ancestors must feel, watching from the afterlife. I get on my train back to Pamplona feeling sad, tired, and sick.

We roll out of the Valladolid train station. *If this is really the end of Toro de la Vega, it'll truly be a Toro de la Peña, a shame for El Mundo de Toro, and for human culture as a whole.*

Chapter 15

Don Tommy-Boy

After the long trip home to Pamplona, I sit in the Café Lorek in Plaza del Castillo, sipping coffee and watching the Pamplonesas pass by. *Fucking been through a lot this summer. One hundred seventy-something runs with a week left. Who knows, if I can find some reses bravas around Navarra, I can clear two hundred runs. So many new friends, so many new towns. The backstabbers? Ha, fuck 'em. It's good to know they aren't your friends, and to get them out of your life. And look at the reward, all these new friends in Spain and Basque Country. I giggle.* A rich and gravelly voice flows from the stone archways.

"Back in Pamplona again… Back where a friend is a friend… Where longhorn cattle feed on the lonely mozos deed… Back in Pamplona again…" Gowen emerges from the shadows and gives me a sound pat on the back.

He wears a shirt designed by a friend of his; it reads: *Trump/Putin '16, Make Tyranny Great Again.* "They're for sale, kid, if you want one."

I cough up $20 for one.

We go through Gowen's regular day in Pamplona. People guffaw and stop dead in their tracks, gaping at the shirt as we giggle. Tom has some friends in the CIA; he knew about the Russian interference long before it made headlines.

We head up to his favorite restaurant, on the second story of a fancy building near one of the corners of Plaza del Castillo. It's a beautiful restaurant with white-cloth-covered tables and a nice balcony.

Niche, the owner, walks out of the kitchen; she's a pretty, older woman with short hair. She sees Gowen and shouts "Tom!" and comes over and kisses him and hugs him. We sit down, and Gowen gets up and goes into the kitchen and comes back with a bottle of wine.

We sit and chat, and an older couple walks in, and Gowen waves. "Ata! Come here."

The guy is older and heavyset, with short curly hair; he walks over.

"Bill, meet my friend Ata." Then: "Ata, this kid ran one hundred encierros this summer."

Ata guffaws. "Imposible! En un Verano? No!"

"No, no," I giggle, "Just runs, not all of them were encierros."

"It's great to meet you," Ata says and shakes my hand eagerly.

"Great to meet you too," I reply.

The couple went off to sit, and Gowen grins at me mischievously. Ata, Ata, where have I heard that name before? Then it dawns on me. *That's fucking Atanasio.* "Is that Atanasio, the bull runner?!"

"Yeah, that's Ata, the seventh bull. Well, that's what Carney used to call him anyway."

"Holy fuck." I look over at Ata as he pulls the chair out for his wife to sit. *That guy might be the greatest bull runner ever. And I just met him and didn't even know it.* Gowen's like that though, no pageantry, no BS, just, hey this is my friend, meet him. Gowen hates the hand job stuff that most of the regular foreign runners play into. For Gowen, Spain is just about friends, music, fun, and stories. And if there's enough time, maybe some bulls.

Later when Gowen and I go out to smoke on the balcony, I stop by Ata's table and shake his hand again.

"Maestro, es un honor."

He giggles and shakes his head humbly.

♉

That night Maria, Tom, and I head to Novallas, the same town I ran way back in June, the one that definitely wasn't Novallas. They hold a capea, and I run the bulls down a twenty-yard callejon into the ring several times. We watch the excellent recortadores. Tom gets that mischievous look in his eyes and giggles.

"Go on out there and show 'em what you got, kid."

"No way, I ain't no recortador."

"Well if you're scared, that's fine. I mean, you can run a hundred encierros in a summer, but a little bull dodging? Naw, no way."

I roll my eyes at his antics.

Then at the end of the capea they let all the bulls and vaca loose into the street, and I run them down to the corrals, and then they come back and we run them again, and then one more time as they return to the corrals.

JuanPe writes me, inviting me to Lodosa for their bull-on-a-rope festival; I ask if Tom can come and he says yes.

The bull-on-a-rope event is exponentially more chaotic and dangerous than an encierro. I have never been to one; all I know is that the bull has a thick rope tied around his horns that runs about fifty feet long, and when it is released from the truck it is completely free. There is nothing keeping the animal from going anywhere it wants to go.

That night, Tom pulls out his copy of the famous Matt Carney USA sweater. It's a white sweater with a red stripe across the chest and USA written in blue in the center. Carney started wearing it during the Vietnam protests to show his pride in the USA in a time of unrest.

"Kid, I want you to wear it for your last runs this summer."

"Wow, Tom, thanks."

JuanPe picks us up the next morning in his minivan and we head out to Lodosa. After we park, I pull JuanPe aside.

"JuanPe, Tom is a great runner from the seventies, he used to run with Atanasio."

JuanPe shrugs and kind of brushes off what I'd said.

We head to the square in front of town hall. Barricades line the square, and a truck backs up to an opening in the fencing. They pull a rope out and string it through the crowd.

Everyone around us begins looking at Tom nervously. He's over seventy years old and cannot physically run or dodge or do anything if the animal chooses to come at him. He is literally at the mercy of the animal, and the ability of the runners around him to protect him.

"Would you like to watch from this balcony?" JuanPe asks, pointing up at the two-story-high balcony on the town hall.

"No, I'm OK right here."

They prepare to open the doors to the truck. *Oh shit. Tom?! I gotta get him somewhere safe.*

"Tom, come on, let's get you up on the fence."

"Naw, I'm fine!"

I put my arm around him and start to lead him to the fence when the door swings open and the brownish-red bull explodes out with a thick rope tied around his horns. He tears around the crowd, somehow missing the scattering people. He comes our way, and I dive in front of Tom as the bull swings his horns at me and blisters past, with JuanPe and other runners on his horns leading him up the street as the rope whips around behind him. The rope-holders chase after the rope, trying to grab hold of it.

Afterward Tom and I go to the square across the street full of bars and restaurants.

"What was that crap, you trying to get me on the fence?!"

"I was trying to protect you, Tom!"

"What's this trying to protect me crap? I'm fine!"

"Tom, what if you get gored or killed! All the blame'd be on me!"

"Like hell it will! If it's my time to go, it's my time to go!"

"Alright, you gotta absolve me of any sin if something happens."

"You are absolved. I know what I'm doing, and if something happens, it was my time."

"All right." I shrug.

We shake hands on that, and I go and find JuanPe as Tom stays behind, muttering to himself, or maybe the sparrow that's sitting on the bench with him. JuanPe informs me the bull seriously injured two runners. He gored one badly and tossed the other one, who landed on his head. A big trail of blood leads to a nearby bar, where the medics are rushing in and out.

They put the bull on a truck and we pick up Tom and head to the Plaza de Toros. That's when Tom starts to really shine. All the older guys in Lodosa realize who Tom is, and then phone calls start coming in to JuanPe. JuanPe guffaws as Tom answers the phone. *Oh yeah, it took an hour and now Tom is the new king of Lodosa. Figures.*

They take us back behind the scenes in the Plaza de Toros. They transition bulls through these little concrete channels, using a spray of water from a hose to entice them to move. They lasso ropes on their horns, then use a knife on a long pole to slice other ropes off of them. A worker clips a bull's horns with a device that looks like bolt cutter. Then they load one bull up a ramp onto a truck. He can't get through the small opening; my chest tightens with his claustrophobic struggle. Then it eases as he squeezes his huge horns through the narrow passageway and disappears inside.

JuanPe drives us home. Tom and JuanPe talk merrily and really hit it off, which is nice. I'm glad; they're two of my favorite guys in the world of the bulls.

Back home at Tom's I get online and pull up some runs in the area. Zizur Mayor is only fifteen minutes away. Then Olite is about forty minutes away. *I can hit 'em both. Maybe I can get it close to two hundred runs if they're reses bravas.*

♉

Pulling a hard right, I exit onto a roundabout bridge with two huge metal arches looming above. I park and walk through the suburb until I find a long barricade full of teenagers watching. The sounds and shouts and bells of a bull run rumble on the other side.

I climb in. Hundreds of teenagers fill the street, walking around nervously. A big vaca rounds a corner and we all run, leading her up the way. I try to get a feel for the course. I walk around it. *It's a rectangle! Forty yards by eighty yards. With a corral in one corner. It's like a fucking racecourse.* I run into the young Indian kid I'd run with in Puente la Reina. We nod to each other with grins.

They release a vaca, and we run her eighty yards down a straightaway and dive out to the fence. Another fourteen-year-old Basque kid with floppy hair runs past with the vaca hot on his tail. He shouts to the other boys, who dart out of his way. *Man, that kid's got passion! He's like a mini-Aitor!* The animals dash round the course in chaos. Some of the teens are budding recortes, and make turns with them. These kids are pushing each other's limits to get close and control the animals. *This is how the Basque runners get so good. It's like the minor leagues for San Fermin. By the time they get to run in Pamplona they've run the horns of five hundred animals, or who knows, maybe way more!* I run the horns of ten different vaca before I climb out and head to Olite.

Giddy with the action, I drive into the night. *They aren't all encierros, but I've got one hundred ninety-two runs now. If Olite is anything like Zizur Mayor, I'll crack two hundred tonight.* I zoom through the winding rural roads.

The humongous Royal Palace of Olite looms over the town as I arrive. It's known as the Palace of the Kings of Navarre. It's an elaborate castle, with several tall towers and a cathedral connected to it.

After zigzagging the narrow streets like a loose bull, I find the course and climb in. I walk down a hill to the corrals in a squat little building just outside the old section of town. The course climbs a hill out of a park, then turns and passes under a beautiful stone archway into a triangular-shaped courtyard. A big, square, red, wooden wall sits before the door of a business like the little walls that line the exits in the bullring. The courtyard empties onto a long narrow street. I walk the two-hundred-yard street. It enters a huge main square with a circular fence in the center and a circular platform inside the fence. *I like that little courtyard.* I walk back. A family and a few little boys hang out behind a chest-high wooden wall. *Maybe I'll run them up the hill through the archway and dive out behind the little wall.*

They release the first two vaca; they ramble up the hill. I run and lead them through the archway and into the courtyard. I parallel the wooden wall and cut hard out into it as the vaca hooks for me. The little boys giggle and point at the vaca that disappears into the long street. One of the little boys goes and gets me a sausage on a stick from inside. I thank him and quickly eat it between runs. I continue to run the vaca very close, into and out of the archway as they replenish the animals every fifteen minutes. In my seventh run in Olite, I run the horns of a brown vaca very close. She nudges my butt with her snout. *Fuck lady, give me a break!* I nearly lose balance before I dive out as her horn brushes against my hip. I hyperventilate behind the wooden wall. Four of the teenage boys I'd been running with come over to me.

The leader, a curly-haired kid in a black T-shirt, frowns at me.

"You are running too close," he declares, as his friends agree, nodding. "You're going to get hurt."

I humbly nod.

"Sorry," I say and pat him on the shoulder.

The very next set of animals we run, the leader with the black shirt runs a little closer to the vaca's horns, and all five of us run to the far corner of the little square where the barricade stands. She viciously throws her horns at us and follows us to the barricades. We hit the fence. I just freeze, gripping the barricade. The boys leap up. The vaca hooks like crazy as the boys scamper up the barricade. Her horns hit their feet and legs as they frantically climb. She suddenly dashes away. They all check their legs and feet for injury. Their hands tremble.

"Are you all OK?" I ask.

"Yes, I think so," the leader replies.

I grin and wag my finger at them.

"You guys are running to close to the vaca! You're going to get hurt!" I giggle.

"OK… OK…" the leader says.

They break into laughter as we pat each other on the back and the spectators chuckle at us. I walk into the street to watch for the vaca to return. I pat the USA on my chest. *I just passed my two hundredth run, fuck! What a trip. I hope this makes you proud, Matt Carney... I'm done counting. It was never about the stupid number. It was about the pueblos. Two hundred runs in one summer. Well, that does some justice to how many bull runs there are in Spain every year. Fuck, I've run over three hundred times total in my life.* I giggle. Committed Basque and Spanish runners run three hundred runs in a year or more. I look at the eager leader of the little group I'd been running with. He pulls his sweaty curly hair back out of his face as he watches for the vaca to return, grinning with his friends. *That kid'll have more than three hundred runs under his belt before he turns eighteen. The numbers don't mean anything. What matters is I got a taste of the pueblos, a real true experience with them. I'll never forget it.*

We run for another half hour until they shut it down for the night. I grin walking back to my rental car. I don't have a clue how many times I ran, and I don't fucking care. All I know is I ran great vaca with some brave kids in Olite, and I loved every second of it.

♉

The next day, Tom and I head to Sanguesa and meet up with our friend Carmelo Butini. We get lost and make it with only a few minutes to spare. We climb on the course next to the corrals. Carmelo stands with his three friends in the center of the street forty yards down. I leave Tom with Carmelo and try to run the later stretch. The rocket bursts before I even get to see the whole course. I get on the fence hoping to see the others. Chaos surges up, and I try to jump down and run, but they blister past me. *Shit, this is only town I've run in this summer that I didn't run the horns in. Well sometimes it's better to be the wise old bull that refuses to charge when it's unsure.*

Tom and I eat breakfast and head to Olite. We pull into town; it's bustling with the reses bravas about to begin. *Man, I hope the same kids will be there! Knuckleheads.* We park and walk to the course. I slip through the barricades.

"Hold my cocktail." Tom hands it to me and slips through.

"No!" A pretty and elegant older woman yells from the barricades and points at us. "Hey! He can't run! He's drunk."

"No, he isn't. He isn't going to run, he's going to stand behind the wall over there."

She continues to fuss as we walk up the hill toward the courtyard. As we get to the archway, a police officer catches up to us and escorts Tom off the course. He unlocks a metal door in the barricades and makes him step out.

"Well Tom, why don't you stay right here? I'll run them right past you," I say as the cop disappears up the street.

Tom hands me his cocktail and starts climbing up the barricades. I sigh, and he gets to the top. "If you don't catch me, I'm gonna..." Then he falls on me. I catch him. I walk him to the wooden wall in front of the door and we stand behind it, waiting.

"Are you gonna run this time, or just let 'em fly past like in Sanguesa?" Tom chides me.

"I'll run," I giggle.

"It's embarrassing. Jeez, I talk you up, then you run like a big wimp. I mean, I thought you were good at this."

I giggle.

"I mean, I loaned you the Carney shirt, and this is what I get in return?"

"Fine, Tom, I'll put on a real big show. I mean, if I get gored, will that make you happy?"

"Well that'd be a start, kid," he giggles and winks. "You know I don't give a crap if you run or not, right?"

"I know."

He pats me on the back. There's so many layers to our friendship: sometimes he's my guru grampa, others I'm his mom, and oftentimes we're both mischievous twelve-year-old knuckleheads. And sometimes like right now, he's an older brother to me, jabbing me with his horn tip any chance he gets.

"Don Tommy-Boy, you're something else, you know that?"

"Me?" He grins. "I'm just an old guy here to watch young guys like you get in big trouble."

I laugh—patting him on the back. Don Tommy-Boy... my new nickname for Gowen. In Spain and Latin America "Don" is put in front of a highly-respected elder's first name, and calling him Tommy-Boy is my way of saying that deep down, he's still just a boy. I have the utmost respect for Gowen; he's arguably the greatest American bull runner since Matt Carney. But I also want to celebrate his boyish nature. In the end, we are just two goofballs who love Navarra and bulls.

"What was that lady's problem? This is my first cocktail of the day."

"I know, but we both look drunk, the way we're yakking and laughing like a couple nutjobs."

"You're the only one here that's on psych meds, kid."

"Yeah and I'm the only sane one!"

The rocket goes off, and a young bull and vaca round the corner; we wait behind the wooden wall.

The young bull, a Novillo, approaches us, and Gowen takes his red raincoat and attracts him. He charges the wall and batters it with his clipped horn tips. The bull searches for Gowen with his horn. I grab hold of Gowen's shirt, ready to grab him away if the bull snags him. The bull's snout is getting in behind the wall. He inhales Gowen's scent deeply. *He wants you bad, Don Tommy-Boy!*

The bull finally shoots off down the long street. I go out to check his route and distance. *I'll put a show on for Gowen and run him back into the square, and hopefully redeem myself.* I chuckle and look back, expecting Gowen to be back behind our little wall. But he's standing a few feet behind me holding his red raincoat—smiling and squinting in the sunlight.

"Tom! They're coming back, man! Get back to the wall, he's coming back!"

"What? No, I'm fine. I'm gonna stand here."

The bull and vaca begin galloping our way.

"Tom, please get somewhere safe!"

"Stop trying to protect me!"

Fuck! I sprint toward the charging bull. *I gotta run him really close, and hopefully he won't see Gowen.* I pick up the bull and vaca and wave my paper in their faces, running them close. As we approach Gowen, he flaps his red raincoat.

"Tom! No!"

I swipe my newspaper at the horn of the bull. He turns, seeing Tom, and twists his head, sniffing and looking back at Gowen as we pass.

"Aye," I shout at the bull, and he focuses back at me.

With the bull on my ass, I run back to our wall and dive behind it. The bull looks at me behind the wall. I swear to you, I look into this bull's eyes and see him thinking, remembering the guy with the red coat. His eyes spark excitedly as he turns and trots right back toward where Tom stands in the street.

I follow the bull, shouting and clapping, trying to get his attention. The animal saunters right up to Tom, drops his head, and barrels into him. Tom seems all right until the bull digs his horn into the back of Tom's knee and flips him into a terrible cartwheel. *No!* I rush up. *Fuck!* Don Tommy-Boy goes for a ride, flipping head over heels; it ends with him unconscious on the sidewalk. *My god, he killed him!*

The bull continues to try and gore Tom's crumpled body. I close in and grab the base of his nearest horn. The bull seethes and lunges at me, tossing me backward. I stumble but stay up. Then he charges at me.

Come on, let's go! I dash away, hoping he'll follow. He stops, his hooves screeching on the cobblestones. He looks me in the eyes with a sadistic glare that says "I can't catch you, but I can fuck your friend up some more." *No, please don't!*

He turns back, scoops Tom up onto his horns, and throws him at the nearby door. Tom's limp body flies through the air upside-down and collides with the door with a deep crack. *Jesus Christ!* The big wooden door breaks wide open as Tom falls back to the sidewalk unconscious. *That's it, motherfucker, I will fuck you up if I have to!* I stomp into the animal's space again, screaming and waving my arms as the other runners rush in from all around. The bull looks me in the eyes as I cock my fist to hit him. He cowers backward from me and dashes off down the street with the vaca behind him.

Tom lies unconscious, not making a sound. The animals run off toward the big square. *Fuck, they're gonna come back.* I quickly grab Tom under his arms and drag him into the open doorway, then close the broken doors behind us. They won't close completely. *Fucking hell!* The bull and vaca return, trying to find Tom. Their horns tips hit the door.

I smash the door shut.

"Go the fuck away!" I scream, and they finally disappear. And for a moment, we are alone in the dark entryway.

I look at him lying in the low light coming in from the cracked open door. Tom's blood oozes from several places; it pools on the white tile floor in the quiet. It is smeared all over my arms and hands. *What did you do, Tom?* Regret fills the darkness. The silence seems to stretch on and on. *My god, is he breathing? Is he dead!* I kneel down over him to listen.

Then out of the long soundless void comes this deep long groan: "Ahhhhhhhhh." *Thank God, you're alive!* I take his hand in mine.

"I'm here, Tom. It's gonna be OK." Others come to help as Tom wakes. His eyes light up with that crazy old look of his. He immediately squeezes my hand.

"Help me up."

"Tom, it's OK, the ambulance is coming."

"Help me up, goddamnit!"

Are you fucking kidding me? Hell no! I'm glad you want to stand, but I ain't helping you up till you been seen by medics! He continues to yell at me to help him stand up, and then tries to sit up. Another guy comes in to help and puts his knee on Tom's chest to keep him from getting up. Tom's eyes bug out as he glares at him.

"You motherfucker! I oughta…" Tom growls at him. The ambulance pulls up and the medics move in. *Fuck, our bag!* I run over to grab our backpack from behind the wall. I come back around the corner and see the two medics holding Gowen's hands and pulling him to his feet. *Oh my fucking god!* His legs tremble and shake, wobbly like a newborn calf's. Blood drips down his grimacing face. *Oh my fucking god!*

He glares at me. "See! I told you I could stand!" he growls.

You crazy fucking bastard. How on earth did you just stand up? You've been unconscious for a full minute. Your seventy-one-year-old body's been rag dolling around like you were in a fucking washing machine! He stands proudly before me, grinning like a triumphant toddler. That is the greatest act of pure toughness I've ever witnessed in my whole damn life.

They help him onto the stretcher. Gowen starts cracking jokes and hitting on the female medics. I get in the ambulance with him.

"Tom, I'm going to go meet you at the hospital."

"No, stay with me. Wait, which hospital are we going to? Hospital de Navarra?! OK, go kid. Meet me there."

"OK." I hop out.

As I walk through the town toward my car, my chest pulses with joy, the joy that Gowen is alive and will be OK. I find my phone in Gowen's red coat pocket. The screen is completely shattered. *Jesus!* I laugh as I check it out. *It still works!* Some voice rings in my mind. 'What happened, Tom?!' I burst into laughter. I can't believe it. *How the hell did he stand up?!* I pass the woman who'd gotten Tom kicked off the course.

"I told you to get him off the street! Now look, we had to cut our party short!" she gripes.

"Sorry." I shrug.

When Tom Gowen gets something in his head there's no way to stop him. He's a fucking force of nature. I drive to Hospital de Navarra in Pamplona and find Gowen in his room singing, telling stories, and bantering as the doctors and nurses work on him.

The young bull we later find out is named Mandarino inflicted three horn wounds. The one on Gowen's forehead is probably the most impressive-looking. Mandarino took the clipped tip of his horn and peeled Gowen's head open like somebody peeling a mandarin with their thumbnail. Mandarino also gored Gowen in the shoulder and behind the knee. The worst injury is probably the ribs, which doctors later diagnose as fractured, front and back.

No one suffers like Gowen; he makes some of the most hilarious noises you will ever hear. As the doctor stitches his shoulder he lets out a loud moan, then turns it into a jolly song.

His jokes and hilarious banter continue. He gets crabby at a few points and really digs his horns into me, but we weather it all.

After the young doctor finishes his work closing Gowen up, I come over and look at his work. Gowen grins at me; five wide shiny staples start at his forehead and step up into his thin white hair. His flesh glows neon red. I've never seen a wound like this.

It's like his skin is just a clear sack, and the living creature inside is visible for the world to see.

"We want to keep him for observation," the doctor tells me.

"I'm not staying in this hospital another minute, I told you already I've got a little concert to play tomorrow night at the Toki Leza."

I shrug, the doctor shrugs, and Gowen signs himself out. Gowen can't really walk because of the horn wound in the pit of his knee, so I take him in a wheelchair to the car, then to Hotel La Perla, where he gets a room because they have an elevator and he is friends with the owners and staff. One lady is really rude to me and delays our booking, but Gowen later straightens her out. I wheel him around in a wheelchair that night, and his friend takes him to dinner, and I crash.

♉

The next day I sit having my morning coffee at Café Lorek. Gowen's deep baritone rises behind me. I spin around as he slowly walks over.

"My god, Tom! How the fuck are you standing? I can't believe it. You are one tough motherfucker."

"I'm fine, kid," Gowen says. "Just peachy."

That night we head over to the Toki Leza, Gowen's favorite music bar, a couple blocks from Plaza del Castillo. It's a funky, long bar with a stage in back. The owner/operator looks kind of like a Basque Elvis. Gowen convinces a young woman who he'd met and charmed a few days before to meet him there. She is obsessed with Janice Joplin, and Gowen of course knew Joplin.

Gowen convinces her to get up on stage and sing some Joplin, something she hasn't done in a while. She rocks the house. I giggle listening to her sing. *Fucking Gowen's like that, he draws your best stuff out of you.*

Then Gowen gets up on stage. His face winces with the pain, but also with a serene kind of pride and joy. He sings one of my favorite songs, a John Prine classic, "Angel from Montgomery," in his deep rich voice like a bull's bellow. I've been listening to that song since I was a little kid. My parents used to blast John Prine on the weekends while we were cleaning the house. As Tom's deep voice floods into the long room, suddenly the song isn't about an old woman longing for something more in her life, it's about Tom. It's about me.

"My old man is another child that's grown old…"

Yeah, he is my father in some way. Shivers soar through my whole body. *My god, how did he survive that mauling, let alone make it back here the next day to sing? What a fucking legend.*

"Make me an angel that flies from Montgomery… Make me a poster of an old rodeo…"

A poster of an old encierro… An image of Aitor blazing down El Pilón with a cast on his wrist flashes through my mind.

"Just give me one thing that I can hold on to… To believe in this living is just a hard way to go…"

I been listening to this song my whole life. And I even knew it was about me; it's about depression, sadness, and loss. It's about holding on to the old days, trying to get through the doldrums of this life. *That's what this whole summer's been about, maybe. Trying to escape this prison of society I'm stuck in. It's about Tom, and people who suffer like us.* Tom's deep rich voice sends my mind racing through his life, Vietnam, all the suffering, all the loss, the encierro, Matt Carney and Harry Hubert, the seventies, both of his dear friends passed on, and one day Tom is gonna leave us too. *You gotta cherish him, Bill. He's your true friend, and he's only got so much time left.* I sit at that barstool in the Toki Leza in awe. I can't help but love this man, who's at once a maestro of the highest regard and a young playful child... *Viva Don Tommy-Boy.*

♉

As I pack my bags that night, I find out Aitor Aristregui is in the hospital having trouble breathing. He's been running in Guadalajara and with all the battle and struggle that summer, he ends up in the hospital. I write him on Facebook.

"Take care, Aitor. I hope you heal quick."

"Gracias, Bill."

My heart aches for Aitor. *He took it to the limit. Hopefully he just wore himself out and needs a rest.* My mind flashes through all his amazing runs, killing it in Pamplona, leading the entire pack out of the tunnel in Lodosa, flying down the mountainside in Falces like frickin' condor, zooming through half the course in Sanse and all the way down Estafeta, always just a few feet before the horns of the bulls, linked with them like a true minotaur, half-bull, half-man—a god of the encierro. *There's no way to deny it, Aitor Aristregui had as great a summer running with the bulls as anyone in history. And he did it for his grandparents. What an incredible person: kind, humble, always leading with his blazing comet of a heart, ready to sacrifice it all for his culture. I'm so glad I was here to see it, what a fucking honor.*

As I lie down in bed tired and sore I think of that lone bull, the lone bull from Cuellar who escaped for all of those days into maybe the wildest freedom a toro bravo has ever felt. My heart aches for him; such a special life he had. In a way the encierro in Cuellar didn't end until that farmer shot him dead. *A nine-day-long encierro. It was an honor to run it with you, my friend. It was sad you had to go that way, but maybe there's a poetry in that too. You died fighting for your freedom. Alone but free. I respect that. I guess I got my taste of freedom this summer too. I guess I'm ready to go back to the real world. To my life.*

The next morning Stephanie Mutsaerts brings Nacho, the *Diario de Navarra* writer who put me on the cover way back in the beginning of the year, to have a coffee with me and Gowen at Bar Windsor. We talk. He wants to do a story about my adventures that summer. We do a little interview that goes over nicely. At the end of our talk, Nacho looks at me from behind his black-rimmed glasses; his thick eyebrows are trembling.

"What does it take to run over two hundred runs in one summer?" he asks.

"Pasion por los toros," I say, and grin.

He looks me intensely in the eyes, gives me a thumbs-up, scribbles his notes, and hurries off to write the story.

About a week later a nice article appears in *Diario de Navarra*, with the big photo of me galloping with the entire pack of vaca down the steep cliff in Falces on the back cover. In the image, my face is tense and fearful as they thunder behind me. The lead vaca is fierce; her sisters are afraid and curious as they bunch up on each other arching their heads up to see me. And now I'm more intoxicated with this taurine dream, this thunderous, primeval stream of man and beast, than ever before.

PART III

Regresar

Chapter 16

Into the Ranches

I fly back to Volcán, in Panama, to be with Enid.

In my first day looking for an apartment, I walk over to a big white-walled mansion to talk with the owners; Enid heard they were looking for someone to live in their guesthouse.

The owner, Al, greets me at the gate; he's a tall old man with a big white beard. He's from Georgia and has retired with his wife Paula in Volcán. They were lucky; with only a few hundred thousand, they were able to purchase the million-dollar estate with its fantastic landscaped garden, huge five-room home, and big three-bedroom guesthouse garage. Al and I make a deal: I will provide security and help maintain the property in exchange for free rent in the guesthouse.

Enid and I move in. The guesthouse has a nice balcony that looks out toward the gigantic Volcán Barú, the highest mountain in Panama. Across the street there's a family who lives in their woodshop; they have three kids, three dogs, thirty roosters, geese, turkeys, rabbits, and a wacky goat. Every morning I wake, go out onto the balcony, and write, with the scent of the sap and the sound of the blade rhythmically slicing through the lumber, and the massive green mountains looming above. I have to say it is as close to paradise as I've ever been.

I continue to publish stories with *MEL Magazine*, and that funds my adventures. (Some of them you'll have trouble finding because I wrote them anonymously. I plead the fifth. OK, I'll admit to "The Legend Of The Slap-Boxing Wife-Swappers of Panama.")

My goal is to write two books in two years: *The Pueblos*, and the sequel to my novel *The Old Neighborhood*, which came out a couple years ago. I power through discovery drafts of both and sign with an agent who is placing books with big New York houses. Enid and I are doing good. Things're nice, and we're happy.

♉

That winter, a documentary filmmaker reaches out to me for help doing a documentary on San Fermin; he wants do a portion of the project about me. He seems like a good guy, so I say yes. I also still want to help present the culture positively to the English-speaking world.

The plan is to get eight Spanish runners to give me advice on running eight different sections of the course, one for each bull run of fiesta. I get Stephanie and JuanPe involved, and things start coming together. I decide to head back to Pamplona, and to get there early so we can do some filming before fiesta.

When I arrive in Pamplona, the director and his bitchy producer are being idiots and clashing with JuanPe. JuanPe and I have gotten eight runners to give me advice on running the different sections. I try to mediate, but it is falling apart. Stephanie threw a party the week before to explain the project to all the runners, but it backfired when the runners started bickering. When JuanPe found out I invited Aitor to take part, he didn't go to the party because of their unresolved issues. Aitor didn't show up either, I assume for the same reason.

Then an article comes out announcing the budget being over $100,000 (a chunk of the director's recent inheritance). The other runners find out JuanPe is getting paid for his work as a story fixer. Half the runners demand money and quit. We scramble to find replacements. I haven't asked for money. I don't like profiting from fiesta-related things. It feels wrong. I got involved out of the goodness of my heart, because I believed in the director. But I am already regretting it all. He is not the guy I thought he was. In fact, he is an arrogant, loudmouthed prick.

The director, Stephanie, and I meet up with JuanPe at a café in the town hall square to make a plan for the replacement runners. We sit at the tall tables with the midday sun pouring down on us. The portly director is trying to communicate with JuanPe through Stephanie's translations. It is going well when suddenly JuanPe's mood darkens. He turns to me with pain in his face.

"Do you want to run with me in Telefonica, or with Aitor?" JuanPe asks me, agitated.

"Both!" I reply, surprised by the tension in his voice. "One day with you, one day with him…"

He nods, but his brow furrows.

"Come on JuanPe, what's wrong?" I pat him on the shoulder.

"Nothing," he says as the conversation shifts. *It's really bad between them.* I wince. *This is so tragic.*

We conclude the meeting and I head back to one of Stephanie's fancy apartments, sit down in a plush velour chair, and get online. I go through the footage from San Fermin 2016 on sanfermin.com. *How bad is it?* The first morning of fiesta 2016, Aitor leads the first bull for a hundred yards as JuanPe runs a few yards in front of him. Then in the tunnel, Aitor and JuanPe tangle. Aitor shoves JuanPe, and JuanPe falls hard and has to roll sideways to avoid the hooves of the galloping steer. *Fuck! That was really fucking bad! Well, maybe the second day was better.* I click around and can't find good video of their run the second day. The still photos show the two colliding again, with Aitor leading a bull into JuanPe's back again, this time in the middle of Telefonica. *Again? Jeez!* I roll my eyes as the crew goofs off in the big high-ceilinged room.

Groaning, I scroll around and click on to the third day of runs. In the video, Aitor links with a bull at the top of Estafeta. JuanPe squeezes in front of Aitor and takes the lead from him. Aitor yells at JuanPe and hits him with his newspaper as JuanPe takes the bull into Telefonica. The bull passes JuanPe, and Aitor screams again at JuanPe as he positions to run a later bull. *Jesus Christ!* I grip my head. *How did I not notice this last summer!? It is a damned tragedy!* Aitor leads the next bull as a huge pileup of a dozen people forms in front of him; Aitor leaps, and sails over the pileup like an Olympic hurdler and long-jumper in one. *Holy shit!* He lands in full sprint and guides that bull through the tunnel into the arena. JuanPe runs the horns of a later bull into the ring behind them. *Well, they both did good, but where's the harmony?! This is so fucking sad.*

A pretty dark-haired woman appears in a window across the way. She sips a coffee, then disappears.

OK, what happens next, guys? I find the video of the fourth day; they clash again and seem to be yelling at each other, when suddenly a brown bull lunges at JuanPe, slings his horn inside JuanPe's shirt, and knocks him up in the air. Aitor slaps the bull with his newspaper in an attempt to distract him. *Good, Aitor helped him!* The bull gores the runner beside JuanPe with his other horn—flipping him in the air. *Jesus!* Somehow the bull's other horn doesn't wound JuanPe, and he dashes ahead, miraculously keeping his footing. *The nine lives of Juan Pedro Lecuona.* I laugh. JuanPe leads that bull all the way into the ring with Aitor behind him, linked with another bull. *Well, that one was good. Aitor helped him. OK, they weren't all bad.*

The director runs through some video of the Miura ranch they'd taken the week before. I take a look over his shoulder; two black bulls with massive horns perch behind the elegant wooden barricades that shape the ranch. *Well, JuanPe opened that door for you guys, so he's doing something right.*

Scrolling through some pages, I pull up the fifth day. JuanPe runs the horns of a brown bull and then stumbles and falls as Aitor thunders past, leading four bulls a hundred and fifty yards into the ring. *Jesus, Aitor, what a year you had!* They bump each other on the sixth again, and Aitor finds his way into the pack of the first four bulls. *Another collision, shit!* Another day, they nearly tangle again but instead JuanPe slips in behind, as Aitor leads the first bull and JuanPe guides the next two. *Fuck. OK, that's better, at least they didn't tangle every day!*

A chubby little boy climbs out onto a balcony across the way, excitedly looking down and pointing at something below on the street and yelling back into the apartment.

You two... My mind flips back to the time I interviewed them both together in Joe Distler's apartment in Pamplona back in 2014. Aitor was just twenty years old, fresh off his first few years of running; JuanPe had his arm around Aitor's shoulder like a proud uncle. *Remember that, guys?* I sigh and click play on the video of the final run; they are on opposite sides of the street, leading the same three bulls. One new guy runs between them, in all white with a green penuelo. *That's that guy, the recortador, Pablo! Pablo Bolo! Fucking Bolo is becoming a figure at the end of the course.* The flow of runners squeezes JuanPe out into the fence, and Bolo and Aitor run the bulls into the ring. When the bulls enter, they all fall into the sand. Total chaos erupts as Aitor and Bolo run out into the sand before them. I go back into the footage, trying to find Bolo's start. Way back on Estafeta, I see Bolo dash onto the horns. *Bolo had a run for the fucking ages!* Bolo leads, then loses it, then accelerates, leaping over runners, nearly falling. *Damn!* Bolo cuts around runners, jumps again, and somehow lands sure-footed. *How the fuck?!* Bolo miraculously gains command of the same bulls again. *Ohh man, Pablo Bolo is special.*

All the images of their runs flicker through my mind. I shut my computer and lean back into the plush tan couch. *The encierro tells a story. Is this the story here? JuanPe is passing the torch to the younger guys, Aitor and Bolo? So bittersweet.* I gaze out the window along the pretty balconies. I wonder what it was like when Julen passed the torch to JuanPe. Julen was more historic, forty years of greatness, but there's no question JuanPe has been the most excellent runner in Telefonica for the past twenty-five years. I've heard Julen was a real firecracker when he was younger. I wonder what was it like when Atanasio passed the torch to Julen. *These moments in history, they are so potent, so beautiful, but they can't all be easy, there has to be tension. But it's how you get through the tensions that matters, how you overcome it and return to harmony.* I close my eyes and wince at the emotion stabbing my chest. *Ah Julen... Maestro, how can we get these two back together? Bomber? Any ideas guys?* I can see their faces smiling awkwardly—embarrassed at the situation.

Sighing, I get up and walk to the balcony and gaze down as the Pamploneses stroll the cobblestone avenue below. *This bickering bullshit has to stop, it's ludicrous. My book's whole theme was about this passing of the torch, this legacy of great Navarrese runners moving from one generation to the next. Now that chain's broken by the very thing that set out to display it to the world, my damned book? Well of course there's more to it, but still, Aitor not going to my book event definitely threw some gasoline on the flames. I gotta get those two back together, this is ridiculous.* I grip the iron railing. *I can't stand to see it.*

A white-haired old man walks below with a toddler in his arms talking with him as they look in the windows of the shops.

It has to end. I'll help mend this if it's the last fucking thing I do.

♉

In the aftermath of nearly all of my bull-runner guides quitting the documentary, I start to brainstorm who'd be down for it.

An image pops up on my Facebook feed of my friend Raul Lasierra running in the corrals at Toro Passion where he works as the mayoral, the manager of the animals. Raul is running, his tall frame and floppy black hair swirling in the air. A pack of twenty monstrous bulls gallops in a chaotic pack behind him, their wide horns plunging into the air as they smash into each other. Raul runs in the muddy dirt ahead of them, all alone. *Fuck! To run in a corral in a ranch! That is epic. I bet Raul would be down to guide me.* I reach out to him. He replies with an immediate yes. I ask if he thinks Miguel Angel Perez, the co-owner of Toro Passion, would be interested. He comes back with another yes. *Fuck that was easy!* My mind races through the images of Miguel Angel Perez saving Xabier Salillas's life way back in 2005 when he grabbed Vaporoso's tail as I watched from above. *Of course he's a master with sueltos. He owns hundreds of bulls, his life is bulls.* I always wanted to get to know him better. He was my first maestro, and maybe my most important maestro. My mind flicks through running with Perez with a suelto up Estafeta in 2010. If it wasn't for him, that day never would have happened. *Damn, I've run with Toro Passion bulls dozens of times. It's like we've been linked one way or another all these years.*

The next day we interview Miguel Angel Perez. He walks up: stoutly built, in a white collared shirt, with slicked-back salt-and-pepper hair. His face is stern and serious; his fiery eyes tell you he doesn't have patience for dumbasses. I apologize for the crew being late again. I look up Estafeta; there are twenty loud delivery trucks parked and moving around the street, supplying the many bars. *Oh god, why is this director so obsessed with shooting at the same time every day? Now the shot is ruined. What the hell are we going to do?* The director and crew arrive flustered, throwing the blame at each other, and start to set up sound for us. They refuse to buy clips, so they need to tape the mics to us. The tape doesn't stick and the mics keep falling off. Delivery trucks are driving through the shot. I glare at the director as he fixes the tape on my mic for the twelfth time. *You dumbass!* Perez finally gets fed up, changes position, and we get the shot done.

As they pull the dangling mics off us, I thank Perez. *Oh man, how cool would it be to go to Toro Passion...*

"Miguel, could we possibly come to your ranch and film?" I ask.

"Si," Perez replies.

"Ah thanks!"

"When do you want? Now?" I asked.

Turning to the director I hike my eyebrows. He nods. I go down to the free lot near the corrals and grab the documentary crew van. I roll back up as the crew sluggishly gets the gear ready. *Man, if it wasn't for me driving, you guys'd take two hours getting ready to go anywhere. You're constantly forgetting shit, then you have to walk across town to get some missing piece of equipment. Fucking amateur hour with you guys.*

We arrive at Toro Passion, just outside the town of Al Faro. The ranch is hilly, with many wooden pens full of bulls. The barricades of the pens are made of thick red wooden lagging that is slightly warped and natural-looking. A big tall metal barn sits at the entrance. Perez takes us into the ranch to a concrete structure.

"Bill, I have something to show you," Perez tells me.

I follow him to a stall and peer into the darkness inside. Three tiny black calves watch us from the far corner, their horns just sprouting out of their heads. My eyes bug out.

Perez opens the door and waves me inside. I step into it as they scamper around trying to hide. Then one baby bull stands defiantly, snout high, brandishing his horns at me as I squat down to their height. *OK, OK, big guy. I see you, you're tough.* He sniffs in my direction as his brothers cower behind him. I pick up a few fresh strands of golden hay. *Maybe I'll see you out on the street in a few years.* I offer the hay to him. *Remember, I'm the nice guy that tried to feed you.* He digs his tiny paw into the bedding. *OK, alright, you're not hungry.* I look up at Perez at the door as he watches me, grinning.

"Thank you," I tell him, with warmth swirling in my chest.

We follow him up onto a walkway above a series of small pens. From up there we can see two huge pens full of big beautiful bulls. One of the stupid interns starts asking idiotic questions; he is an anti-taurino, actually. (Absurdly, most of the crew are anti-taurinos, including the bitchy producer.) Miguel's broad torso swells and his angular face sharpens as he gives the wimpy intern an angry lecture.

"This world isn't a cartoon! These are bulls, we eat these animals!" Perez says angrily, and the intern wilts before him. I roll my eyes, embarrassed. I can't believe I brought these idiots to Toro Passion. *You'd think when someone is giving you a gift of allowing you into their world that you'd be grateful and kind. But no, they have to bring up their flimsy pop-culture attitude about animals.* As Perez finishes his lecture, I tell the crew in English, "No more anti-taurino bullshit, understand? He didn't have to let us come out here. He's doing this as a gift to me. Show some damn respect." The twerpy intern bows his head, ashamed.

"No Bill," Perez corrects me. "It's important that we talk with the anti-taurinos. It's the only way we can show them the truth."

I sigh and nod to my maestro. He pats me on the shoulder and grins. We look out at Perez's ranch, its hills climbing up and over the back side of the ranch. The various colors of the bulls in the pens before us is marvelous; one is black- and brown-striped like some kind of bovine-tiger mix. I think I ran with that bull in Lodosa.

"It's beautiful, Miguel."

Perez grins.

"Welcome," he tells me, and the tensions seem to fade as we bask in the calls and bellows of the animals all throughout the ranch. The gamy stench of bull dung swirls in the air. *I could live in a place like this.*

Raul Lasierra shows up, tall and geared up for work. He is excited and surprised we made it out. I thank him for the help. I ask him to show the picture of him running in the pens to the crew, and he does. They're impressed. *Fuck, what if we could replicate that with me for the documentary? Should I ask them?* I hesitate. *Man, they've already done so much for me. Should I really ask now? Well, they'll probably just say no, and that'll be that. But this might be my only chance to do it.* I ask Raul and Perez if I can run with the bulls in the nearby pen. Perez and Raul chat a bit. Raul nods.

"Bill, we had a documentary guy get gored here a few years ago in one of our pens."

"Oh, I understand, it's OK." I shrink back.

"But it's you, Bill, you are a mozo. So we're going to do it. But be careful, OK?" Raul tells me as my eyes bug out.

"Gracias, maestro!" I tell Perez, and he grins at me.

Before we step through the fencing, Perez turns to me.

"Be smart, no crazy stuff. If you get in trouble get to the fence," Perez tells me sternly.

"Yes, maestro." I nod.

We climb through the thick red lagging barricades into the huge pen with thirty or so bulls. Something comes over Perez; his body trembles with rage and power. The animals respond, trotting away from him. Perez shouts, whistles, and vocalizes with these intense clicks. The bulls bunch up—their noses high, blinking. He tosses a rock at them, and they trot to the back of the pen behind some trees. I position myself in the middle of the big half-football-field-sized pen. *Shit, if they get on you, that's a long run to the fence.*

"Ready?" Perez shouts. I nod.

Perez sprints into the trees and they come rambling around the bend. The sound of their hooves thundering over the dark red dirt tremors through the ground like an earthquake. Thirty bulls wrapped in a massive dust cloud surge toward me. They stampede close, and I turn and run ahead of the massive pack as they fan out wide. They see me and divert, and run back around behind the trees. We try a few more times, and the crew gets some incredible pictures of me running with them. I look into the viewfinder of the camera. There's me, tiny in the wide shot, in white pants and a white dago-T, with a big old seagull chest piece, and my tan cap pulled down low on my brow. Thirty-something galloping bulls surround me, fanned out in a wide gallop in a rising dark red dust cloud, like a huge avalanche chasing a skier down a mountainside.

♉

We roll up to the Reta ranch a few days later. It's just outside of Pamplona. JuanPe took me there in 2014; it's full of woods and twisting roads that climb up the hills. Breathtaking mountain ranges surround it all.

Several big dirty German shepherds are part of the ranch team. They've got a lot of heart. When JuanPe brought me and some friends to the ranch, I watched them intelligently herding the young vaca in a small stone-fenced pen. They are also very tender dogs. They were very kind to my friend Gustavo's five-year-old son Emilio, who was very afraid of dogs. They accompanied him everywhere he went, protecting him and listing to him telling them things, and by the time we left Emilio wasn't so afraid of dogs anymore.

We open the doors and the big dogs trot up to me; the mother who'd been so sweet to Emilio nuzzles her head against my leg and rubs some scent on my knee as I pet her soft, thick, light-brown fur. *How've you been, old girl?*

Don Miguel Reta greets us with a weathered handsome grin on his dark face. His salt-and-pepper hair swirls in the breeze. He is an average-sized man, but his presence is strong and big, and at the same time warm and fatherly. Reta is the chief pastore in San Fermin; he's always positioned at La Curva, the most complex portion of the course. If there were one single individual leader of all the mozos in San Fermin, it would be Don Miguel Reta.

Don Miguel shakes my hand with his strong paw, and softly pats my cheek with his free hand. He leads us up to some pens where they are doing some work moving the animals. Three adorable puppies with long puffy brown fur lie at the feet of their momma near the pens. I play with the puppies, rolling them on their backs while they give my hands little puppy nibbles. *Sweet little guys. You're going to grow up to be big noble herders, aren't you?* One especially sweet puppy nibbles my wrist as I rub his belly. *You're gonna draw blood, little guy.* He smiles, his long tongue hanging from his lips.

They transition the cabestros through a narrow stall next to us. One of them looks at me and his eye swells wide. He begins bellowing and trying to escape his pen. A memory of a cabestro smashing into my back in Telefonica flashes in my mind. I flew in the air then; my whole body pancaked, and my balls smacked the stones. I cringe and look at him. *Was that you, old boy?* Reta and the ranch hands calm him and progress him into his stall using a pole. Sergio Colas is part of the ranch also; he's a big monstrous runner who runs the middle section of Estafeta. He's one of the greatest Basque runners of all time, even though he's also deaf.

We hop in some pickup trucks and go up to a lush green pasture sprinkled with little white flowers on a long hill so we can take a portrait of Don Miguel with his animals. The pastore opens the gate and thirty head of vaca trot into the pasture with one big old black bull. *Must be a nice life, big guy.* I grin at him as he moves through his reddish-brown ladies proudly. They push the herd up the hill; they want Don Miguel Reta's photo to be up the hill so everyone can see the Pyrenees in the background.

Don Miguel Reta paces nervously; some of these vaca are dangerous and have severely injured people. He only has one of his pastores with him, and the documentary crew want him to put his back to the animals when they are only a few yards away. That is a big no-no when dealing with animals, especially on grass where they can cut and run so well.

"I'll help!" I plead.

Don Miguel Reta looks at me sternly. His handsome fatherly brow flexes as he thinks about it. He goes to the pickup truck and pulls a willow cane out of the truck we rode in on. He shows me how to hold it, gripping the top and putting your thumb over the tip. He tells me to walk down around the pack of vaca to hold them in position.

"Be firm, don't show fear," he says, as I nod.

I slowly walk around the big pack until I am in a good position to keep the pack from running off. After a few minutes the vaca seem to be conferring about me—vocalizing, watching each other, then me. A big vaca finally challenges me. She trots through her sisters in my direction, gets to the edge of the pack, and stomps her hoof. *Oh, you don't think I'm the real thing?* I spread my arms and hold the stick out wide and slowly walk toward her. *Chill out, lady.* She gives me some strange looks, twisting her head to see me from different angles; curious little vocalizations hum in her throat. Then she drags her hoof through the grass, stomps again, and raises her chin high. *Go back to grazing, girly. I'm used to running with your big bad brothers.* As I step closer, her eye widens with fear and she melds back into the pack. I grin—feeling surprisingly confident. *Man, this is so cool that Don Miguel Reta has enough faith in me to hand me a cane to handle his cattle.* I glance at Pablo, Reta's big curly-haired pastore, who stands guard on the other side of the herd. He grins at me; his eyes bulge with surprise as he guffaws. *What? You think I'd get scared, Pablo the pastore? Come on. Ain't you seen my picture in Falces?* I giggle. *Oh man, if she gave me trouble on this grass, I'd be toast. Don Miguel Reta'd have to rush over and save my ass!* I laugh at myself.

As they photograph Don Reta, I daydream about being a pastore one day. *How great would that be?!* Fantasies of me saving runners and whipping steers with my cane shot through my mind, and like a little boy playing right field, I start playing with the stick and drop it! *Hahaha!* I pick it up quickly; Don Reta and the crew haven't noticed. Then I look over at Pablo the pastore; he grins at me and shakes his head as I giggle and blush. *I guess I've got a lot to learn about being a pastore.* They finish snapping the shots, with Don Miguel kneeling proudly with his animals standing behind him, brown against the green pasture with the little white flowers surrounding them, and the thick pine woods lining the sides of pasture with the Pyrenees floating above.

We pack up, and Miguel's kind and pretty wife joins us as we drive up along the hill into the woods and Miguel calls a pretty song to the animals that is nothing short of a bovine language. The vaca trot toward us through the woods, following the truck.

Miguel Reta squeezes my knee and looks me in the eyes. "You are home, Bill."

His words send shivers down my spine. "Gracias, Don Miguel."

We park up on a high hill overlooking the countryside as the sun sets in creamy purples. Don Miguel calls to his cattle and pours little piles of feed throughout the nearby bushes; the vaca return his calls as they close in around us. One tall brown vaca slowly steps into view between two bushes; her twisted horns stretch high above her head as she sniffs the air and returns Miguel's call. A dozen more vaca calmly step into view from all directions, surrounding us. They bow their heads and eat from the small piles.

Pablo the pastore points to one big, red, docile-looking vaca, who's feeding just ten yards from us. "She nearly killed a man last summer."

I look at him nervously. *That's some good information to have, I guess.* Reta's vaca are some of the fiercest in all of Navarra, but in his presence they become like sweet calm puppies. He calls to them like a father, like a loving grandfather, and they return the calls from all directions as they surround us. Pride fills Don Miguel Reta's eyes as he grins at them. I watch him. *Look at the love he has for these animals.* His voice stirs this emotion in me. There is a sweet loving adoration in the tone of his voice as he sings to them—something you hear only when a father talks to his child. I blink back some tears. *Are you really going to cry, Bill?* And there is a childlike love in the vacas' responses, in their faces as they bow their heads to eat, and blink up at the one who must, in some way, be their father. *This is Navarra.* I giggle as my throat aches and joyful tears bead in my eyes. I watch him as he bends to pour more feed into a pile near me. *He's one of the most special people in all the world of the bulls. A father to all of us, and to many of the animals too.* His spirit is much bigger and more powerful than any simple words on a page could ever do justice. Don Miguel Reta is a vital participant in the heart of Navarra.

♉

The Cebada Gago Ranch bulls have inflicted the most gorings in the recorded history of the running of the bulls in Pamplona. In 2016 they gored several people, and one almost gored me when I tried to step back on the course after a bad trampling.

JuanPe got the crew in touch with owners of Cebada Gago, and so we're headed down to Cadiz to film them on the ranch. It is a long ride into the south of Spain. The crew starts complaining about my driving, so I just shrug and let them fucking drive, and nap the whole way.

We make it down there in the wee hours of the morning and go out into the fields to film the bulls I'll be running with in a few days. We drive out on a dusty road as the enormous metal windmills spin all around us as far as the eye can see—climbing up and down the hillsides. Two horsemen gallop the bulls in a lose pack toward us. A big *melocotón* (a peach-colored bull) eyes us as he passes—digging his hooves into the dusty trail and throwing his horns aggressively. The pack goes up a big hill and feeds on the grass while the drone driver zooms his drone above, filming them. Then the horsemen gallop them back past us. We drive in from the fields. We pass other bulls in corrals. They sit in the midday heat, their massive muscular bodies like black mountain peaks as they rest in meditative silence like mountainous Buddhas.

We have a few hours to kill, and go to a nearby beach. And the director crashes Stephanie's van while trying to park it. We get out to inspect the long gash that stretches along the side. I giggle. *They fucking complain about my driving, then he goes and crashes it? Dumbass.*

We head back to Cebada Gago. A bunch of cars full of spectators show up. The herdsmen prepare to load the bulls up to drive them to Pamplona. I go to a stone pond in the parking lot as they get ready to lead a few bulls from an adjacent lot. The horsemen ride up to me and tell me I can't be there, so I get into the truck with the drone driver. The bulls come trotting past us and stop—eyeing us in the truck just a few feet from my window. One is the *melocotón*. His big muscular body heaves for breath. His peach fur fades to a darker brown color near his spinal column. His long tail curls and flicks. I freeze. *Fuck, they'll destroy this fucking truck!* The *melocotón* turns his face—his wide eye watching his reflection in the side of the truck. He sees himself! *Jesus, please don't charge, man.* He stomps his hoof. Luckily the herdsmen trot back over to gather him up. He ambles past—eyeing me inside the truck. *See you in a few days, buddy...* We wrap up the shoot and head home to Pamplona. The documentary crew is late to film them unloading the bulls into the corrals in Pamplona.

♉

The next day I get online. I need a run to burn off some steam and find out about a little run in Carcastillo, a nearby town. The crew wants to go, and we bring Tom Gowen along too. We make it on time and pour out into the sweet little Navarran town.

We get on the course and find a small triangular courtyard for them to film in along the barricades. I lead the vaca down a straightaway to the end of the course. As they batter the fence, I sneak around them and lead them back toward the square with some local teenagers. The crew gets some good footage. They switch the animals and I lead a young black bull toward the courtyard. He breathes heavily at my back. *I gotta cut out!* I sprint to the courtyard. *Just gotta get there and I can escape!* I enter the courtyard and cut right. Instead of the open escape, three fat old men stand in front of the opening in the fence. They try to retreat—squeezing their big bellies through the narrow opening I need to get through. Luckily Tom Gowen waves his red raincoat from the fence across the courtyard, and the young bull dashes toward it and shoots on down the street. I stand before the old men and throw my hands up and guffaw. The whole courtyard full of spectators laughs as the last old man shimmies his round belly through the tight escape in the barricades— yelling at his friends for being slow.

Afterward we start chatting with a big group of rowdy little boys who ask questions and tell me about their town's run. They bring us to a gigante parade, and one of the guys in a gigante costume lets me try it on. I dance around a little bit before we hop back in our car, with Gowen grinning at me proudly.

"Not bad, kid." Gowen pats me on the shoulder.

"Oh yeah, and thanks for the help." I grin at him.

"Yeah, if you woulda been quicker with yours, I wouldn't be in all this damn pain."

"Aye! I grabbed Mandarino by the fucking horn!"

"Yeah, I know you did. You shoulda grabbed him by the tail! Who taught you how to deal with a suelto anyways? The tail! Not the horn! Jesus!"

"Haha, want me to count how many times I saved your ass that day? I got four, so you still owe me three."

"Me owe you? Aren't you the one staying in my apartment this fiesta, for free?! But I owe you? Why don't we discount a few for the rent and call it even." Tom gives me his mischievous grin, his blue eyes sparkling.

"Ahah. All right, all right, Don Tommy-Boy, we're even."

We pull off in the rental and weave through the winding streets out of town. *Well, that was a fun little trek into the pueblos.*

ᛘ

Tony Ho Tran arrives to town a few days before fiesta. Tony is a Vietnamese-, African-, and European-American writer in his early twenties, and a fan of mine; he looks like a big muscular version of Bruno Mars.

I've run into him in the weirdest situations; I actually gave him a ride while driving Uber. He said he wanted to go to Pamplona and run, so I set him up with the Pamplona Posse so he could work and stay for free. He had a blast. He reached out again in the past winter and said he really wanted to learn to run this year. I told him about the documentary, I talked with the director and we invited Tony to be my student in the run. I would teach him basics in Novallas before San Fermín started.

Tony and I drive to Novallas; the crew decides not to come, which really shocks me. We hop in the van and roll out.

"Man! I am so excited!" Tony says, grinning, his spiky slicked-back hair gleaming in the sunlight.

"It's gonna be fun, man." I grin. *I convinced this great kid to take an extra week off of work, come to Spain early to run with me in Novallas, and these idiots don't show? Hey rejects, your documentary is happening…you might want to film it!*

"I can't believe I'm here right now with you, man!" he says as I accelerate onto the highway.

"Me too, Tony." I sigh. *Well, I guess the doc crew not coming to film isn't a big deal. All that matters is you got this kid who's really excited about the culture. That's all that really matters in the end. Fuck this stupid doc, it's probably going to be retarded anyway, with the way they do shit.* We cruise through the Pyrenees as I walk Tony through what to expect.

"Expect the unexpected. They'll do the same thing three times, and suddenly they'll let another animal out the fourth time and completely surprise you. You have to mistrust everything in the pueblos. Ease into it, do what you feel comfortable with. I'll try to urge you closer, but if you panic, then get out. No matter what I'm saying, just escape. We will slowly work you closer and hopefully tomorrow we'll get you running on the horns. But Tony, the most important thing, and the only thing that really matters, is that you're safe and don't get hurt."

"I'm so nervous, Bill! Thank you so much for doing this!"

"Thank you, Tony. I really appreciate you being part of this."

We get on the course with just a little time to spare. Novallas is just as beautiful as I remember it—the tight twisty streets with the little barricades in front of the doorways, and the old ladies standing on the balconies with their grandchildren, with the blue and white flowers hanging from the railings.

We run the first half of the course. A big bad vaca wreaks havoc as we try our best to lead her for long stretches of the course. Tony tries to run close and we have plenty of fun. We meet a wild, older woman who is running with the bulls; her nieces are begging her to stop running and come into the big metal cage we all stand in at the opening of a garage.

"Tia! Tia! Por favor!" they yell after her.

"Tia Brava!" I shout. "Eres Brava!" I mean brava with respect of course; she's brave and fierce like the cattle.

They all giggle. We make friends, and realize later that Tia Brava is my friend Juan Jose Magaña's sister! Magaña befriended me on Facebook after seeing me in Novallas the year before. He is a friendly short and thin guy in his forties from Novallas who owns part of a nearby ranch.

After the run, he joins us, and we all sit at a little patio next to the bull square.

"I have to go and get ready for the fire bull," Magaña says.

"Wait, a real fire bull, or the ones with the guy wearing the suit and the fireworks?" I ask.

"A toro bravo! With fire!" Magaña moves his fingers like flickering flames above his head.

"I have to light the torches, it's dangerous..." he says, nervously puffing his cigarette.

"Can we run with him?!" I ask.

"Yes, you can, he will go into the streets," Juan replies.

Holy shit, I can't believe this. I bug my eyes out at Tony; he giggles excitedly.

"But be careful, it's dangerous," Tia Brava warns. "He won't just gore you, he'll burn you too!"

I giggle, imagining a horn wound that simultaneously singes the flesh.

"You watch, Tia Brava, I'll run the horns of the fire bull tonight. And lead him right into the ring." I grin and point toward her. "I'll do it for you!"

She giggles and sneers at me suspiciously, "OK, OK. Sure you will..."

Night falls, and a truck pulls into the bull square. They tie a thick rope to the bull, and thirty guys drag the bull out of the back of a truck, down the metal ramp to a big wooden post set up in the center of the square. They pull the bull snug to the post as the truck motors out of the square. Tony and I get out there in the sand with the bull and help hold the thick rope, with twenty other guys keeping the bull snug to the big post. The massive black bull tugs the rope, angrily contorting his massive muscular body back and forth. Several officials screw with the two metal fittings with cloth torches on the ends of his horns. Then they are ready. Juan Jose lights his wooden torch; the flame blazes up, tall and violent.

Suddenly a fat guy cuts the thick rope with a serrated knife; with the tension on the rope, the knife slices through it almost instantly. We let go of the rope as the bull wrestles to free himself from the post. The chunks of rope fall free to the sand below him. Juan Jose Magaña bounds in and lights one of the bull's horns. The bull twists free violently, and Juan Jose dives in with the bull completely free on the sand and lights the second horn, then dashes away with the burning horn tips charging at his back.

The bull gallops out into the dark streets, and we go out to run him. He looks incredible in the tight dark streets as the big flames whip up off his horns, sending shadows flickering through the balconies and barricades. He dashes back and forth through the tight streets like some smoldering apparition of Taurus invading Hades. As he starts back toward the ring, I position myself to run his horns, letting the youngsters sift past me. *Gotta show Tia Brava I mean business!* He starts to come, and the street clears, and it is just me and him and those big flames floating above him. One drunk local calls him towards a little red wall in front of a doorway. The bull spins around on him and charges the wall. *Fucking guy! Come on! What are you doing? I gotta pull this crazy run off for Tia Brava!* I bound on my toes, waiting for the bull to turn back toward me.

They send a big old steer to help bring the bull back as the drunken guy distracts the bull one last time. The bull batters the wooden wall before the doorway. His flaming horns come apart in a huge spray of sparks that rain down on the obnoxious drunk guy. *I hope they burn you, hahaha!* Then the fire bull comes toward me, with his horns still burning and smoldering. I run beside the steer and let the steer pass. Then I dash before the bull's horns. As we enter the ring I look up to where Tia Brava and her nieces cheer, and I point to her. The bull's hot horns burn brightly at my back. Her mouth hangs open shocked as she points at me. I cut across the ring as the fire bull enters the middle of the sand and the crowd erupts in applause.

I jog over to Tia Brava and her nieces and say, "That was for you, did you like it?"

"It was beautiful." She grins, with tears in her eyes. "A Dios mio."

Tony and I head back to Pamplona laughing our asses off about all the crazy shit the film crew missed. *Dipshits!*

♉

The next day the film crew comes to Navallas, and they shoot Tony and me running. After a few runs, Tony's confidence wanes. The vaca disappear down the street, chasing runners.

"Tony, you can do this, man. You're a big athletic guy. Just listen to my voice, OK? Think of your outs. You're sprinting full out, that's good. You're scared. That fear will save your life. But learn to control it. Head on a swivel. The most dangerous thing are these kids we're running with, if you tangle with one and fall, that's trouble. But they're good runners, this is their town. Have faith in them, but beware."

"Alright…" Tony says breathlessly.

"Just listen to my voice, I'll get you closer. But remember if you can't handle it, then get out, no matter what I'm telling you. There's no shame in it. The only thing that matters is you're safe."

"OK…"

"Think of my voice as your guide. My voice is battling your fear. You can trust my voice, but the voice inside you is the most important one. I'm urging you to slow down because I know you can do more. But when I say GO! sprint as hard as you can through the fence."

I go out about sixty yards from the metal barricades we've been escaping through. I wait for the big vaca to return. Suddenly Tony comes up and stands beside me. The vaca zigzag the course toward us.

"OK, just wait, face me." We face each other, one shoulder pointed to the vaca, one shoulder pointed toward our escape. "Hands out, in case one of these kids comes up behind you. You will feel him and can avoid him." We both put our hands behind us like feelers.

The vaca trots toward us, angrily throwing her horns.

"Hold… Hold… We're good…" Tony reluctantly holds his ground. "She's not coming hard. She might change speeds, so be ready."

We start to jog sideways—watching her approaching as she closes within fifteen yards of us. Tony panics and turns to run.

"Slow, slow! We're good…"

He slows.

"Look at her, Tony! We're fine, she's under control."

He looks back—fear all over his young face.

She sees us at ten yards away. Her eyes light up and she charges us.

"GO! GO! GO! Get out!" We sprint thirty yards to the fence with her right on our tail. We slip through the vertical bars as she bangs them with her horns. She batters the metal bars, her hooves scraping the asphalt and leaving white marks like chalk. She glares at us, her nostrils flaring in our scent trail.

"You did it, Tony!" I pat him on the back. "You ran on the horns, kid."

"Thank you, Bill." He huffs and puffs. "I can't believe I just did that."

"You got it, buddy." I grin at his exhausted, thrilled, and fearful face. *Yep, that's all you need, that mixture of excitement and fear.*

♉

Juan Jose Magaña brings us out to a nice little ranch a few kilometers away. It is made of pallets and a couple hundred head of cattle. We go around to some pens that are pieced together like a mismatched treehouse. A dozen three-month-old vaca sit in the shady pen. They stomp their tiny hooves at us as we peer down at them. *Cute little gals.* We head home with the sun falling through the mountains. *Nice little adventure in to the pueblos. Man, just a few days till fiesta.*

A guy named Kim arrives as part of the documentary crew; he'd won the Pulitzer Prize for photography. He's a big guy with a round bald head and curious eyes and a humble demeanor. We head off to do some shots of me walking the course. *This guy's so nice and friendly and he's the only one on the whole crew who has anything to be arrogant about. These nutty arrogant pricks, must be that they're insecure or something.* We film with Kim for a little while, then wrap up.

"Hey Bill, I just wanted to say thank you for doing this," Kim says.

What?! Did you just say thank you to me?! Wow. "Thank you, Kim," I reply. "It was an honor to work with you."

I walk off up Estafeta. *After everything I've done for the project—and it's a long fucking list—nobody on the crew has even said "thank you" to me. I giggle. The only guy who says thank you is the only real journalist on the project. Figures.*

♉

The crew has an idea to do a workout with JuanPe and some other runners, just to get us training together. I've invited fifty-nine-year-old legend El Boti, who is my guide for the first morning's run, thinking it will be fine.

We all plan to get together really early in the morning at town hall. But what I don't realize is that JuanPe's really mad at the documentary guys; he got a rich bull enthusiast interested in investing big money to sponsor the whole project and get it broadcast on Spanish TV, and the documentary director essentially ignored him. Plus, the director's been completely ungrateful for all the doors JuanPe has opened for him, like the Cebada Gago and Miura Ranch and various others. So JuanPe's on his last limb with them.

I round the corner into town hall square on time. The documentary crew is running fifteen minutes late, as usual. I walk up and see El Boti and JuanPe standing together in town hall square. They're so different; JuanPe is huge, tall and husky, and El Boti's about five feet tall and thin, with a shaved head. *A true odd couple.* I grin. They speak quickly to one another, and suddenly I realize: they're fighting!

"No pasa nada, I'll go home now!" El Boti says furiously.

"No! You stay! I'll go home, I have things to do!" JuanPe replies.

I giggle. *They can't be serious.* "What's up guys?"

JuanPe turns to me angrily. "I thought you wanted to film with me," JuanPe scolds me. "You want to film with him, fine! But leave me out of it!"

"Wait, I thought we would all film together, just jogging around and stuff." I thought I'd told JuanPe that El Boti was coming, but I must have miscommunicated it.

"No, this is about friendship!" JuanPe yells. "He's not my friend!"

El Boti looks up at him, startled and furious, his big hazel eyes trembling.

Oh shit. I grip my head. *How the fuck did I invite two guys who don't get along to film together in the wee hours of the fucking morning?*

The film crew shows, and JuanPe stomps off. El Boti keeps repeating, "NO PASA NADA!" ("Nothing happened!") But something bad has definitely happened.

I chase after JuanPe and try to smooth it over, but JuanPe is fit to be tied. El Boti is pissed, too. Finally I apologize to El Boti and he goes home. We film, and I apologize to JuanPe for inviting El Boti, and it ends OK.

I walk away from the shoot shaking my head. Imagining JuanPe screaming "Voy a mi CASA!" and grabbing El Boti by his shoulders and picking him up furiously. And El Boti with his legs dangling off the ground screaming "NO PASA NADA!" and kicking JuanPe in the balls. Us bull runners are a little feisty sometimes.

I enter Plaza del Castillo giggling. But really, I just feel terrible that my dumb idea to bring two guys together to train and film for the documentary had sparked something nasty. I sit down at Windsor and order a cortado. *I got some crappy luck with that. I guess it's better to keep guys separate, with the cliques and all that. For all I know something happened between them in the run, or their friend pushed the other one's uncle and he got hurt twenty years ago and they've never spoken since, and here I am bringing them together like: It's going to be fun, guys!* Sometimes I really am a fucking dumbass gringo.

Chapter 17

Another One?!

The rocket soars into the sky above town hall and shatters San Fermines into ten million tiny shimmering enigmatic pieces that flicker down all throughout the city. Every tiny piece will dance and drink and kiss and run and rage for almost exactly eight and a half days before it will settle into the cobblestones of the old section: another glorious layer, another triumphant year. But until then San Fermines is alive. That life will touch every single individual in this swelled-up city; whether it is their first, their last, or their only, this San Fermines will mark them eternally.

Tom Gowen and Maria Huarte welcome me into their beautiful home and I watch San Fermines from above for the first time. Seeing the joyous spray of sangria and the water raining down from the balconies from a new angle.

Tony Ho Tran and I head to the *encierrillo* that evening, to watch them transition the bulls from the massive corral across the river up to the holding pens where they'll wait for the run the next morning. We wait on a grassy patch atop the castle wall with thousands of Pamploneses as the hour closes in.

"It's a totally different experience," I explain to Tony. "The only runners are the pastores. The run happens at nightfall, and they ask the crowd for silence."

In the last few moments before the *encierrillo* starts, the fat director comes cantering down the hill with his camera on his shoulder. His chubby face sweats profusely as he looks around, flabbergasted.

I shout to him, point at my watch and shake my head. *They're late for every-fucking-thing!* He glances at me, then grimaces and continues toward the corrals.

A hush falls over the spectators as a rocket shoots up and pops. The gates bang open and the shouts of Miguel Reta usher the animals toward us, with the steers' bells banging and their hooves clapping the pavement. The steers swing around the bend into view, their asymmetrical horns bouncing before them. Then the Cebada Gago bulls come into view in a distinct wide pack behind them. Three black bulls lead—their wide horns pointing upward triumphantly as camera flashes flicker all around. The crowd unleashes a hushed delighted sigh. *They don't want nothing to do with them steers.* The melocotón trails in the back of the pack. The bulls round the second turn just below our feet and disappear up the long straight hill, following the steers as the green-shirted pastores drive them, slapping the street with their willow canes. Up high on the hill they slow as they approach the wooden corrals.

"That was weird," I say to Tony as we sit in the damp grass waiting for the workers to break down the fencing. "I wonder if that means it'll be steers out front tomorrow?"

"Maybe. They didn't seem to like the steers at all," Tony replies.

"Yeah I hope not, I want to run the bulls, not the steers!"

"I doubt they'll do the same thing."

"I don't know. I hear you can learn a lot from the encierrillo."

Back at Tom's place I lie down to sleep. I wake when Tom comes home. Nervously, I go out to the kitchen and tell him what I'd seen in the encierrillo.

"Well kid, if the bulls were snug behind the steers, then that's what you can expect in the morning on Cuesta."

"OK," I say, sigh, and turn back to my room. "Thanks."

Tom continues, "Or they can do the complete opposite, kid." He grins at me sadistically. "They're pretty much wild animals, remember?"

Shaking my head and laughing, I head back to my room and crash out.

♉

I wake before sunrise and go down to Santo Domingo. As I approach the thick crowd of runners, forty-something guys look up in my direction and whisper. *They must be looking at something behind me.* I keep walking toward them. Then one waves, then another from across the street. *Holy fuck, I know them. That guy's from Iscar. I ran with him in Falces.* I wave back. The dozens of the runners looking at me wave. I grin broadly at them. Little packs of them shout things at me: "Bill!" "Salud carbon!" "Aye, Bill Hillmann!" "Que Paso!" "Mozo!" I scan the dozens of faces. *Holy fuck, it's guys from all over the country, Cuellar, Sanse, Medina, Valladolid, Iscar, Falces,*

Lodosa, Tudela, Tafalla. Fuck, I know them all! They all grin at me as I wind through them shaking hands, like a politician or something—reminiscing about last summer.

I squeeze down the front with El Boti. He is so nervous and agitated. His small white-clad body trembles powerfully as he argues with the police officers. I just leave him alone as I stand beside him in the front line of runners. We sing the last prayer for protection to the idol in the wall and turn around to the neon-green- and dark-blue-clad police line. The rocket soars up into the sky and pops. *Fuck it's so quick.* I bounce, trying to loosen. The bulls pour out of the wooden corrals in front, nothing but tall pointy horns and wide muscular shoulders. *YES! What great fucking luck!* All six bulls fan out wide: just like the night before, except with bulls in front instead of in back. As they rise the hill, one steer sneaks into the pack of bulls. The melocotón gallops snug in the middle of his black brothers. *Look at this, they're way slower than I thought they'd be!* The police line breaks, and El Boti and a few other runners run toward the charging bulls down to the painted line. I position myself beside El Boti. As the galloping pack approaches, the other mozos run. El Boti and I stand our ground. Four bulls flood into the lead. They gallop hard at us up the hill with the melocotón leading in the center, his peach-colored fur undulating atop his muscular frame. We wait. El Boti runs first. I follow. As we round the first bend I look back. The bulls fan out wide, filling the entire street. One bull even goes up on the sidewalk. *Fuck, nowhere to escape!* I turn and run. The crowd of runners ahead squeezes me closer to the galloping horns at our backs. I feel the gravitational pull of a bull linking with me. I glance back. The melocotón locks on me and surges toward me with his coral-colored horns bowed climbing the incline. *You're trapped! Fuck.* I look to the sidewalk as the black bull folds back off the sidewalk into the street. *Get out!* I cut hard out to the sidewalk and smash into a bald-headed runner behind El Boti. We fly into the wall. I land on the back of another runner like I'm spooning him. *Fuck, at least I'm the big spoon! Gross!* The melocotón dips his horns at me and the horn tip passes just a few inches from my arm as he eyes me urgently, his gorgeous silky jaw flexing. His beautiful yellowish-tan body flows past me. *Phew! Thanks, old friend.*

After the pack rumbles past, I hop off the runner I'm spooning with.

"Sorry!" I tell him.

He looks embarrassed. We both laugh, and I help him to his feet. I recognize his spiky hair and collared white shirt as one of the French runners, Sebastian's friend. I check on everyone, and everybody's OK. The director and the female producer walk up. The woman complains she missed the shot of me running. Just like the director, she doesn't take responsibility for her own failure.

"This guy bumped me right when the bulls came!" she complains.

I wince. *Well, maybe tomorrow.*

"And I mean, you only ran on the horns for like twenty yards. Why did you cut out?"

I freeze. "What?" *Bitch, my life was on the line. If I fucking didn't cut out, I might be dead or on my way to the hospital right now.* I furrow my brow and glance at the director for support.

He nods in agreement.

"Yeah, we set up to film you and you barely run the horns?" he says glaring at me.

"Fucking nitwits," I mutter and walk straight between their plump bodies as they stagger backward. I continue up the street as mozo friends wave and wink at me and give me the thumbs-up. *Those documentary idiots are in bed with the toxic foreign runners that I want nothing to do with. I fucking told them I want nothing to do with them, that they've got a history of harassing me, and that piece-of-shit director doesn't give a shit. You gotta get away from these assholes.*

The workers swiftly break down the barricades as I make it to town hall square. *I was stupid to believe in a guy I hardly knew. But that's life. Bad people'll always try to take advantage of you and not appreciate what you do for them.* I bump into El Boti and he grins at me.

I shake his hand.

"Maestro, I'm sorry about the other day with JuanPe."

He glares at me, outraged.

"No, Bill! No! Never apologize for that. That was between him and I. You were trying to do something good. And I agreed because it is good for the culture." His hazel eyes glow as he corrects me. "No pasa nada! OK?"

I nod. He grins and pats the side of my face and gives me a hug.

"Gracias, maestro."

"How was the encierro?" he asks.

"Pretty good, I was right beside you."

"Really?"

"I couldn't have done it without you, maestro."

He shrugs, surprised.

I grin and head up the street. *Man, Boti was really in the zone down there.*

I stick my head in a bar on Estafeta as the TV footage plays across the screen. Boti's gleaming bald head leads the bulls another forty yards after I exit. *Fucking El Boti is a great guy, I regret helping those documentary guys, but at the same time, I don't regret anything I do with passion, and with the hopes it will help positively present this culture I love so much. Fuck it. And now I got a new friend and maestro in El Boti. So good.*

I order a cortado as I watch Aitor's tall thin frame glide in front of the melocotón and lead him into the tunnel. *Fucking legend. Tom and Maria didn't like those documentary guys straight off, and I probably should have considered that a bad sign. They also started complaining about JuanPe and Stephanie. I keep trying to be positive with them, but they're showing no appreciation and no respect for me and my friends, or the culture.* My cortado arrives; the earthy rich scent hits my nostrils. On the TV screen, Aitor falls into the sand as he enters the arena and the melocotón kindly avoids him. *Another gem, Aitor! Those fucking doc guys, they've shown zero professionalism. They're always late, and constantly repetitively messing up simple tasks like putting a mic on somebody.* I sigh as the bulls thread up Estafeta, with Sergio Colas's massive body leading as he screams at the runners ahead of him. *But if the worst thing that came of it is that I got to hang out with my bull runner friends, make some new ones, and go see a lot of great ranches and run some small towns with Tom and Tony then hey, it's a win.* I take another sip and watch Pablo Bolo lead two sueltos into the tunnel and through into the arena with his green penuelo flapping in the air. *Fucking Pablo, that fucking guy is possessed!*

♉

The morning before Brevito gored me in 2014, a dark premonition fell on me as I warmed up on a side street near the course. I jogged looking down at the pavement, humming Nam Myōhō Renge Kyō as I gazed at the litter on the dirty pavement. Then I passed over a tiny dot of blood. Then another, and another. The dots grew until I found a big dark red puddle. I stopped, looking into it at the reflection of my dark form. I pushed the thought from my mind and soldiered on.

♉

Arriving at Santo Domingo, I feel great, light and ready. I set to run with Xabi halfway up Santo Domingo. Weaving through the crowd I find Aitor, Xabi, Mikel, David, Cristian, and the guys. Xabi looks seriously sick; his face glows pale like he's going to pass out or vomit. I grin at him.

"Xabi, que paso, amigo?"

He sternly turns to me.

"It's so fast here, it's so fast! When you see the bull, just get out! He'll be on you in a split second."

"Xabi, it's just another encierro, brother! Relax!"

"Suerte." Xabi hugs me, grips my face, and kisses me on the top of my forehead. He whispers a prayer, and heads off to prepare. I linger near him, warming up. *Fucking Xabi, he musta had a bad dream or something.* I giggle.

The rocket pops. I watch the narrow channel, one side a plain tan curved wall, the other topped by a mass of spectators leaning along a steel railing. There's a slight pause, then the thick clot of mozos begins to trickle around the slow curve, past the red and gold idol of San Fermin in his little cove in the stone wall. Turning, I run in the center of the dark cobblestone street up a long slick hill. Other runners crowd around me. Frightened shouts erupt behind me as the runners thin out, bailing to the sides.

I glance back as hooves clap my way. Two pointy horns emerge out of the mass of running bodies. A lead silky grey bull zigzags the street furiously, gouging his horns at the runners as he gallops up the hill. Then he melds back into the mob of runners behind me. Wind whirls in my ears as I turn back ahead and struggle to hold the center of the street. A wave of exiting runners pushes me right. I cut right to maintain balance. *Hope he passes in the center. Then I can run alongside the pack.* I look back; I can see the thick pack of animals further down the stones. *I got a few seconds.* I aim my sprint at the center of the street. Suddenly the runner directly behind me screams and dives out. The lead animal's horn passes within an inch of his back. Something hard jabs into my butt cheek. The hard thing pushes the waist of my white running pants down—revealing my yellow underwear. *What's that?!* I glance back. The lead, dark-grey bull's horn pushes into my butt. I look down; the base of his girthy horn is beside my hand. *No way! He's already under me!* The bull violently dips his mighty head. His hoof claps beside my red Air Jordans. His horn digs in near my asshole. *No! Not there! Fuck, jump!* I leap as he lunges upward, sending me flying straight up into the air above him. Painless. The sound of a knife jabbed into Styrofoam courses through my ears. *Fucking again?!* I twist midair as his muscular grey back undulates in gallop below me and he shoots past. The dark sidewalk soars toward me. I reach my hand out and break my fall. My palm strikes the wet stones; my shoulder and elbow collapse. My hip bangs hard, then my side and my head both whack the cobbles. Bright electric white flashes through my head.

The herd thunders past. I shoot to my feet angrily. *Motherfucker!* I feel myself for wounds. *I'm fine. How the fuck did he gain on me that fast!?* I feel my pants; they aren't ripped. Mozos rush up yelling urgently, trying to pull me to the medics. I refuse, still looking back for blood. *Nothing.* A pack of sweeper steers thunder up, with one grey straggler bull snug inside them. I try to run them, there's no opening. I dash beside them. Then they're gone.

More runners rush to me. Three of them forcefully take me by my arms and escort me across the street. I step through the barricades. The medics pull my pants down. I grab my naked dick and balls in my hands and look down. My underwear hangs down between my hairy naked thighs. Dark red stains the yellow crotch. *Fuck, he did gore me.* I lie down face-first on the stretcher, trembling.

Suddenly my friend Cristian, the big burly Basque runner who works as a gigante for the parades, rushes up. "Bill! Are you OK?" he asks worriedly.

"I got gored, Cristian." He holds my hand as the medics inspect the wound.

"I hate to do this to you," the medic says, smearing lube on his gloved finger. "But I need to stick my finger in your anus so I can see if it has been perforated."

"Crap, alright." I squeeze Cristian's hand and grit my teeth as the medic does the nasty thing he has to do.

The medic dabs his finger onto a sheet of medical paper and looks at me. "Good, no blood! You are very lucky my friend."

Well that's one of the oddest things anyone's said to me after intercourse. But seriously, fuck, if it perforated my asshole I'd be in the hospital for months like Carmelo was. Fucking colostomy bag and everything. I'm one lucky motherfucker. Shit. I gotta call Enid before this story breaks and fucking CNN starts talking shit. My phone is in the bookshop.

"Cristian, can you please go get my bag? It's in the bookshop. Please! I need to call my wife. The little red bag!"

"OK, I'll try to find it!" Cristian disappears as Xabi materializes.

Xabi holds my hand. "Bill! Are you OK?" he says, tears trembling in his eyes.

"I'm alright." I grin. "It's tiny!"

Xabi burst into laughter. "You crazy asshole!"

"What?! It's nothing!" I laugh. "It's hardly bleeding, I'm gonna run again tomorrow!"

He laughs and fights back tears and grips my hand.

"You crazy motherfucker."

The medics load me into the ambulance, and just as they are about to shut the door, Cristian appears with my bag.

"Bill!" He hands it to me.

"Thank you, Cristian!!!! You are a fucking great friend! You're a fucking giant FRIEND!" I shout as they shut the door.

I call Enid, it goes to voicemail. "Baby, I'm fine, I got hurt, I got a small goring but I'm fine. I love you. I'm sorry…"

As we drive over, the medics ask me the most important question you'll be asked if you are ever gored: "Are you in pain?"

No, I'm not in pain. But wait, they're going to stick their finger in the wound when I get to the hospital. My mind flashes to my first goring. The doctor in the hospital asked me if I was in pain. I told him no. Then he stuck his entire blue-gloved finger inside the wound. It felt like his finger was a sparking electrical wire. I screamed and contorted. When he was finished he grinned as he said, "You're in pain?" "Yes!" I told him. Then he shot me with morphine and I didn't feel pain again for a long time. *Fuck that I ain't going through that again!*

I look at the medics waiting for my answer as the ambulance rushes me through the Pamplona streets. "Yes! I am in pain!"

The medic shoots me with morphine and pats me on the shoulder.

Inside the hospital, they wheel me through some white hallways. We pass a corridor, and about seven hundred camera shutter clicks fire down the hall, trying to get an image of me. *Oh boy, here we go again.* They wheel me into an adjacent hallway and leave me there. I am alone in the quiet. *You know what'll go down now. They'll come after you.* My stomach aches, hollow at the thought of the world turning on me again. Loneliness, a deep, dark loneliness overtakes me. *What are you doing with your life, man? Nobody cares... You're just some sideshow freak, some viral news item, a target for animal rights weirdos.* A memory of the emails and DMs they sent me when I came out of surgery after my first goring: "I wish you would have died." "I hope you die." *You fucking people don't even know me.* Tears well in my eyes as I plunge deep into the stretcher cushion. An iron blanket of sadness lies atop me.

"Bill..."

I turn to see JuanPe walk up to my stretcher with his running pants rolled below the knee. Concern on his handsome brow. I spark up and look him in his eyes. *JuanPe, he came; right when I needed a friend.*

"Thank you, JuanPe."

He reaches out and takes my hand in his.

"Are you OK?"

"Yes, my friend. I'm alright now."

He takes my bag and follows me as the medics roll me into the big white operating room.

The doctor enters, they transition me to the operating table, and he has me roll on my belly.

"I'm sorry to tell you this, but I need to do something to the wound."

"I know. You gotta stick your finger in it."

"This isn't your first goring?" he asks.

"The third," JuanPe chimes in.

"Haha yep, my third wound. Feel free, I'm on morphine."

JuanPe chuckles and holds my hand as the doctor prepares to inspect the depth of the wound. The doctor sticks his finger into the hole, which is basically right next to my asshole. I tense up, gripping JuanPe's hand. *Man, that sank in a lot deeper than I thought it would. Thank god for the morphine. Didn't feel a thing.*

"How bad is it?" I ask.

"It's deep."

"Really, I thought it was little."

"It is small but it's deep. I have to check your anus again."

"Oh, boy."

JuanPe shrugs and continues to hold my hand. The doctor does the nasty thing for the second time, twisting his finger all around inside as I groan and almost puke. JuanPe tries not to laugh. I giggle after the doctor is done. *That was pretty horrible.* No blood again. They wheel me into the main waiting rooms. JuanPe steps into another room to check on a friend.

Suddenly Dennis Clancy walks in in his buttoned black running shirt. His friend, a shorter muscular Basque-American guy in a long-sleeve American flag shirt, follows him in, grinning.

"Thanks for coming, guys!" I say.

Dennis recognizes the guy in the bed next to me.

"Do you know who you're right next to? That's Bill Hillmann, he's a fucking great runner," Dennis says.

I grin.

"Hi, my name is Ander," the friend says. "Man, it's nice to meet you." We shake hands.

"Nice to meet you too," I reply. *Who is this guy, and why the hell did he feel the need to come visit me in the hospital?*

"I just wanted to come to check on you and say that I really respect what you do," Ander says, sounding genuine.

"Thanks." I shrug. *Nice dude.*

Then Xabi, David Lerga, and Aitor round the corner, grinning.

"Cabron!" Xabi hurries over and grips my hand.

"Cabron!" I reply. "I'm fine, man. I'm gonna fucking run tomorrow. Watch!"

JuanPe walks up with a little grimace on his face making sure Xabi isn't messing with me. I grin at him and reassure him.

"Voy a corer a mañana, JuanPe!" I tell him as he chuckles.

David Lerga comes up and says "Bill," in his big deep voice. "Que paso?"

"I didn't see the fucking bull, what can I say!" I tell them.

They burst into laughter. Then it dawns on me. *Aitor is here. And JuanPe is here. Man.* I nod at them. Xabi and I watch as they smile awkwardly and chat at the foot of my bed. *Come on, guys. Make up already.* JuanPe reaches his hand out and squeezes Aitor's shoulder. Xabi and I look at each other. Our eyes bug out as we start giggling.

"Did you see that?" Xabi says.

"Can you believe it!" I grin.

"They made up!"

All I had to do was get gored to make two of the greatest Navarrese runners in history, who'd hardly spoken to each other in over a year, to make up. What a fucking trip. I watch them grinning and chatting. *Their friendship broke in part because of me and the book, and somehow because of my goring their friendship mended. Only in fiesta...*

I have to take a leak, so they bring me over to the bathroom in a wheelchair. I stand and shuffle into the little bathroom. *Shit, I can walk.* I come out and brush past the nurse with the wheelchair and waddle toward my bed.

"Aye Cabrones I'm fine! Look, I'll run tomorrow!" I say. I waddle around in goofy circles as the guys laugh. Aitor grins, his big angular face flexing as he shakes his head "no." His grandfather's face bobbling around on his chest as he laughs.

They come to bring me to surgery. JuanPe holds my bag and walks with me into the big circular operating room. *Damn, I couldn't have a better person having my back going into this.* They do the epidural, a nasty little prick in my spine. Then the numbness swirls through my butt and legs. Then they put me in this stirrup chair, the kind they use for pregnant women about to give birth. *Well I guess the bull impregnated you! With bits of horns and an infection. Should this be considered an STI?* My legs are spread and my feet are up in the air. The surgeon sits before me with his blue mask and cleans the wound, pulling out slivers of horn. JuanPe says goodbye and heads to work. They rig me with a drain capsule and wheel me to my room. Tom and Maria come in and visit briefly, bringing my charger for my phone.

Well, I'm ready this time. I look at my cracked screen. *Fucking Gowen. Mandarino left his mark to this day. Last time around you didn't have a phone, remember those days? You took on the whole damn world, and all the lies they tell about this culture. You used a bunch of linguistics concepts you didn't even know existed, and by the end of the summer you'd confronted the lies and attacks, and spread the truth of the culture to tens of millions of people globally. You'd grabbed the global conversation by the horns. Fuck, it might be the greatest thing you ever did in your life, to defend this culture you love so much. Well, here comes round two.* I plug in my phone and post my cell number and email on my social media accounts.

A young, pretty journalist named Lisa Segarra shows up to my room with a Spanish photographer. She is serious, professional, and excellent.

"What outlet are you with?" I ask.

"AP," she responds.

Holy fuck, this story will be published in the biggest outlets around the entire planet. Tens of millions of people are listening right now. Every single word you say is important. I watch her as she checks her batteries in her recorder. *She's young, she might be an animal rights activist. But look at her, she is a real journalist. She won't pull a Jeanne Moos on you and backstab you.* I take a deep breath and start to field her questions. The photographer shoots photos of me as we talk; because my IV is in the nook of my right elbow I have to have my arm extended to reply to friends and well-wishers, so it looks like I'm taking a selfie. I show them a shot from Santo Domingo on my cracked screen, with the whole herd closing in and El Boti and I at the starting line. I try to express all my love and joy for the encierro to her. I mention as many of my Spanish maestros and the runs in the pueblos as I can. And I tell her I plan to run tomorrow. She thanks me for the interview.

I shake her cool elegant hand before she goes.

"Thank you," I tell her. "You're a real journalist. I've been burned before. I respect you."

She blushes a little as they leave.

The story hits within an hour.

TIME is the first outlet to pick it up. I read it on my phone.

"One of the two Americans gored Saturday during this year's second running of the bulls in the Spanish city of Pamplona is swearing that he will run again before the festival is over."

I giggle. *OK, here we go, now everybody will be on you.* The story shifts to the other injured runners. *OK, not bad, you were right about her, she's the real thing.* I continue reading. Suddenly the full picture of me leading the bull with Aitor that was the cover of *Mozos* appears. Is this real?! She writes about how Hemingway's *The Sun Also Rises* inspired me to come to fiesta.

"It changed my life. It made me want to be a writer, to run the bulls, to come to Spain," he said. "When I got here everything in the book was still here, but a thousand times more. And it just keeps getting more interesting. People think this is just crazy people running. There is real art. If you pay attention, you can see it."

Oh my god, that sums it up fucking good! Damn! That's a fucking billboard quote for the culture! My eyes race across the screen: "Hillmann claims to have participated in over 300 bull runs across Spain at traditional summer festivals." *Fucking great.* I raise my fist triumphantly. *The whole world knows it now. There's more to the culture than just San Fermines. In this day and age with all the lies out there, the crummy politicized journalism. This is a total utter fucking triumph!*

I get on Twitter to share the story and see in the Twitter sidebar the list of Top Trending World News Stories. Her article on me is sitting at number one. I glance down the list and see an article on Trump's antics at the G20 sitting at number three on the list. *Holy fucking shit. You did it, man, this is massive! Millions of people around the globe are reading this right now! Now you gotta get back out there and run! Prove to the world that there's more to the run than a stupid thrill for tourists.*

Even if one of my books becomes an international bestseller, it would probably still only reach hundreds of thousands of people. But this AP piece is reaching tens of millions. It's my best chance to spread the truth of the culture, to fight the negativity about the encierro with something positive. Whether I like it or not, I am a spokesperson for the culture. I can, and have, single-handedly altered the conversation about the culture worldwide for the better, and in these situations, it is my duty to do so. If I clammed up or refused to talk, I would be wasting a massive opportunity for the tradition. Some people think it is noble to not talk to the media, and that's fine. But if we don't talk, then the only voices that get heard are the animal rights activists and their lies.

Pablo from outside Medina del Campo peeks his head around the door with his bashful grin.

"Pablo!"

"Bill! Que paso mi amigo?" he giggles.

"Todo bien no pasa nada!" I giggle as he comes in and gives me a hug.

A TV crew from Antena 3, a national Spanish station, sneaks into the room. We film a little segment chatting, reminiscing about running the tunnel in Iscar and the embudo in Medina del Campo.

Then the documentary crew shows, late as hell, as usual. They cheer me up, and I start running around the room and hall to show I can do it while they take pictures of the open back of my hospital gown and my new underwear that looks a lot like a diaper. The nurses eventually kick them out.

Later they bring a grungy American kid into my room from surgery. He wakes up and pukes. His name is Jack Capra; he's in his early twenties and was living in Paris when he came down to run with the bulls just like Hemingway. Sentido, the bull that gored me, gored him too. Sentido really caused some damage today. I help translate with the doctors to get his belongings brought down to his room. His mood brightens as the anesthetic wears off from his long surgery.

"I don't even know what happened," he tells me.

"You haven't seen the video?!"

"There's a video?!" he says, swallowing back some puke.

I pull it up and we watch the video of the goring on my phone. I go flying up in the air and a few seconds later Sentido tramples Jack; his arm flings upward as he goes down and the horn pierces his forearm. In the split second Sentido is goring him in the arm, another bull beside Sentido sticks his horn in the same hole.

"Damn! That's one of the most bizarre things I've ever seen. You got fucking got DP'd by two bulls!" I tell him as he giggles.

The phone keeps ringing, and we give raucous interviews well into the night before we drift to sleep.

♉

In the morning dark, I wake with a tremendous gravity pinning me to the bed. *You gotta run.* I try to sit up. I can't move. *You'll never be able to run like this. Who were you kidding? Now you told the whole world you were going to run and you ain't.* I blink back some tears and drift back to sleep.

The door to my room opens. I rouse as Miguel Reta and his wife walk in quietly with concern in their faces. They walk to me as I reach out my hand. The both take my hand and look at me warmly.

"How are you?" Miguel asks.

"I'm OK. Thank you so much for coming."

"When you feel better, come home, come to the Finca," Miguel whispers.

"I will…" I say as they leave quietly.

I feel terrible. *Fuck, you were kidding yourself to think you'd run today.* Exhaustion and dull pain ache throughout my body. I float in a morphine cloud. The doctors have taped a clear plastic drain capsule a little larger than a big marble between my butt cheeks. It's kind of resting against my taint. The drain capsule creates suction and has a little rubber tube running from it into the wound to extract blood and pus. Most people think goring wounds require a lot of stitches. They don't believe me when I tell them I only had three stitches holding my huge thigh wound together back in 2014. Actually, the doctors can't close a goring wound with stitches; it's a puncture wound and needs to remain open and heal from within. Having to sit on the hard plastic drain capsule is somehow cutting the circulation off to my left testicle. I adjust it. *Fuck, you ain't running today. You'll be lucky to run again at all this fiesta.*

As the morning light brightens my room my friend Alfonso, the cultural guide, shows up with a steaming cortado below his excited grin.

"Alfonso!"

"Bill, I thought you could use a boost," Alfonso says, handing me the cortado.

"You're the fucking best!"

I take a sip. Energy courses through my body. *I feel like a new fucking man!* I stand and walk round. *Fuck, maybe I can do this!* The surgeon comes in with a nurse. He has a full beard and watches me sternly.

"Can I leave?" I ask the surgeon.

"I saw the news articles. You can sign yourself out if you want," the surgeon says very stoically. "We can't stop you."

"But surely he can't run again!" Alfonso chimes in.

"I don't want him to run," the surgeon replies. "But he is a grown man. He has to decide for himself."

Tentatively, I walk around. *How bad is it?* My back and pelvis stiffen as I step around. *I mean, your pelvis is seriously bruised. But your legs are good.* I hop on my toes. *Something's wrong with your shoulder. You got this drain capsule crushing your testicle every time you sit or lie down, you got the infection to fight, but other than that you're good to go.* Tom Gowen had to play his concert at Toki Leza after his dance with Mandarino, and I gotta run after my little boogie with Sentido.

"Alight, let's do this," I say, and gather my clothes.

Alfonso drives me to pick up my prescriptions: antibiotics and ibuprofen and some stronger painkiller. The teller rings me up, then Alfonso hands her his ID. She glances at me, then swipes it.

"Un euro," she tells me.

"What?! That'd be a couple hundred dollars in America!" Alfonso grins at me.

"This is Spain, Bill." He pats me on the back as we leave.

We roll through Pamplona's winding streets closing in on the heart of the city.

"Fuck, it's Fuente Ymbro tomorrow, isn't it?"

"Yes, then the next day it's Jandilla."

"Fucking I don't want my first run back to be with the Jandilla. I gotta run tomorrow."

"Bill, this is crazy, I really don't think you should do it," Alfonso complains.

"I know Alfonso, but I have to."

"Why?" he asks.

"It's an opportunity to show the world that the run is about more than just adrenaline or adventure."

"What is it for you, Bill?"

"It's something that changed my life. It's the most beautiful culture in the world, I love it very deeply, Alfonso. It's something I'm willing to die for. And if I can physically run, I'm gonna be out there."

"Bill, you are outrageous, I love it." Alfonso grins and grips my shoulder.

We pull to the edge of Plaza del Castillo. I start to get out. *This'll be a fun walk.*

"No, Bill. I'll drive you to the door." We pull up to a police officer guarding the entrance.

"This is Bill Hillmann," Alfonso tells the officer. "He was gored yesterday, he lives here." The officer peeks in and sees me; his eyebrows pop up. He waves us through. Alfonso pulls up in front of Bar Windsor. I get out with a little bit of pain in my back.

"Thanks so much, Alfonso," I tell him, gripping the door.

"I wish you well, Bill," he says with a grin. "Be careful tomorrow, mozo!"

I grin as he drives away. *He's a such a sweet friend.* I head toward Tom's red door. *What a guy. The people of Navarra, man, best friends you'll ever have.*

After a painful climb up to Tom's place, I lie in bed and check my email. NBC's *Today* show writes, wanting to do a segment on my return to running. *Fuck, this is great! This is really going to show people how much passion real runners have.*

Enid calls. She doesn't want me to run the next day. We begin to bicker over Facebook video chat.

"Why are you doing this stupid shit!" she asks.

"Look, I have to!"

"You don't have to do anything!" she screams. "I love you, isn't that enough? Can't you just stop now!"

"Look, everything is riding on me running tomorrow. The *Today* show is following me around. Don't you see, if I do this it will show the world that there's more to this tradition than just a stupid been-there-done-that vacation!"

"But why, William? Why does it have to be you?"

"I don't know, it's my fucking destiny! Look, I need you! I don't care if you don't understand! You're my wife, I need your support!" A spike of pain stabs my back; my whole being seems to drain into the mattress. "I'm exhausted, Enid. I'm in pain. I'm in the middle of a war with the world media. It's been building to this moment for the past twelve years, and I'm about to fucking win, but I need you!"

I see her crying in the little rectangle of my phone screen, back at home in Panama. "I can't. I just can't! I don't want you to die."

"I'm not going to die, Enid. I just need you. Can you be there with me through this?"

"OK… OK, just be careful."

"Thank you."

"I love you."

"I love you, too."

We end the call. I lie on my little bed in Gowen's small spare room. *It's so hard to explain to her. She just wants me to come home safe and alive, but I was fucking born for this.* I go out on the balcony. *I hate fucking selfies. But fuck it. It's the best way to show everybody I'm out of the hospital. Sentido knocked me down, but I got back up and I'm still fighting.* I take a pic overlooking the heart of fiesta. I post it to Facebook and write a post in Spanish:

"If you are a runner in San Fermines, you have to be prepared for war; war of the mind, war of the spirit and war of the body. And now I'm in all of those wars…"

I look out over the masses of partiers dancing and drinking in the afternoon light. A few people spot me from down at the plaza. A guy shouts and points up at me.

"Bill!!!!" he yells, and gives me two thumbs up. *Is that that Ander guy?* I wave back. *Fuck.* I head back into the apartment. *That was weird.*

NBC's *Today* hires a Spanish crew that starts following me around getting B-roll for the segment. We do an interview on the course, and I do another one with Reuters, and some Spanish station. I fall into bed exhausted around midnight.

Tom and Maria wake me and bring me into the kitchen. Gowen grimaces at the little kitchen table. His blue eyes sparkle as he puffs a cigarette.

"Bill, you are getting yourself into trouble with JuanPe," Tom says in his gravelly voice.

"What do you mean?"

"We talked with him in the hospital, and he is very upset about not being paid by the documentary guys."

"Fuck, OK. I'll get it done tomorrow. I'll make them motherfuckers pay."

Gowen grimaces at me, glaring into my eyes urgently. "You got to, kid. Your friendship is in jeopardy. You understand? The Basque people, when they become your friend, it's for life. You just can't lose this man as your friend. Make it right."

"You're right, maestro. I will." I head back to my room and check my email, I have to ignore the dozens of outlets that are writing me, because I'll never get to sleep if I don't. The *People* magazine reporter who interviewed me the last time I got gored reaches out again with questions. She asks me if I have anything going on this year, or anyone else she should talk with, or anyone to get photos or video from. I throw the documentary guys a bone and mentioned them. She says she'll reach out to them.

A producer at CNN is hassling me about video of my goring for a segment they want to do. CNN's Jeanne Moos really screwed me over when I got gored in 2014. I jumped through hoops to get a cell phone into my hospital room and Skype with her. Then she turned around and did a horrible hit piece on me. And even though later in the summer, Al Goodman did right by me with a follow-up segment on CNN International, I am getting the feeling this new producer is more of a Moos type. She keeps saying there is no video footage of my goring. Then she says that she found me in the video wearing a baseball cap later in the run. I finally send a video clip giving her the exact second that I go flying up into the air on Sentido's horn. She replies with: "Wow that's a nice attitude." So I tell her: "If you're too useless to find a simple world news clip in a video that's all over the internet and I'm the one producing this segment, I better be getting paid as a producer!" She stops bothering me.

Lying back on my little bed, I sigh. *You sure did get yourself in big, big trouble again, Bill.*

♉

I get a little sleep and head out in the morning. I walk down the stairs and push open Gowen's red door. The cool dank morning air greets me. The NBC *Today* show crew stands leaning against the stone arches in front of me. A Reuters reporter walks up from the side. Another Spanish TV crew hurriedly rushes up from across the plaza. *Well, I guess it's all eyes on you, tough guy.* I wave to them all timidly. *Fuck, I need a coffee.* They swarm me and tell me to just do what I'd normally do if they weren't there. *Fuck, normal is kind of over now guys. I got a fucking drain capsule hanging outta my ass!* I giggle and head toward the course. I grab a coffee at a bar, and another TV crew filming for a Chicago station waits for me near the entrance of the course at town hall square. We do a brief interview.

"How are you feeling returning to run just two days after being gored?"

"I feel a little better after that cortado, but to be honest my hips and legs are killing me. I'm really stiff. I don't know what I'll be capable of. I hope I can run," I say, and shrug. "I'm here 'cause I love it. I love this tradition. It's part of me."

The director of the documentary walks up and looks at me pompously.

"Don't forget, we're the ones who filming you first! You owe us," he says.

I glare at him and grin disgustedly. *Motherfucker, without me, you had nothing, and nobody'd ever have noticed your pathetic little project. You owe me!*

I ignore him and enter the course with three TV crews and a couple more photographers. *Well, if the runners are supposed to be anonymous, then I really fucking failed at that.* Upper Santo Domingo is pretty empty. *I'll warm up here.* The TV crews set up across the street. Behind them, a big crowd of spectators sit and stand along a wide outdoor staircase. I glance a little ways down Santo Domingo to where Sentido gored me. *Fuck man, do not get gored again!*

Several cameras film me. *Fuck, maybe a few million people from around the globe are watching, or will be in a few hours. No pressure or nothing guys, thanks.* I stretch my aching hips. They're supertight, I stretch harder against the pain as it percolates in several different spots. *Fuck, they hurt.* I bounce a little, gather myself, and jog up the Santo Domingo toward town hall square. The crowd watching from the steps erupts in cheers. I look over. *What the hell's going on?!* They point at me and watch eagerly. *Fucking are they cheering for me?! This is nuts.* I walk back down, bounce a little, then jog back up. The crowd erupts in applause again.

"Bill Hillmann!" one drunk guy yells in a thick Spanish accent.

I giggle and try to run hard but my back and hips burn. *Well, you're good enough to run alongside them, and hopefully the adrenaline'll loosen you up when the bulls are coming up the street. Is this the right thing to do? Is this about ego? Is this crazy? Are you a media whore? An attention junkie?* The faces of nervous runners pass me. *Naw man, look. This is your way to show the world how much the run means to you. And if it means this much to you, then there's got to be something deeper happening here in San Fermin. You're doing this to show the world that there's a real deep culture here in Spain.*

The police escort the TV crews off the course and I head down to say hi to the guys. I approach Aitor, David, Cristian, Mikel, and Xabi.

Xabi sees me, and his eyes light up angrily. He steps in my face and berates me. "And this fucking guy, I told you they'd be faster than you think!" he says, throwing his hands in the air exasperated.

I grin, embarrassed. "Perdoname, Xabi," I say sheepishly as the guys giggle. Xabi grimaces, not accepting my apology. "Perdoname," I urge him, reaching out to hug him as he pulls away from me. "Perdoname..." I groan and grab him around the neck. "Perdoname CABRON!" I yell. He finally concedes and lets me hug him as the guys laugh and pat us on the back. I whisper in his ear. "Your friendship means a lot to me, Xabi. Thank you for trying to help me and teach me. You told me good things. I just didn't realize."

"You didn't listen!" he says, tears trembling in his eyes.

"I listened, but I didn't realize how fast they were going to be."

"But I told you!" Xabi counters me.

"You did, you did." I pat him on the back. "It's my fault I got gored. Not yours."

The tension in Xabi's arms loosens and he hugs me back—his strong shoulders heave.

"Be careful," he tells me.

I grin. "I'm really fucked up."

"Then don't run!" Aitor shouts at me angrily.

"No, no. It's not that bad," I whine.

"If it's that bad, Bill, don't run!" Aitor scolds me, his eyes tremble.

"It's not, it's not, it's OK," I tell him. I take a deep breath. *Damn, these guys really do care about you.* I look at their concerned faces. I feel like a fucking suelto about to break from the pack and go out and do something big on my own. *OK, guys, look, I can't explain it, but this is good for the culture. People are going to follow this story all over the USA, and they're going to love it. It's going to help the culture, trust me.* Then to myself: *Fuck, you don't want to make them look bad. Well, then don't get hurt again!*

We walk down to the idol of San Fermin. I look up at him in his gold and red robe with his golden hat. *San Fermin, can you give me a pass today? If I get gored again, this won't look so good. My wife will divorce me for sure. I'm trying to do right for you and this beautiful fiesta of yours, so please look out for me this morning.* I sing one prayer to San Fermin and walk back up to the beginning of town hall square. JuanPe walks past, looking worried.

"JuanPe!"

He sees me and comes over.

"I'm sorry about the money, I didn't know. I will get it today, I promise."

"Bill, all that matters is you are OK," he says and grips my traps with both hands.

"Suerte, hermano!" I tell him.

He squeezes my hand with both of his, closes his eyes, and whispers a prayer.

Watching him walk away, bouncing on my toes. *I will get him that fucking money today if it's the last thing I do.* The rocket goes off. A white blur of runners flash past me in a panic. They push me into the thick wooden barricades. I fight my way off of them. The bulls round the bend down on Santo Domingo and disappear into the running bodies. I try to dodge the young runners blasting past me on either side. I hear a crackle and a hard banging bell around one of the steer's necks. I turn and sprint, hugging the edge of the glob of runners crammed in front of the barricades. A hefty runner bursts into my back and yanks my shoulder, tearing past me. My core muscles collapse, and a sharp pain stabs into my pelvis near the hip. I lose stability and dive into the crowd near the barricades. The first of the Fuente Ymbro soars past, his hooves reaching out in front of him majestically. His mighty horns stand tall, stretching up toward the sky. His muscular side gleams in the morning light shooting through Mercaderes. The street opens as the bulls and steers sail past. I gather myself, break into sprint, and run alongside them. Their eyes dart around in their sockets, looking at me curiously as I run beside them. The sounds of the camera shutters click all around us. Then I dive to the fence and they're gone.

The spike of pain scolds my hips as I limp around, groaning. I hop as the pain intensifies. *Is this gonna stop?!* I can hardly breathe. Panic constricts my lungs as I fold over at the waist and scream. Then one of the photographers from the documentary walks up.

"Did you run?" he asks goofily.

"Yeah, if you have pictures of the herd, you got me for sure."

"I don't think so," he says.

I grab his camera and flip through the photos. Three images of me running alongside the pack materialize. My arm is reaching out towards the black beasts as I look them in the eyes. *They're fucking gems!*

"You're so fucking good, man, why don't you do more journalism? *The Today Show* will want these, so stay in touch."

I head up the street. A Spanish TV crew grabs me for an interview. I am trying to say nice things about the Spanish and Basque runners and their culture. David Rodriguez stomps up angrily, the green patches at the chest tremble.

"Bill! You shouldn't have run so soon!" Rodriguez shouts angrily in my face. "It was ugly! You should have rested!"

"Perdoname David." I sigh. "You're right. I'm sorry."

He frowns and walks off. *Fair enough, I guess I'm taking a few days off.* We finish the interview. *Well, it fucking took everything I had to get through that.* I climb back up the stairs to Tom's apartment in the shadowy stairwell. I make slow and painful progress. *I guess I agree with you, David, but it's something I had to do. I showed the world there's more to the tradition than just the silly tourist view. There's people like you David, people deep inside the heart of the tradition who would do anything to keep running.* I lie on my bed as the adrenaline wears off and two weird lumps form on either side of my pelvis. My lower stomach bloats. *What the fuck is going on with me?* The pain and exhaustion flood back. I try to sit up and two daggers of pain stab my hips. I scream. *Motherfucker, what is going on with you?!* I climb out of bed and walk to the bathroom. The drain capsule nestled in my butt crack blocks the poop from coming out. I have to push the shit out, so I nudge the capsule out of the way. The shit smears around the capsule, inevitably seeping into the open wound. It's so bad down there, I have to take a shower afterward.

Chapter 18

JuanPe

Alright motherfuckers, I've been a bill collector before, *you don't want to be late or come up short on me even now when I'm at half-strength. I'll still bounce you down some stairs.* I step painfully toward the documentary crew's apartment. *You owe my friend JuanPe money. And you're gonna pay.* Exhaustion and pain slow me as I climb up the stairs to the apartment the crew has set up their headquarters in. I walk in to the living room. They busy themselves throughout the apartment.

"Hey," I go, "where's JuanPe's money?"

The director looks at me befuddled.

"I told him to send me an invoice."

"You write the invoice right now," I tell him, walking up to him.

He throws his hands up, flabbergasted.

"Look," I say. "I ain't leaving here 'till I have the money."

"I'm not giving it to you. How do I know you'll really give it to him?"

"You got the cash on you right now?" I glare at him.

"Wait, I'm busy with something," he says, looking over one of the intern's shoulders.

"Naw, you're going to do it right now," I growl at him. "The money is late, you been treating him like shit. So stop whatever the fuck you're doing and get JuanPe's money."

Everyone in the room stops what they're doing and look up at me uncertainly.

The producer gets up, sipping a cup of tea.

"Bill, chill, what's up with you, man?" she tells me. "Have you heard yet? *People* magazine is doing a piece about us, and we're telling them it should be on you."

"What?! Are you nuts?!" I ask her. "The only reason *People* magazine even knows you exist is because *I* told them about *you*."

"OK, OK," the director says and stands. "I'll go down and get the cash."

I walk down the hall and wake up the wedding photographer with the shots that NBC *Today* is requesting. He's asleep. I wake him up and he drags his feet sending the files to NBC *Today*.

"I don't even know why I'm doing this," he whines.

"They're going to fucking pay you for them. You know that, right?"

"How much?"

"I don't know, ask them!"

After a few quick messages they negotiate the price and he sends the shots.

I walk down to the cash station with the director. He takes out the money. I double-check the count and he's given me twenty euros extra. I count again and hand him the twenty back.

"Keep it," he tells me.

"Naw, I don't want your fucking money," I say, and head off to Plaza del Castillo. I sigh. *Good riddance, motherfuckers, I hope I never see you fucking idiotic egomaniacs again.*

♉

Painfully, I walk back to Tom's and write JuanPe that I have his money; I tell him I'll meet him after the bullfight.

After a rest, I gather some energy and go down to the bullring. I try to sit up but scream out as daggers of pain stab into my pelvis like the horns of a wrathful bull. I pant, trying to calm myself. *It's time. It's time to meet JuanPe. Get the fuck up motherfucker!* I raise my knee and thrust my body upright in the bed and twist around, growling from the pain. I stand up in the shady small room with the sunlight oozing in from behind me through the open windows looking out onto Plaza del Castillo. I see myself in the reflection of a mirror. Deep shadows cut through the creases of my pale thinned-out face. *You'll be back in bed in thirty minutes, Bill.* The deep exhaustion aches in my shoulders and back. *You can do this.*

I'm a pretty simple guy. I work with my hands. I break concrete with rivet-busters, and build and repair concrete sewers and bridges. It's some of the lowest, dirtiest work on earth. I'm a street brawler; I've been in and out of jail plenty. I'm not a big shot. I'm not important. I'm just a working-class knucklehead. But as I walk out of Tom's apartment into Plaza del Castillo I step into this dream world where I am not me anymore. I am someone people know and like, and maybe even love.

Rounding the corner, I step onto Estafeta with fiesta flowing strong. *OK, you gotta walk two blocks there and two blocks back.* I hurt pretty bad; the infection is draining me. I feel about as weak and miserable as I've ever felt in my whole crazy-ass life. I look up and a few older local couples watch me walk past. A balding man raises his glass of white wine toward me.

"Bill Hillmann," he mouths with pride in his eyes.

I don't even know that guy, do I? I double-take. *Naw, I never seen him before.* I approach a whole group of rowdy partiers on my left and every face turns and smiles at me. Some wave. I wave back awkwardly. *What the hell is going on?* Three guys across the way turn and see me and stop me.

"Eres Bill Hillmann!"

"Si." I giggle, *"Como estas, amigos."*

"Si puede toca un foto?"

"Si. Si tu quieres," I tell them.

They crowd around me and take a photo with me.

"Estas bien con la cornada?"

"Si gracias, un poco dolor, nada mas."

"Dispacio, amigo."

"Gracias necisito ir, buen día, amigos."

I continue up Estafeta. *That was weird, I've never seen those guys in my life. Well, not that I can remember anyways.*

I look up the chaos of Estafeta as dozens of partiers outside the bars turn to look at me, grinning. A beautiful woman with long sandy blonde hair grins at me, steps up to me, and touches my face softly. *Is this real?* Everyone wants to touch me and wish me well and take photos with me.

"Bill Hillmann!" I turn to see Chapu Apaolaza standing with Tom Turley and a few others. I step up to them.

"How are you with the *cornada* and everything?!" Chapu asks, his big furry beard sprouting out on his cheeks.

"It wasn't that bad, but I think I'm sick. My body is really bad, my hips."

"And you ran today?" Turley asks.

"Yeah just a little bit in town hall," I say dismissively.

"Just a little!" Chapu echoes me as the group giggles.

"I was beside them for a few yards, not much," I giggle as Turley grins at me mischievously. "I gotta go guys, have a good day," I tell them. "I gotta go see JuanPe and give him something."

"Take care of yourself," Chapu says like a big brother.

"I will, I'm going to sleep after this." I put my hands up like pillows to my cheek as they grin and wave.

The people continue to grab me and accost me, giving me love and wanting pictures with me as I wade through them trying to get through Telefonica. *You gotta get JuanPe this money. He took all this time away from his family and spent his own money for this documentary project, he's owed, and you ain't letting this cloud hang over you another second. It ain't right. JuanPe lost his job, his family lost both grandfathers. My god, he's gone through hell these past few years. JuanPe deserves this damn money, for him and for his family.*

"Bill!" I turn to see my big gregarious friend Carmelo Butini; he eagerly approaches me and shakes my hand with both of his.

"Carmelo!" I say. "How are you?"

"Good, good, and what happened with the *cornada*?" he asks.

I shrug and grin, embarrassed. "I didn't see the bull! What can I say, Carmelo. One second I'm on the horns, the next I'm gored and flying up in the air."

He bursts out laughing.

"But that's San Fermin!" I say.

He reels back from me startled; his eyes turn serious and bug out. "Exactamente! You know, you took a cornada, it's just the encierro, brother." He guffaws and shakes my hand eagerly again. "This is exactly it, Bill."

He hugs me and we say goodbye and I continue past the Hemingway statue. I give him a glance. *Well old man, I probably ain't gonna win the Nobel Prize, or even the Pulitzer, but I might be leaving my mark on this town.* My limp becomes more pronounced as the pain swirls through my pelvis. *Shit, it's sure as hell left a few marks on me.*

"Bill Hillmann!" A little ten-year-old boy in all white with his faja dragging on the ground runs up to me.

"Hi." I shake his little hand.

"Papa, can we take a picture?" he asks his father, who walks up holding a toddler.

His dad grins, and I nod yes and bend down through the pain to take a picture with him.

"He took a goring the other day and came back and ran this morning!" the little boy says, and I painfully stand and wave goodbye.

Suddenly my friend Rafa materializes with a few friends.

"Bill!" he says and gives me a strong hug.

"Remember in the *montón*?!" he asks, and my heart swells remembering carrying Jon Jeronimo Mendoza's dying body with him to the surgery room. Emotions swirl through me; I try to say yes, but I am too choked up to say anything. I nod as he introduces me to his girlfriend.

"You have to come to Valencia this August for our town's fiesta. We will make a big paella for you!"

"I would love to Rafa, but I don't know if I can."

"One day you will come to my town, my friend. You will stay with us, we will have a great time!"

"I hope so."

"How do you feel with the cornada?"

I grin, looking at him as the sun falls through the thick leafed trees along the Paseo de Hemingway. *Rafa, I feel like I'm dying, but talking with you here makes me feel fucking immortal.* I blink back some tears. "Rafa, I feel better than Jon Jeronimo Mendoza did that day, I can say that. I'm grateful I'm standing, my friend."

He grins, pats me on the face. We say goodbye and I continue.

It's as if there are waves of people pushing against me, keeping me from getting to JuanPe. But each one of their smiles and waves and well-wishes inject this joy in me that keeps me standing as the weight of the infection hangs on me like a lead suit.

"Bill!" I turn to see Don Miguel Reta standing with a group of people chatting. He grins at me with a deep pride and love on his dark weathered face.

I reach my hand out and he takes it and squeezes it. This powerful energy seems to rush up through his hand into my arm and explodes in my heart. I look him in the eyes and there's nothing to say; everything is there in that simple gesture.

And finally I am at the doors of the horse patio. I text JuanPe, and he materializes at the door in his white Murrillo uniform with his broad grin. I hand him the envelope full of his money.

"This is not important, Bill. You need rest, this could have waited," JuanPe says, and hugs me.

"JuanPe, I'm sorry this happened like this. I didn't know they hadn't paid you for your work. If I would have known, I would have done this sooner. You're my dear friend. Thank you for doing what you did. Thank you for being there for me in the hospital when I needed a friend. Thank you for everything."

JuanPe hugs me.

"Gracias a ti, Bill."

"I'm sorry, JuanPe, I'm really tired. I have to go back and go to sleep."

"Bill, gracias," he says with a grin. "Take care of yourself. You look pale. Rest, please."

I start back along the bullring. Our friendship's safe, not because of the money, but because I did the right thing to protect our bond, even if it wasn't my problem. *JuanPe put a lot of work in. He spent money he didn't have to spend; he did it for them but in some part he did it for me, and for his culture. And now it's all right, and now I can sleep.*

I start back through the sea of people exiting the bullfight. Another group of them rushes up excitedly. "BILL HILLMANN!!!! *Eres increible! Eres loco! Tengo mucho respecto por ti."* More photos. "Gracias… gracias…" I tell them as I fight back tears and patiently give them all they ask of me. They wish me well, they ask if I am OK. A group of young runners I recognize from the pueblos in Navarra rush up. The little Indian kid from Puente la Reina squeezes through them and up to me. His dark face peers at me worriedly.

"Bill Hillmann, are you OK?!" I want to tell him: No, I think I might be dying. But I grin and nod. *If I die today it would be a great day to die.* They pat me on the back as I continue through Telefonica as brilliant shivers swirl through my chest.

They never stop coming up to me. They bring this energy to me, like little cortados. But still I know it will fade soon. I keep trying to get through the well-wishers. My body aches, the pain spikes, and the exhaustion takes hold. Then a new group of well-wishers rushes up and hugs me and brings me a new boost of energy. It's like they're healing me, like they're a series of waves of healing washing over me, and they keep coming. On Estafeta suddenly Raul Lasierra, the mayoral at Toro Passion, steps in my path and folds his arms across his chest; he pops his chin up and his floppy hair bounces on his brow.

"Bill Hillmann!" he says with a grin, holding his hand out before me to make me stop.

Then he motions to a dozen of his friends, Josechu and a dozen guys I recognize as runners from all over the country. They mob me, they hug me, they steal my hat and make me take a big group photo with them. I am in the front row, and they try to make me crouch down with the others in the front row. I try to bend, but the pain spikes in my back and hips; they push me down and I cringe into a crouch for them as they snap a few shots. Across the street Chapu and Turley see me and point and laugh. I ask for my hat as they urge me to stay. I apologize and tell them I want to, but I have to sleep. They flop my hat back down on my head and pat me on the back as I continue down the last stretch of Estafeta. The people watch me; I grin and wave. My vision begins to tremble and fade out. The people watching me, their faces morph and turn sad. *Don't be sad, it's fiesta!* Every step on the cobblestones seems to expel all the energy I have left down into that ancient beautiful street. The world tips over on a hard tilt. I stagger sideways. Suddenly Pablo Bolo appears with his spikey hair and green penuelo.

"Bill!" Bolo says. "Are you sick? You need to go back to the hospital!"

I try to speak but I can't. He grabs me by my shoulders. His eyes widen.

"I'm OK," I stammer.

"You are not OK!" he says, touching my face. His eyes tell me how bad I must look. "Please let us help you!"

He takes my arm and slings it over his shoulder. His friend converges on us and puts my other arm around his shoulder. They carry me a few yards toward Tom's place. Tears well in my eyes. *Why, why do you guys care about me so much?* Their hands seem to ward off the dizziness and weakness, and after a few yards, I stop.

"I'm OK guys, thank you, I am almost home. Just enjoy fiesta for me, OK?" I say.

"Are you sure?"

"Yes, yes, I just got a little weak."

They look at me startled and worried. I assure them with a nod, and they go back to their girlfriends, who are waiting behind them.

"Thank you," I tell them and round the corner to Gowen's red door. I open it and step into the dark silent shadowy hall. I climb a few steps, then sit down on them. I lean forward, putting my elbows on my knees, and I hold my face in my hands. *I don't deserve this, this love. These people, they don't even know me, why do they love me? I'm not who they think I am. I'm just a little construction worker from Chicago.* Tears stream down my face. The love of the people of Pamplona and all of Spain swells in my chest. *I love you. I love all of you so much. Viva San Fermin...* I sit there in the dark with the warm tears pouring down my face—alone in the quiet in San Fermines.

After a few minutes, I get my shit together and climb up the stairs and walk into the kitchen. Tom sits at the table drinking some wine out of a small glass.

"JuanPe has his money."

"Good work, kid," Tom says with a grin. He raises his glass toward me and sips it. I drift down the hall, lie down in bed, and I sleep for a long, long time.

♉

My phone ringing wakes me in the middle of the night. I roll over and find it. I answer.

An Englishman's voice comes through the receiver. "Hello, is this Bill Hillmann?"

"Yeah, who's this?" I say as the exhaustion blurs my voice into a mumble.

"I'm a columnist with the *Chicago Tribune*. I'd like to dedicate my whole column tomorrow to you and your story."

"Wait, you're with the *Tribune*?" I ask. "You sound British."

"Yes, I've been living in Chicago for several years now."

"OK," I sigh. "What do you want to know?"

"Well, you know there's been a lot of commenters chiming in online, and I wanted to know if you can answer why you do this?"

Delirium swirls through me as I try to explain that humanity has been running with large game for at least two million years, ever since *Homo erectus* ran African buffalo in the Oldivia Gorge. I hear laughter, him and one of his colleagues laughing in the newsroom. A flash of rage shoots through me. *You're fucking with the wrong suelto right now, motherfucker. You know what I just been through? I got a drain hanging out of my ass. I might be fucking dying from this infection. I just told CNN off, you really think I give a fuck?*

"What I really want to know is, have you read any of the comments on these articles? What do you have to say to all the people commenting on these articles about you?" he asks.

Pshh. Oh, they got jokes? Motherfuckers in glass houses shouldn't be chucking stones. I grin. "All I really gotta say is, all of you can eat a huge...fat...nasty...dick." I giggle as the pain sprouts up along my tailbone. "You're boring, pathetic, fat dumb people who vote for Donald Trump and have no interests except McDonald's and malls." A stab of pain digs into my hips. "Come on, you know it, you're from the UK. The whole world knows America is, by and large, full of idiots. These dipshits commenting on these stories, the most interesting thing that happened to them this year is probably somebody shouted at them 'cause their dog was barking." I laugh as something stabs into my shoulder. "They have no understanding of this culture. Why do they comment at all? It's an ignorant attack on someone's cultural identity. I'm not going to listen to that shit from them. Learn some respect. I love these people in Spain, and this culture."

My heart swells thinking about all of them: JuanPe, Aitor, Xabi, Cristian, my friends that helped me. I go on: "The Spanish and the people from Pamplona are the most incredible beautiful people. This culture of bull running, when guys like Aitor and JuanPe are leading bulls, it's high art, it's like ballet!" My mind flicks through the faces I passed on my walk to the bullring earlier that day. "These people know what I've done, and what I've been through. I can't even walk down the streets in fiesta. People are showering me with love, grabbing me and asking for photos with me. Some of the greatest bull runners from Pamplona were at my bedside, and I'm supposed to give a rat's ass about what some boneheads in America think of me? Fuck you, bitches!" Another dagger stabs my pelvis as rage flashes through my torso.

"You know what PETA people are?" I ask. "They're miserable idiotic stuck-up losers who have no friends." The reporter chortles. "They're arrogant, and they hate human beings so much they put animals over their fellow man. Oh, but they still put themselves over animals. They watched too many Disney films; they completely lost touch with the reality of being human.

We are apes that kill and eat meat; we are bloody animals." Red flashes through my vision. "I tell them, 'Oh, attacking and lying about a foreign culture you know absolutely nothing about is, by definition, racism!' They say, 'Oh, well you're a speciesist!' Dumb motherfuckers, of course I am! I am human, I literally kill and eat other species, and wear their skin as clothing. Human beings are the apex predator of Planet Earth. You think we could become that without being speciesist?! Ya morons!"

I seethe with a kind of wicked satisfied chuckle that only a great and complete rant can give you. Then: *Wait, who the fuck are you talking to right now?*

"Who the hell is this?" I ask.

"Kim Janssen, *Chicago Tribune*," he replies.

"Oh man, I probably shouldn't be talking to you right now." I hang up.

Fuck, what kind of journalist asks questions like that? Well, that oughta make for a fucking riot of a story. The exhaustion from the infection swirls through my back as I sink into the mattress. *Did you just fuck up? Fuck it, no one will take something like that seriously. You're obviously playing around. It'll read like one of those wacky Mike Royko talks with Slats Grobnik.* I guffaw and burst into laughter. *Did you really just say all that shit to a national newspaper? You are a fucking idiot!* I cringe lying there on my back watching the ceiling as fiesta bustles outside the windows. *You asshole.* I sigh, then start giggling as the exhaustion finally swallows me whole and I delve into the soft comfort of sleep.

♉

Trying to listen to David Rodriguez's advice, I lay low and heal up for a couple days. The infection and pain settle down some. On the twelfth, I go out on the balcony overlooking Estafeta with Maria and Tom to watch the encierro. I grip the railing as the music fills the street and the runners begin to round the curve. *Damn, this is the first time I watched an encierro from a balcony in Pamplona in twelve years.* An image of Miguel Angel Perez saving Xabier Salillas from Vaparoso flashes through my mind. *It's only my second time ever.* The runners fill the street as the families watch from the balconies. The rocket pops and everyone starts the bouncing stampede. The bulls thunder around the bend and shoot up the street, four lean black bulls out front. My friend Jack Denault eases out in front of the lead bull's bobbing horns in his white collared shirt and short running pants. It is like my vision zooms in and time slows to an almost halt. He dashes ahead of the four bulls, leading them perfectly up the center of Estafeta. The thrill of it explodes in my chest.

"JACK!!!!!!!!!!!!" He turns to his right to escape, but the bull next to him gains on him. A horn sneaks up under his arm as he tries to cut back left. "NOOOO!!!!!!!!"

The lead bull digs his horns into Jack. He topples to the cobblestones as the animals trample over him. *Fucking looks like he got gored!* I run downstairs to the last place I saw him. Runners mill the streets: no medics, nothing. I walk to the intersection. Jack is standing there arguing with the medics.

"Jack! Are you OK?! Were you gored?"

"No," he yells. "No, I'm OK."

"Thank God." I go to hug him, but he resists.

"Well, I'm not OK," he seethes. "My shoulder is really hurt."

"Well, go to the hospital, man!"

"No!" he yells angrily. "I'm not going anywhere without Victoria. Will you go get her for me?"

"Yeah, where is she?"

"She's at Txoko."

"OK." I hurry toward Txoko, looking for Jack's wife.

Victoria stands there alone, her face worried, holding her arms across her chest with her reddish-brown hair draped over her shoulders. A couple of the guys stand with her, trying to keep her company. I hurry toward her. *Be calm, so she'll be calm.* I take a deep breath.

"Victoria. OK, listen, he is fine." I reach out and hold her softly by both shoulders. "He wasn't gored, he's OK," I tell her calmly.

"Well, why isn't he here then!" she says angrily.

"He told me to come get you." I put my arm around her shoulder and we start walking back toward Estafeta.

"I don't understand why he isn't here!" she says.

"The medics are trying to get him to go to the hospital," I explain.

"Why won't he go!?" she yells.

"Because he's refusing to go anywhere without you."

"He has to go to the hospital." She starts to cry, and I try to console her as we hurry toward Jack.

"He's OK, he was really lucky, he's going to be fine."

We round the corner to Estafeta and I point to him.

"He's right there, if you want to run to him he's right there."

She hurries to him and they hug, and Jack mouths *Thank You* to me.

"You're welcome," I say as the guys rush up to him. I look at Jack's torn pant leg. *Looks like a horn did that.* "That pant leg is ripped... You're lucky, Jack."

They head off to the hospital. I walk off and find Aitor and Xabi, and we chitchat and wait for everyone else in front of the café near Telefonica. David Rodriguez stands in front of a nearby café in his white gear and green patches. I sigh and walk up to him.

"David, perdoname for running so soon, you were right," I say.

"It's ugly," David scolds me. "You were so hurt."

"I know. I'm sorry, but I was hoping to run tomorrow if that was OK with you."

"Naw." He turns his back to me.

"David, por favor! I've been in bed for two days, I feel better now."

He pauses, considering my request. His young daughters ask, "Who is that guy, Daddy," and point at me. I wave at them; I'd met them before in Sanse.

Then David turns back grins and says, "OK, OK you can run."

"Gracias David, gracias maestro!"

He giggles and we hug.

I walk back over, and Xabi looks at me like I'm totally nuts.

"What the hell was that?" Xabi asks.

"What? I had to ask him something..." I reply.

Xabi giggles and shakes his head; he has a befuddled look on his face. I ride with him to Huarte so we can all have breakfast. The pain and exhaustion suddenly surge back as I eat. I observe the others as they goof off over breakfast. *They're such a great group of guys, so wholesome and heartfelt.* At the end, I drop a fifty-euro note on the table.

"No no! Bill!" Xabi says.

"No!" Aitor pleads.

"Es un regalo!" I glare at Xabi angrily. "Es un regalo," I growl at Aitor. They glance at each other and quiet down. "You guys are very, very good people. I'm very grateful for what you did for me."

"Thank you."

I look at Aitor, then Xabi, then David. "You are great friends." They pat me on the back.

The fifty pays for most of the table. We head back to town on the bus. They are going to the hospital. I want to go, but the exhaustion grips me. I walk home and go back to bed. There is nothing I can do. If the exhaustion comes, I sleep. If I feel OK, I go out to the street. My body, the infection, and pain are the boss.

I run the next day, but I'm really incapable of running. It's just too much. I dive to the side and an old man trips over me. I apologize to him as he scolds me for getting in his way. As I apologize and rub his back, my friend, a good Basque runner named Isidro, comes up and laughs at us.

"Are you crazy?" he says to the old man. "Do you know what this guy went through this fiesta?" He points at me. "Just that he's out here is a miracle!"

"No, no, I shouldn't be running." I look the old man in the eyes. "Lo siento. I'm sorry."

I limp away and bump into El Boti puffing a smoke in Plaza del Castillo. His energetic personality and serene seriousness hypnotize me as he talks about the fear.

"It's so powerful. I can't think about the encierro all year. I do everything I can not to think about it, or else I am awake all night full of this, this fear!" he says, smoking. "I don't smoke all year, now here I am smoking!" He guffaws as I giggle and spark my cigar. *A maestro like you, so humble to talk about his own fear. Wow.* El Boti continues his urgent speech, his hazel eyes glowing as his clean-shaven head gleams in the morning light. *I think I'm gonna start running Santo Domingo with you.* There's something spiritual down there with those guys, flowing beneath the idol of San Fermin with the bulls at their backs.

♉

The night before the last run of fiesta, I write a post on Facebook to the runners: "I wish I could be with you on the street tomorrow, but I will be running with you in my dreams."

When I fall asleep, I dream of the encierro. The bulls charging up the street and El Boti turning at the line, his small body zooming ahead of the massive black bulls, leading them up the way, and as he cuts to the wall, Chapu dashes before them; his eyes light up above his furry beard as he springs out of the way of a bull that leaps up at his back. Xabi takes the lead, his muscular frame powering through the bailing bodies before he shoots to the to the wall where Cristian Yodi waits. Cristian runs them through town hall; his giant body plows through the mob of runners with the horns of the bulls at his back, then David Lerga thunders in front of them down Mercaderes, pacing with them coolly, his face in a tight grimace. He hugs the inside of the curve, and then Raul Lasierra picks them up, his tall thin frame and long gait scooting them up lower Estafeta and then out of the curve. Then Fernando Del Valle in his purple striped shirt scorches ahead of them, leading them through Estafeta, and David Rodriguez with his bold green patches at the chest gathers control and ushers them through Estafeta as Sergio Colas blisters in front of them and brings them to Pablo Bolo, who scoots in front, twisting back to maintain connection as his green penuelo whips in the air, and he passes them to JuanPe with his pants rolled at the knee, and Aitor thin and agile bouncing through the air like a gazelle, and my two dear friends run together, steaming toward the arena like the old days. Someone whispers: "Your friends."

I wake up as the bulls thunder below Tom Gowen's windows down the hall. I climb out of bed and into the hallway feeling horrible and tired and sick.

"What happened? Is everyone OK?" I ask sleepily.

"Yes, everyone is OK," Maria says from the couch as she watches the encierro.

"Is that Aitor?" I see Aitor falling in the slow-motion replay in the tunnel. "Is he OK?!" I ask.

"Yes, I think so," Maria replies.

"Are you sure?" I blink wearily, holding the doorjamb. "Is everyone OK?"

"Yes." She looks at me, confused.

"OK. OK, thanks." I limp back into the room, fall into bed, and sleep.

An hour and a half later, I wake up to five angry messages from JuanPe. "Where are you?! Aitor is hurt! He needs you!"

I jump up and run around like my head is on fire.

"What the hell's wrong?" Tom asks.

"Aitor's hurt!" I shout. "Oh my god, I got to get to the hospital!" I run out the door, down the steps, and across Plaza del Castillo; I jump in a cab and shoot straight to the hospital.

Once I get there, I run inside to the information window.

"Which room is Aitor Aristregui in?"

"He's not here."

"Wait, is he at the other hospital?"

"No, they already released him."

"Thank god. OK, he is OK." I go and sit down in the waiting room, still hyperventilating; I take a picture of myself in the hospital and send it to Aitor with the message, "I'm here at the hospital, where are you?!"

"I'm in Plaza del Castillo!" he writes back.

I laugh and jump a cab, right back to the exact place I was when I found out he got hurt.

The guys come out of the overhang right by Tom's door. Aitor looks sick and somber.

"How are you?" I ask Aitor. "Are you OK?"

"I am…" He shrugs. "I am…"

"I didn't know, I'm sorry. I would have come right away."

"It's OK, Bill."

We stand right next to Tom's apartment.

"Do you guys want to go up to my friend's apartment? It's like an encierro museum."

"Yes," Aitor says. "Let's go."

"It's a lot of stairs though. Are you sure?" I ask Aitor.

"Yes, I'm OK," he says. "I want to go."

I call Tom and write him a few messages; he doesn't reply. *Fuck, he's got a strict rule about bringing people up to his place.* I scratch my chin as they watch me, waiting.

"I know he's up there," I whine.

I push the buzzer a few times.

"Fuck it, let's go."

We climb up. Aitor is lagging a little behind. The guys try to help him, but he refuses their help. I wince watching him painfully climb the stairs. *Maybe we shouldn't have gone up.* I knock on the door. Tom throws the door open angrily.

"What in the hell is this?!" Tom explodes at me, his face red. "I specifically told you no one comes up here without my prior approval!"

"Tom, I'm sorry but I wanted to bring the guys up to meet you and see the apartment," I whine sheepishly.

"Ohh boy, you really fucked up now." He straightens up, glaring at me. "Maria is the shower, for chrissake!"

"Tom, this is Aitor, Xabi, Cristian, and David. They're the runners I've been telling you about."

"That's not Aitor, Aitor is hurt!"

"No, he's OK," I tell him.

"No, yes I was hurt," Aitor says. "My knee is hurt. But the medics released me."

Tom grimaces at me. "You fucker, you!"

I look at the guys. "I'm sorry!"

Xabi grimaces at me and shakes his head angrily. *Fuck, he's pissed! Aitor might have climbed all them stairs for nothing!*

"You motherfucker, you!" Xabi says, and clenches his fist and cocks it back at me like he's going to punch me playfully.

Tom opens the door to the bathroom. "Maria, we got company."

"OK," she replies.

"Come in." The guys walk in wide-eyed, looking at all the pictures and the balcony that opens onto Estafeta. We walk the hall. Tom describes the blown-up black-and-white pictures. He points to the big one of James Michener and the two guys getting gored on Santo Domingo. Tom yuks it up a little and says both the gored guys died.

"No! That's not true! I know the names and dates of every death in San Fermín!" Xabi confronts the exaggeration.

I cringe and try to shush him. Xabi looks at me angrily.

I whisper, "Solo cornadas... solo cornadas..." grinning.

Xabi chills out. Then Xabi sees the balconies looking out onto Plaza del Castillo and hurries over, guffawing.

"Balconies on Estafeta and Plaza del Castillo! Don Tom, I want to buy your apartment. How much?!" he yells.

"Well, I don't know... how much you got?" Tom replies grinning.

We all giggle, still looking at the pictures. I knew those two knuckleheads would get along. Maria gets dressed and comes in, and her and David hit it off. Xabi guffaws again and hurries back out onto the balcony.

"It's the best apartment for San Fermín I've ever seen!" he shouts.

"Who is that guy?" Tom grins.

"That's Xabi," I say. "Pronounced 'Shobby.'"

Tom grins sadistically. "The guy's name is Shabby?"

I burst out laughing. Leave it to Don Tommy-Boy to bust the balls of the biggest ball-breaker in the gang.

"What? What did he say?" David asks.

I get my shit together. "'Shobby' sounds like 'Shabby,'" I say, laughing. "In English, a shabby person is someone with bad clothes and an ugly house."

"But it's not true," Aitor says. "He dresses really well and has a nice house!" We giggle.

"I know, that's why it's so funny! He's like a model, with his perfect hair and nice clothes."

We all laugh. Xabi comes back from the balcony; we all look at him awkwardly.

"What?" he asks.

"Bad news, Xabi, Tom says your name sounds like 'Shabby.' It means a person with bad clothes and an ugly house."

"No! Really?!" Xabi says, and looks like a sad puppy.

I pat him on the shoulder. "You bust everybody's balls all the time. How's it feel, Shabby!" I pat his chest as Tom grins.

"It's Xabi, not Shabby," Xabi whines, fighting back a grin.

We start to head out. *Fuck, I hope I didn't fuck things up with Tom, bringing these guys up unannounced.* I tell the guys goodbye, so I can apologize to Gowen.

Xabi guffaws, "But I didn't pay for my ticket to the museum yet!" He rolls his eyes at me as they go down the steps.

I sit on the steps as Gowen and Maria start down.

"Tom, I'm really sorry."

"Oh no, you fucked up this time, kid! You really fucked up..."

"I just really wanted them to meet you and see the place."

Tom grins looming over me. "Kid, you know I'm just fucking with you, right? Go catch up to your friends."

I burst into laughter. "Thanks Tom!" I shout and hurry down the stairs and head out with them.

Cristian says goodbye in the bright sunlight of Plaza del Castillo, his giant frame slouching a little in sadness.

"My giant friend," I tell him, and give him a big hug. "You know I'll never forget what you did for me."

"Bill." He pats my back. "It was nothing..."

The guys and me go around toward Mercaderes. David says his goodbye to us on the street he runs; sadness falls along his muscular brow. We all hug him. *Fuck, fiesta is really over.*

Then Xabi, Aitor, and I walk up Estafeta slowly, the street still thick with revelers. Suddenly Aitor's face turns pale grey. His tall frame staggers slightly sideways. *Fuck!* I grab him by the shoulders.

"Are you in pain, Aitor? Are you OK?!" I ask urgently.

He fights back tears. His body's limp and weak in my hands. Xabi hugs him, then takes Aitor's arm and puts it around his shoulder. They turn up the street before me. They walk together, their arms around each other's shoulders up the dark cobblestones of Estafeta with the balconies rising into the heavens above them.

I follow them with this great sadness and exhaustion weighing me down. *Should I grab his other arm and put it around my shoulder? But what if it makes it harder for him to walk?* An old man's voice swirls through my mind. *You are the witness...* The great sorrow of the end of fiesta fills my chest as I look up at the channel of blue sky as two of the brightest spirits of their generation help each other up the way. *Look at them, two of the young runners, the torchbearers, carrying the flaming torches of their tradition. The great runner and the great colorful spirit.* Aitor bumps his head against Xabi's. *Do you see how Xabi will protect him?* I nod and blink back tears as a gleaming thread of light spills through the soft clouds above. The sweetest joy mixes in with the sadness and overtakes it. *What a beautiful friendship. I'm humbled by the honor of being part of this walk. Thank you, San Fermín, for this and for our friendship.* We step into Plaza del Castillo and Aitor gives me his phone.

"Bill, will you take a picture of us?"

"Of course." I take the camera as they grin sadly in the bright midday sunlight in Plaza del Castillo. I see them in the viewfinder, the tall thin Aitor with his grandfather grinning on his chest and his arm around the shorter stout Xabi, with his spiky hair glistening in the sunlight. I click a few shots of two best friends clinging to their last moments of fiesta together. We look at the pictures and smile. We hug and say goodbye and we all go our separate ways. I guess that's what I've been trying to do all along, take a picture of them with these words; I hope I've done my duty.

I still don't know how bad it was in the tunnel that morning. I don't know that Aitor nearly lost his life.

☿

In the afternoon I go to see the death of the majestic animal these people love and worship—the beast that has given me so much pain and the purest of joys. JuanPe brings me through the back of the bullring. I thank him.

"Have you talked to Aitor!" JuanPe asks angrily, pain stretched across his brow. "Have you seen him?!"

"Yes, he's OK. I saw him."

JuanPe turns away from me and gets on the phone, still upset. He walks down into the tunnel, talking with someone. Then he hangs up and texts someone. I watch him with my heart aching. *Bill, you hurt him. You let him down.* I tell myself it's OK now, Aitor's fine. Down the tunnel I can see Padilla drawing a black bull to himself with his red cape. I walk over to JuanPe and put my hand on his shoulder. He winces at me.

"I'm sorry I wasn't there. I was asleep. I thought he was OK," I tell him. "But he's OK, it's all OK now. I was with him."

"Don't tell me it was OK." JuanPe's eyes tremble. "You weren't there!"

"OK, I don't understand, JuanPe. What happened?!"

The crowd's roar builds as the big black bull leaps through Padilla's cape, his forelegs kicking up in the air.

"It was so bad!" JuanPe says; his big torso trembles.

"Wait, wait, what happened?! I really don't know! I've been sick, I don't know what happened!"

"It was very bad this morning. I had to grab the horn tip to pull it away from Aitor," JuanPe says angrily.

"What?!" I'm stunned. "Are you serious?"

JuanPe angrily pulls his phone out and shows me a photo. The image is one of the greatest images I've ever seen and maybe will ever see in all my life. It's a shot that someone sent him from inside the tunnel. The black Miura bulls are crushing Aitor and JuanPe into the wall. They are both falling, and the horn of the lead bull is pressing into Aitor's spine near the neck. JuanPe is reacting with split-second reflexes; he's grabbing the tip of the horn and pulling it away, keeping the bull from goring and maybe paralyzing or killing Aitor.

"Oh my god! You saved his life!" I yell.

"I don't know," JuanPe says. "But I tried to help him."

"My god, this is the greatest photo I've ever seen, JuanPe. You saved him!"

We look in each other's eyes. The torment of the life-and-death moment he'd experienced a few hours earlier shows in his trembling face.

"I didn't know." I hug him. "Thank you for saving him. JuanPe, thank you for saving our friend."

JuanPe tells me the full story of that morning with Aitor, and I observe it from several photos and videos. Aitor enters the tunnel leading the first set of big beautiful black Miura. JuanPe is in the tunnel, leading too. Aitor and JuanPe tangle as the herd swings wide, crushing them into the wall. The horn of the lead bull digs up under Aitor's armpit. JuanPe, in the most important moment in his entire career as a runner, reaches out and grips the tip of the horn and pulls with all his might. He keeps it from penetrating Aitor's back, but the horn slides up and digs into Aitor's spine at his neck. With his last bit of balance and strength JuanPe pulls up again and lifts the horn out of Aitor's spine, saving Aitor. They fall, and Aitor's knee hits hard on the stones. Then JuanPe pulls Aitor into the safety of the chamber along the floor of the tunnel. Aitor is very grey and in shock. JuanPe is not one of those Basque guys who shows a lot of affection with friends. But here, JuanPe bows his head and kisses Aitor on the forehead—this runner from the new generation, this boy that JuanPe helped lift to greatness. He holds Aitor's hand as the medics work on him, and he stays with Aitor until his friends and family arrive.

This is a moment that can only be described as magic. The two greatest Basque runners of their generations, with one passing the torch to the next in a last-second gesture of kindness of generosity. There's no question Julen, who years ago passed the torch to JuanPe, is looking down at them from the afterlife with pride and tremendous joy.

This is why I will always return to Spain; it's not just for the friendships and the bulls and the adventures. The magic of San Fermin has touched my heart deeply. And maybe I'm the only one from outside the culture who can truly see it. And maybe I'm crazy. But I'm in love with this tradition, and I know I will always come back, hoping to once again feel this magic.

Chapter 19

My Healthcare Odyssey

Things begin to fall apart as I travel home to Panama to be with Enid.

I suffer through the four-hour bus to Madrid, the seven-hour flight to Newark. I cut in front of a line of seven hundred people to squeeze through customs and limp quickly to my five-hour flight to Panama City, Panama. The pain and exhaustion have their grip on me as I board the six-hour-long night bus from Panama City to David City, Chiriquí. I can't get comfortable even though I'm in the biggest, best seat, the front top row of the double-decker. My tailbone is twitching and sending little sparks of pain into my groin. My bus rolls into town around twenty-four hours after leaving Pamplona. Enid stands outside the bus; her beautiful brown eyes look into mine and her smiling round cheeks gleam deep brown. I climb down. We hug. Her body throbs as she cries in my arms.

"I'm sorry, baby. I love you," I tell her. She takes my hand and we walk down the rowdy David City street in the morning light as the families set up their makeshift street market shops and the hungry street dogs trot and cut between the pink and white taxicabs.

We check into a nearby hotel room, and since we haven't seen each other in a month we immediately have sex. As we make passionate and somewhat violent love, my hips, pelvis, and groin burn in pain. After we do it another time, the pain worsens. I try to lie back and get comfortable. *What the fuck is going on? I should be healing up by now.*

♉

We arrive in Volcán, and Al and Paula greet me with a few lighthearted jokes about the goring as I look at the beautiful manicured lawn with the sweet birds chirping and the big dark volcano looming over the white wall surrounding the property. As I drift to sleep in our cozy bed that night, I grin to myself. *It's all over Billy-boy. You did it again. And now you can just rest and write and be with her.* I rub her soft back under the covers.

A jolt of pain sparks me awake in the hours before sunrise. I moan out and grab my hips. *What the fuck is going on?* I roll over and try to find a position that will stop the pain. It starts to worsen, slowly building like a tide, rising and engulfing me. The throbbing pain gets so bad I begin to panic. It builds slowly, then spikes. I tremble, gasping. *Is this going to fucking stop?!* It subsides, only to thunder back worse a few minutes later. *It ain't stopping. Fuck you gotta get some painkillers.* It peaks again, feeling like the tip of several bulls horns are entering me and twisting around inside. I wake her.

"I'm in a lot of pain," I say, breathing hard. "I'm scared."

She takes me to the local hospital. IVs are popular in rural Panama. If you sprain your ankle, they give you an IV. Have a cold, a weird rash, a toothache? You guessed it, IV. When I enter the white, one-room emergency room, all the patients have an IV, even one of the nurses. You'd think they'd be good at administering IVs. They ain't.

My nurse, a bossy, chunky lady in all white, stabs the IV needle into my hand and digs it around. I scream and writhe until I pull a Duran.

"No! No mas!" I yell at her.

"You are very sensitive!" she scolds me, and walks off to torture someone else.

She comes back and finally jams in a really bad IV and tapes it to my hand. When she leaves, I hold it up and look at it. IV fluid and blood leak all over my hand and the bed. *You ain't complaining, or else this crazy chick is gonna come back and start stabbing you again.* Other voices scream in the adjacent rooms as she moves on to new patients.

Though the facility is very state-of-the-art, with X-ray machines and sophisticated equipment, they don't have the technicians to run the machines. They also don't have the pain meds and antibiotics I need, so Enid goes across town to the drugstore to get them. She comes back and they connect the medicines to my IV. The pain from my hips slowly subsides, even though half the medicine is leaking onto my bed. I glance at the wet white covers and chuckle. *Well, hope you're feeling better too.* I pat the covers.

We go home, and within a few hours the pain in my crotch returns. Anger gets the better of me. I hop up. *All you need to do is some squats and this shit will straighten out!* I stand in the center of our dark apartment, and as I angrily dip, my groin tightens. *Fuck, that didn't help. Maybe you need to stretch your back.* I arch my stiff back and yank it to get a deep stretch. A pop jolts in my lower back, then my nerves come alive with electric twitches near my tailbone. *Oh.* I sit on the bed. *You fucked up now!* Within an hour a pain rushes in, so severe I can't stand, let alone walk.

I lie in the bed trembling. *Are you fucking paralyzed? Are you dying? Jesus, what the fuck is happening to you?* Enid goes out, trying to figure out how to get me to a real hospital. *What the fuck did you do to yourself?*

♉

We borrow a wheelchair, and Enid wheels me to a cab that takes us back to the big city of David, to a private hospital. That's when the money starts flowing.

Everything in the private healthcare system in Panama is payment up front. Except for the doctors; you pay for them right after they look at you. Each regular one is twenty bucks, and specialists cost a hundred. Doctors and specialists flood in to see me for little or no reason, and the bills start stacking up.

We pay five hundred up front for the X-rays of my hips and pelvis. They come back negative. They want an MRI, which is twelve hundred bucks. I ask what the bill is; they tally up the five doctors and specialists who saw me and bring me a bill. I cough up over a thousand bucks for the visit, and we go back to the hotel.

As I lie flat on the hotel bed, my tailbone begins to tingle, and spasms shoot into my right groin. Enid gets me hot water from the hotel restaurant in a rubber water bag, and I put the bag on my throbbing groin. The pain cools. Then my left hip spasms. Every time I move the bag, the pain migrates to some new horrible place.

At two a.m. we get in a cab back to the private emergency room. They pull out a huge syringe with a metal plunger with the loops for the fingers. The metal creaks as she pushes half the morphine into my vein. She waits a few seconds, then injects the rest. I only remember waking up in my hotel room the next morning.

The pain thunders back. I fall into fever. In the delirium I scream and moan. *Are you dying? Is this how you die? OK Bill, this really could be it. You gotta write your last words.* I think back to Spain. *Fuck, that stupid trip rant. Oh god, is that really gonna be the last thing people read about you, ranting and raving about your frustrations with Americans? Fuck that.* I get on my computer and write an email to the *Trib* reporter. I write that I love America, and that I don't regret what I said, because sometimes we have to hold a mirror up to the faces of people we love so they can see themselves and become better versions of themselves. And that if I never walk again, or something worse comes of this, I want everyone to know that I don't regret running, I did it with passion for the culture I love.

The *Trib* runs it with a crappy cheap-shot headline. The headlines for both stories are misleading. Kim Janssen asked me directly to respond to the zany people who commented on the stories; I didn't just start ranting for no reason. The stories themselves are OK. But the headlines are unethical, and done in poor taste. Still, I feel better about it all.

My body, however, is worsening, I am only sleeping while on extreme painkillers. The fever comes and goes. I fall into a hopeless kind of fog. I vaguely understand what's happening around me. I am extremely weak and tense waiting for the next bout of extreme pain to swirl up on me. I am losing hope that they will figure out what is happening to me. We return to the private hospital and they suggest we go to the regional hospital, where it will be almost free.

♉

The regional hospital is a high-rise concrete structure. It looms above us as Enid helps me to my feet. Dozens of worried people mill in front of the glass doors. After basically carrying me to a bench, Enid has to fight for a wheelchair.

We wait two hours to enter the regional hospital's emergency room. I wilt in the wheelchair. I didn't think it would be like this. The pain, fever, and exhaustion have put me into a dreary half-sleep state. I squeeze Enid's cool hand as she sits beside me. It's like I'm on a bad amusement park ride and there ain't no getting off it.

Finally, they call my name, and Enid wheels me in through the tattered wooden swinging doors. We enter a small room with three doctors in it. Every few minutes an alarm goes off and someone yells "Code Blue!" and the three doctors run out to save someone's life. After several Code Blue interruptions one of them—an exhausted, agitated young doctor with short black hair and clear-framed glasses—gets back to my entry paperwork. As he finishes it, an elderly woman in a purple flower-patterned housedress dies right behind me in the hallway. The doctors rush to her. The doctor that did my paperwork straddles her, pushing rhythmically on her chest: a crunching of ribs, suction like a plunger slurping at a stopped-up toilet. Her mouth leaks white fluid. After several moments, they fail to resuscitate her and they let her go right there in the hallway next to us. Her daughter and grandson scream at the wooden swinging doors as the security guard tries to pull them out into the lobby.

They wheel me into another long hallway full of people in hospital beds and sitting on blue plastic chairs that line the walls. They all look like they are dying. We sit there for a while without many answers. Then people actually begin to die. So many people die that I lose count. Over the next seven hours, stretchers with zipped-up body bags slowly float past us to the elevators, on their way down to the morgue. I try not to look at them. I try to sleep. The pain worsens. The exhaustion is so heavy. I break into sweats, then shiver. I watch a black body bag slowly float past me. *Are you going to fucking die in this hallway?* Enid urges me to be patient; she places her cool brown hand on my veiny wrist. I receive no care. I dream of ghosts murmuring all around me. The moans of an extremely thin old man in a stretcher near me wake me up. His pale arms and legs tremble violently. He stares up at the light above him as if it were the gates of heaven slowly opening before him.

A dark-skinned Jamaican guy wearing a cheap fedora, black sunglasses, and a blue hospital gown walks the halls with a drugged grin. He moves in a ghostly way. No one seems to acknowledge his presence. *Are you fucking hallucinating?* I look at Enid.

"Can you see him?"

"Yes."

Then the nurses start to yell at him. "Go back to your bed!"

He laughs and replies, "No…I am hungry! I am going to get food." He walks past us around a corner to a stand that sells potato chips, and continues to go back and forth for hours as I doze.

The sound of a man's wavering voice wakes me. A portly guy sits in a chair across from me. Bandages cover burns on his arms, and a big ash smear covers his shirt. He tells a story, staring blankly ahead of himself. He tells the story as if he is telling it to no one, as if he was telling it to himself. The women sitting around him weep.

"The car was engulfed in flames. I pulled the boys from the car. They were burned very badly, they were not breathing."

Two more stretchers approach from far down the hall as he speaks. Small body bags sit atop the stretchers. A middle-aged woman walks into the hall trembling beside me; a friend holds her. They stop at one of the small blue bags. She looks down at it, horrified. Her body convulses.

"My son…my son…" she cries.

Everyone in the hall cries, even the man who moves the bodies to the morgue. I try not to look at them. Because when I look at them I see a grey apparition of the young boy flowing up out of the bag and hugging his mother. I try not to feel the utter horror of both of their losses. Their misery and love seep inside me. *There is true suffering in this world, Bill.* Tears roll down my cheeks.

After ten hours in the hall, a fat, bald nurse wheels a big cart to me and gives me an IV, but no pain medicine. After another two hours, my legs grow rigid in the wheelchair.

"I have to get out of here," I tell Enid.

"No, we have to stay, they're going to help you," she pleads.

I scream at the nurses. "Aye, I need a bed! I need a fucking bed!" The Jamaican guy approaches with a bag of Fritos. "Give me his fucking bed! He doesn't even want his!" I yell.

This thrills the Jamaican.

"Yes! Yes! He wants the bed and I want the food. Give him my bed! And give me food!"

The nurses refuse to bargain with the Jamaican but decide to give me a recliner chair. They wheel me down the hall, where I expect to find the curtained rooms of an ER. Instead I enter a big square room filled with over a hundred hospital beds, all of them full of dying people. Some of the people look like they are already dead; others moan and tremble. An old man lies with no blanket in dirty white underwear. Strange blue and purple rashes dot his emaciated body. His mouth hangs open as his eyes dart around fearfully, watching something floating near the ceiling.

Enid and the male nurse help me to my feet. My legs refuse to straighten. They have locked in a deep bend from sitting so many hours in the chair tense with pain. My legs tremble as they refuse to straighten. After several moments they partially straighten. They flop me into the mauve recliner. I pant, horrified. *What the fuck is going on with your legs now?!* I struggle to sleep under the gigantic blaring AC unit. At nine a.m. they feed us baloney sandwiches and Styrofoam cups of some milky rice drink. An hour later a furious bald middle-aged man marches into the big room, yelling obscenities at all the nurses as they try and fail to stop him. He finds his frail, dying mother across from me and picks her up in his arms. She reaches up and touches his face softly.

"I thought I would never see you again, my baby," she says weakly.

Tears wet his face as he carries her out so she can die at home with her family.

The head nurse, an old woman with a kind face, tells me the MRI machine is broken but should be working in a few hours. I can't imagine staying there any longer and we leave.

We take a cab to a private hospital that will do the MRI for $500. We have it done, and a doctor brings us into a small room and tells us that my liver, spleen, and lymph nodes are enlarged. Enid translates, tears falling down her exhausted face. *Are you fucking dying?* They give me more pain meds and antibiotics. I am running a fever. The doctor tells me he wants to keep me and potentially do surgery on me. *Oh no, you ain't getting no surgery in this fuckin' hospital.* Enid looks into my eyes, horrified. Tears drip down her round face.

"We gotta go home."

♉

My dad cashes in some miles for us, and we fly home. I'm coping with the pain until the third flight, when two airport workers surprise me and do a full lift from my wheelchair and smash my head into the overhead bin. *Thanks a lot guys! I coulda gotten in the damn seat myself, but thanks.* The pain fires up again. My brother picks us up at the airport and drives us straight to the ER on my family doctor's orders. I feel horrible but relieved to be back in the American healthcare system. The relief ends quickly when they figure out I am one of the tens of millions of Americans who don't have health insurance.

This mean old lady nurse in blue scrubs keeps coming to my room and asking viciously, "Why are you here?!" I start to reply and she screams over me, "BUT WHY ARE YOU HERE?!" Her wrinkled ugly scowl trembles with rage.

"I CAN'T WALK!" I yell at her. "I am in horrible pain, I have an infection, my organs are enlarged, that's why I'm in this emergency room."

She leaves angrily.

Another nurse comes in and injects me intravenously with Dilaudid. The room starts spinning. After a few minutes it stops and the pain dissipates.

Then they send me downstairs for a CAT scan. The technician is like a blonde-haired Xena warrior princess, if Xena were having a mental breakdown. She conducts the test. As I'm transitioning back to my stretcher, she starts to help me and yanks me. I slide half-off the table onto the gurney. Sharp pain stabs my back, pelvis, and groin.

"Why did you do that to yourself?!" she yells at me.

Bitch! You did it to me! "Enid! Help me!" I yell between screams.

Enid appears at the door. The blonde Xena lady roars. "Don't come in here! It's like huge magnet in here!"

"What the fuck are you talking about, you fucking nutcase!?" I scream at her.

I slide myself on to the gurney and she pushes me out of the room. "I'm calling security!"

"Good, I want to talk to them and I want to talk to whoever the fuck hired you."

Security comes and we head back to the emergency room. The doctor comes in.

"Well, we can't figure out what's wrong, so we're going to send you home."

"Home? Why did I even come here!? How the hell am I going to get in my parents' house? Somebody's gonna have to carry me up the stairs!"

He caves, and they decide to keep me for observation. Sleeping with my legs and back inclined helps my back incredibly. The groin and pelvis spasms stop.

The next day a physical therapist comes and teaches me how to get up and down steps with crutches. I feel good, and I go home.

But once I'm there I fall right back into a fever and pain. I try to mimic the hospital bed by putting pillows under my knees, but it doesn't work; my spine starts twitching and the spasms start. After two days of that, I go to the general practitioner, and he gives me antibiotics and some powerful narcotic pain and inflammation medicine.

I ask him, "What's wrong with me?"

"Well, I don't know, you got some kinda bruisy teary thing in there."

I implode. *You crossed the damn continent for that diagnosis?* I use my crutches to head out. *You're not coming back, fuck all this whole fucking medical system. It's a damn joke.* I painfully climb into the car.

♉

Over the next few days I slowly start to improve. I begin to walk with a walker. After a week home, I can get up the stairs with the walker.

I convince Enid to go back to Panama so she doesn't screw up her Peace Corps volunteer status. The day she leaves, I sigh, sitting in the basement alone. *You gotta start driving for Uber again.* I look around the messy basement full of our lives we left behind when we moved to Panama. *If you have to sit down here in this much fucking pain, feeling fucking worthless and miserable, you're gonna fucking kill yourself. You still can't walk without a walker, but maybe you can just use the walker to get in the car.* I head outside on the walker, make it to the trunk, open it, and put the walker in. Then I brace myself with the car to slowly limp to the driver seat. I turn the app on and drive away. *Ever have a handicapped driver? Well, here I come. And I got a story, too.*

The next day I wake up and suddenly I can kind of walk without the walker. My dad takes me to get a massage; we see there's a physical therapy place down the hall, and we walk in. The physical therapist is young and muscular, with short buzzed brown hair; he's named Ian. He greets me with a handshake. *Well, this guy seems nice.* He looks me in the eyes and winces like he sees the torturous hell I'm going through. I giggle. *Does this guy actually give a shit about you? Well, that's the first medical person that has made you feel that way since you been home.* I figure, fuck it, it's worth a shot, and I book an appointment.

We start good old-fashioned therapy: stretches, deep tissue massage, exercises, heat, cold. I begin to show progress after a couple weeks.

I'm driving rideshare, sixty hours a week, and one night spasms spark off in my back every time I take a deep breath. I pull over to a gas station at Addison and Ashland, struggling for breath. I get out and sit on the little concrete curb next to the pump. *Jesus, now it's my back and lungs! What the fuck?* The spasms spike like someone is stabbing me in the back. I scream. *Fuck.* I struggle to breathe; every time I take a full breath, it fucking stabs me again. *Should I call an ambulance? Should I?* The spasm digs into my back. *Fuck!!!! Jesus fucking hell.* I sit there gasping for breath, bracing for the next spasm for an hour as they keep coming. The gas attendant walks up and asks if I need an ambulance. *Should you call an ambulance? Fuck no. They'll just waste your fucking time, treat you like shit, and send you home.*

I get back in the car. I figure out that if I lean way in over the wheel and crumple my folded right arm into my chest, the spasms stop. I drive home across Chicagoland like that. Then I get out and head into the basement and collapse on the couch. *Guess I should take a day off.*

♉

The next morning my misery fills the dark, dusty basement. I get up and disrobe to get in the shower. In the mirror my body is pale; my arms and chest are withered. *Man, you've lost twenty pounds of muscle, at least.* There's a massive indentation under my belly button, like the muscle has just dissolved. Then it bulges lower into two lumps in my pelvis. *What did you do to yourself?* My whole body is kind of racked to the side at the hips. *You can't even stand up straight.* I twist to see my profile. A huge long indentation runs along my right butt cheek, where the muscle has just evaporated. *Are you crippled now? Is this gonna be it for the rest of your life? Well, it is, it is. You wanted to be a bull runner. What the fuck are you going to do, cry about it?* I glare into my trembling blue eyes in my hollowed-out face in the mirror. I think of the guns upstairs in my dad's closet. *You can't sit here alone in your fucking parents' basement on these horrible painkillers and anti-inflammatory depressants. You're gonna blow your brains out.*

I shower and go back out to work.

Afterword

After several weeks of ups and downs, Ian and I work through it. I'm feeling better physically, and I'm filled with gratitude for Ian's help. His manager enrolls me in a financial assistance plan, and I pay fifteen percent of what I think I have to. All of this reinvigorates my hopes for the healthcare system in the USA.

On our last day, I'm complaining about my lower back and Ian, who wasn't allowed to work on it because the script my doctor gave him was for my pelvis and hips, finally says to hell with it and takes a look. He feels around on my tailbone and lower spine. He steps back startled, and grimaces.

"What is it?" I ask.

"A few of your vertebrae are seriously compacted." He takes a deep breath and exhales slowly. "If you get script for that, I'll work on it."

"I'm leaving tomorrow, man," I guffaw. "But thanks, without your help I don't know if I woulda made it." I head out.

I jump in the car and go home. *Is that's what it's been all along, your lower back? Makes sense. The pain wasn't from swelling, it was nerve pain, it was spasms. You've been trying to tell everybody that! Not one fucking person listened! Ah, the hell with it. It's getting better, you can walk now.* I head inside to pack up. It was probably a dozen different things that caused the pain. What a bizarre fucking injury.

♉

I fly back to Panama and get back to the writing. I'd hoped to write two books in two years, well, I finish three new drafts of three books over the next few months. I've never written more or better at any time in my life. It feels like a little taste of what Irvine Welsh's life must be like. Constant writing, new books in multiple stages, new projects coming in. And maybe if I play my cards right, I can sign with a big house in the States and take a giant leap in my writing career.

I apply to the University of Louisiana at Lafayette's PhD in Creative Writing program, and they accept me: a fully funded teaching assistantship. I'll be teaching two courses a semester and taking three over the next four years. My article for *Vice* about my goring and healthcare odyssey goes viral around the globe.

Meanwhile Enid completes her Peace Corps service, and we take a big trip through South America: Columbia, Galapagos, Machu Picchu, Lima. We end up spending a month in Mexico City, where I finish this book.

Then one day Enid isn't feeling well, and takes a pregnancy test. It shows positive, and it fills us with such an incredible joy. Our family is finally beginning. For a week we go around dizzy with the idea of our child. Then the baby dies inside her. Part of me dies with them, part of us. We never do recover from that loss of the manifestation of our love. We hang on for another year, but we finally succumb, and get a divorce.

Enid is a great woman. She was everything I needed in those fourteen years we spent together. She saved my life in so many ways. We went through so much together that I never could have overcome without her. She was there for me through it all. I will always love her. But I got tired, I just couldn't do it anymore. I wasn't strong enough to keep fighting for us.

I meet someone, a Basque girl from Pamplona. I fall in love. She loves me, she loves the bulls and her culture, and she is teaching me things. I am seeing the culture through a whole new set of eyes. She is beautiful, sweet, wise, and so positive. She has that special magic that only the people of Pamplona have. She is everything I ever dreamed of.

A voice warns me a few days before I fall in love with her. It is an old man's voice. It tells me that someone will come into my life and change everything. It tells me not to be afraid. It tells me things I can't tell you yet. Everything he tells me starts coming true.

I don't know where my life is going; I've stopped trying to steer it. But if the old man is right, it will revolve around Pamplona, this city I love so much. I can't wait to return to fiesta for another taste of its otherworldly magic, the magic of San Fermin and the bulls let loose on the streets of Spain. This tradition has embedded itself in my soul; it's a part of me now.

About Tortoise Books

Slow and steady wins in the end, even in publishing. Tortoise Books is dedicated to finding and promoting quality authors who haven't yet found a niche in the marketplace—writers producing memorable and engaging works that will stand the test of time.

Learn more at www.tortoisebooks.com, find us on Facebook, or follow us on Twitter @TortoiseBooks.

CPSIA information can be obtained
at www.ICGtesting.com
Printed in the USA
FSHW011325191220
76852FS